Disability Harassment

Disability Harassment

Mark C. Weber

NEW YORK UNIVERSITY PRESS

New York and London

NEW YORK UNIVERSITY PRESS
New York and London
www.nyupress.org

Library of Congress Cataloging-in-Publication Data

Weber, Mark C., 1953–
Disability harassment / Mark C. Weber.
p. cm.
Includes bibliographical references and index.
ISBN-13: 978-0-8147-9405-0 (cloth : acid-free paper)
ISBN-10: 0-8147-9405-X (cloth : acid-free paper)
1. Discrimination against people with disabilities—Law and legisla-
tion—United States. 2. Harassment—Law and legislation—United
States. 3. People with disabilities—Legal status, laws, etc.—United
States. 4. Students with disabilities—Legal status, laws, etc.—
United States. I. Title.
KF480.W43   2007
342.7308'7—dc22   2006030952

New York University Press books are printed on acid-free paper,
and their binding materials are chosen for strength and durability.

Manufactured in the United States of America
10 9 8 7 6 5 4 3 2 1

To Joanne, Sam, and Jane

Contents

Preface

This book discusses the harassment of individuals on the basis of their disabilities. Its central focus is on the legal remedies and policy reforms that can be advanced to address the problem of disability harassment. The analysis is not strictly legal, however. It seeks to build on the insight of many writers in the disability studies field that people with disabilities are members of a minority group in America. Though disability may define the group, what imposes limits on individuals is not necessarily disability itself but the artificial environment of physical and attitudinal barriers that people with disabilities must negotiate. Harassment is a manifestation of the attitudinal barriers.

The book will consider the courts' approaches to the problem of harassment, particularly the application of an analogy to race and sex harassment and the development of remedies under the Americans with Disabilities Act (ADA) comparable to those applied in race and sex cases under other civil rights laws. It criticizes the limits of that approach, which so far has provided remedies only in a few, extreme situations and left the vast undercurrent of harassing activity unaffected. The book suggests that other provisions of the ADA should be applied and other legal remedies developed. It also takes up special problems of harassment in the public schools and the legal response. It discusses possible challenges to the constitutionality of expanded legal protections against harassment. It also explores other policy measures to diminish harassment and end isolation of people with disabilities, thus considering social as well as legal changes.

A note to readers who are not lawyers: a major goal of this book is to demystify some of the legal analysis of disability harassment. Nevertheless, I found myself unable to avoid employing legal jargon without adding hugely to the length of the description of court cases. To understand the description of the cases, it is helpful to know that cases begin with a complaint filed in a court. The complaint contains the story of what happened to the plaintiff at the hands of the defendant and what remedy—damages, an injunction, possibly something else—the plaintiff wants the court to award. Most often, the defendant responds to the plaintiff's complaint with a motion to dismiss, saying that even if the complaint's version of what happened is correct, the plaintiff loses because there is no violation of the law for which the court can order a remedy. The assumption, then, is that what the plaintiff said is correct. If the court denies the motion to dismiss, it is saying that if what the plaintiff alleged is right, then the defendant has violated the law and some remedy may be awarded. Frequently, lawyers refer to that sort of decision as one upholding the claim. It permits the case to proceed to trial.

In many cases, sometimes ones in which the defendant has previously moved to dismiss and had the motion denied, the case proceeds with further factual development. The parties, that is, the plaintiff and defendant, conduct depositions, submit affidavits, and identify documents that can be used as evidence at trial. If at the conclusion of this process one of the parties, typically the defendant, believes that undisputed facts disclosed so far mean that the plaintiff cannot win, it will move for summary judgment. The relevant standard is that no genuine issue of material fact exists. That means that there is no factual dispute for the jury or judge, if the case is heard by a judge, to resolve by hearing live testimony. In other words, on the basis of indisputable or undisputed facts, no reasonable finder of fact could decide in favor of the other side. At this point, the assumption is no longer that everything in the complaint is correct. Nevertheless, all inferences that reasonably could be drawn are to be drawn in favor of the party opposing summary judgment. If the judge denies a summary judgment motion brought by the defendant, once again the judge could be said to be upholding the claim. The court upholds the claim on the basis of the facts developed and presented to the court, both those that are undisputed and those that could be found to favor the plaintiff if a reasonable jury is so persuaded.

Although this book, like other legal sources, describes the allegations of the plaintiffs in cases decided on motions to dismiss or motions for summary judgment as if they were fact, they may not be. It is simply that the judge, for making the decision, must assume that they are fact. If a motion to dismiss or a motion for summary judgment is decided against the plaintiff, no one will ever know whether the plaintiff's version of disputed facts was right. Even if the motions are denied, many cases settle, and so again no one knows what really happened. In any instance, a reader should take descriptions of cases in this book with the understanding that the facts may not be right. The legal analysis depends on making the assumption that they are, but it is always an assumption.

A further note: the federal courts in the United States are organized into geographic circuits. Each trial court, known as a district court, has a court that sits in review of it. These reviewing courts, except for two that sit in Washington, D.C., are identified by numbers. Thus the Seventh Circuit embraces district courts in Illinois, Indiana, and Wisconsin, the Second Circuit the district courts in New York, Connecticut, and Vermont, and so on for the other numbered circuits. These courts are below only the United States Supreme Court and so are powerful legal actors. As a matter of shorthand reference, this book will adopt the legal terminology of referring to a given numbered circuit court as, for example, "the Second Circuit," rather than spelling out the entire title "Second Circuit Court of Appeals" or "United States Court of Appeals for the Second Circuit."

Now a final note: sources of law, of course, include both state law, either written in statutes or unwritten, as with much of the law of civil liability for negligence and intentional wrongdoing, as well as federal law, principally statutes passed by Congress and federal constitutional provisions and principles. Sometimes state courts apply federal law and sometimes federal courts apply state law. The reasons that is so are largely outside the scope of discussion of this work. Where I think it is important for the reader to be able to identify whether the source of law is state or federal, I provide specific information, usually in an endnote. The three basic sources of federal law that I discuss in this book are (1) the Americans with Disabilities Act of 1990 (ADA), found at 42 U.S.C.A. §§ 12101-12213 (West 2006), which bars disability discrimination in private employment (title I), state and local government activities (title II), privately operated public accommodations (title III), and telecommunications (title IV); (2) section 504 of the Rehabilitation Act of 1973, found at 29 U.S.C.A. § 794 (West 2006), which forbids discrimination against otherwise qualified persons with disabilities by recipients of federal funding; and (3) the Individuals with Disabilities Education Act (IDEA), found at 20 U.S.C.A. §§ 1400-1487 (West 2006), which requires states that receive federal special education funding to provide children with disabilities a free, appropriate public education in the least restrictive environment.

Significant portions of the material in this book appeared in an earlier form in three law review articles: "Exile and the Kingdom: Integration, Harassment, and the Americans with Disabilities Act," 63 *Maryland Law Review* 162 (2004); "Workplace Harassment Claims under the Americans with Disabilities Act: A New Interpretation," 14 *Stanford Law and Policy Review* 241 (2003); and "Disability Harassment in the Public Schools," 43 *William and Mary Law Review* 1079 (2002). Thanks to the editorial staffs of those publications for their contributions to the work. Thanks also to the research assistants at DePaul College of Law who assisted with the articles and the book. They have been many over several years, but Elizabeth Graham, Sara Mauk, Janet Brewer, Victoria Napolitano, and Catherine Tetzlaff deserve special recognition. Thanks also for research support from DePaul College of Law and for the support of Dean Glen Weissenberger on this project.

1

Harassment Narratives

Disability discrimination is not mere thoughtlessness or failure to accommodate the needs of people with disabilities. Much disability discrimination consists of overt physical and verbal abuse, the conscious effort to subordinate people who as a group hold less power and social standing than the majority. This chapter presents accounts of people with disabilities who have been subjected to disability harassment. The cases are the smallest tip of a very large mass, but they demonstrate harassment and how it operates to impose stigma, to form and perpetuate stereotypes, and to enforce subordination on people with disabling conditions.[1]

Stories of Stigma

Ricky Casper had a mental impairment that reduced his ability to learn.[2] Supervisors at his maintenance and assembly job repeatedly made fun of him as stupid. One called him a "tax write-off" and told him that his children would grow up "acting . . . slow and stuff." He threatened to come over to Casper's house and have sex with Casper's fiancée in order to show her what good sex was. Another supervisor exposed Casper to streams of profane abuse and constantly forced him to redo work unnecessarily. A third made him work while co-workers stood around and laughed at him. Workers called him "Rick Retardo" and "dumb ass." One supervisor asked him why he had an assembly job because "you can't read or write or do math."

Sandra Spragis Flowers had a different kind of disability and a different experience of imposed stigma.[3] Flowers, a medical assistant, was diagnosed with HIV infection. When her supervisor learned of Flowers's condition, she stopped going to lunch and socializing with her. Instead, the supervisor began a campaign of eavesdropping on her, intercepting her telephone calls, and hovering around Flowers's desk. The company president suddenly became distant and refused to shake Flower's hand; he would go out of his way to avoid her office when going from one part of the hospital to another. Flowers was subjected to four drug tests in a week, written up twice and placed on probation, called names, and subjected to other humiliations. Eight months after the supervisor learned that Flowers was HIV-positive, the company fired her.

Charlie F. was a fourth grader with attention deficit disorder who was prone to panic attacks.[4] Every week, his teacher held sessions in which she asked her students to discuss their feelings. She repeatedly asked them to discuss Charlie and his behavior, and every week they joined in criticizing and humiliating him. He lost the confidence he had gained in school and his academic progress flagged. The barrage of ridicule was accompanied by taunting outside the classroom and fistfights. Although the teacher instructed the students to keep the sessions a secret, the truth came out. Charlie's parents moved him to another school, but even three years later, children from the class still taunted him when they ran into him on the street.

In their pathbreaking article in 1988, Michelle Fine and Adrienne Asch challenged the conventional view that stigma arises from an individual's impairment rather than from "human-made" barriers.[5] Their work referred to Erving Goffman's observation that the discomfort and anxiety that people without disabilities feel in encounters with people who appear disabled lead those without disabilities to impose stigma on those who have them.[6] The narratives given here illustrate how people without disabilities, typically people with authority or practical power, impose stigma on a person with a disability who has no effective power to defend against the oppressor. The supervisor or the teacher cannot accept that the person with a disability is different, even though the difference has no bearing on the person's entitlement to a job or schooling. The lack of experience working in an ordinary relationship with people with disabilities and the general absence of people with developmental disabilities, or HIV infection, or neurological impairments from the mainstream of ordinary life act as barriers to the acceptance of the employee or student as an employee or student. Instead, the person is a manifestation of a disability, and the discomfort of dealing with that manifestation causes a reaction of ridicule, shunning, or abuse, or of encouraging others to ridicule, shun, and abuse.

The mechanics of stigma differ with individual instances and particular disabilities. Few people have experience working as an equal or in an ordinary supervisory relationship with a co-worker who has a developmental disability. Perceiving someone in Casper's work role as a liability to the general effort, as a write-off, is all too easy given the pervasiveness of exclusion of people with mental retardation from ordinary work. In ordinary experience, people with mental retardation work, if they work at all, in sheltered settings or in self-contained crews.[7] Work is medical treatment, not employment. The supervisor's verbal harassment of Casper and his singling him out for extra tasks convey a not very subtle message to quit the job and disappear. What the supervisor perceives as the cause of the discomfort is the person rather than the rarity of the experience of having a person with a developmental disability in a position of productive activity. The supervisor's urge is to make the discomfort go away by hounding the person with a disability to quit, not by altering the work setting to add enough workers with developmental disabilities so that their presence is no longer a shock.

The harassment of Flowers in reaction to her HIV infection illustrates another aspect of disability stigma, the fear of infectious disease. But the reality is that the connection between discriminatory barriers and stigma is much the same as in Casper's situation. HIV infection is something that happens to other people, drug abusers or sexual minorities. Certainly, someone with the disease is not expected to be in the workplace, conducting affairs in an ordinary way. That the illness does not affect the person's performance in role does not matter. In fact, it may exacerbate the discomfort that others feel. Fine and Asch collect studies indicating that people without disabilities appear to experience more discomfort in dealing with a person with a disability who manages tasks competently than with one who fills the anticipated role and needs help.[8]

Aspects of popular imagination associated with HIV also contribute to the stigma placed on people with the infection. Symbolism commonly used in discussing disease from HIV includes that of an invasion of the society and the person and that of divine punishment for sinful behavior.[9] These additional meanings or metaphors attached to HIV infection contribute to the isolation and stigma that other individuals impose on the person who has the disease. Flowers experienced a reaction to disability that traces back to biblical times: the shunning of those perceived as disfavored by the divine and as threatening to the healthy.

Charlie F.'s experience provides an example of how someone in authority takes two of a child's characteristics, severe distractibility and anxiety, and uses them to single out the child as the object of attention, and soon the object of hostility, of the group. The disability is not sufficient to cause the stigma. Rather, a person with power makes a conscious decision to act in a way that leads others to impose stigma on the person with the disability. The social structure of ordinary school renders the person with a disability out of place in the mainstream. In Illinois, where the events took place, the rate of children with disabilities who are excluded from general education classrooms 60 percent of more of the day is 40 percent higher than the national average.[10] Special education children are supposed to stay in special education classrooms. Challenging that expectation carries a price. Those in the dominant group experience a threat and react by ostracizing the person they perceive as breaking the rules.

Stories of Stereotype

Some other instances of harassment illustrate the pervasive use of stereotypes. People observe a disability and assume that the person with that impairment fits a stereotype of someone who is lazy or deceitful or worse. Mitchell Harshbarger worked as a foreman for a power company in a job that required him to lift boxes weighing two hundred to three hundred pounds.[11] He suffered a series of injuries to his elbows and underwent surgery. He returned to the job with a permanent restriction of lifting no more than forty-eight pounds. A few months later, he tore his rotator cuff, went on light-duty work, had more surgery, and spent time off work. He returned to a light-duty position, eventually with a restriction that he lift no more than twenty-five pounds with his right arm and not reach above his shoulder. He attempted to negotiate entry into another job slot, but his employer ultimately terminated him instead. While Harshbarger was on light-duty work, his supervisor taunted him in front of co-workers for being "lazy," "crippled," and "worthless" and asked him, "Where is your dress?"

Neil Haysman worked in a grocery store.[12] He injured his back and knee when a forklift pallet fell and struck him; the injury exacerbated a preexisting emotional impairment. About ten months after he returned to work in an light-duty position with a part-time schedule created for him, the store's manager and assistant manager started a campaign in which they harangued him in front of the other employees, accusing him of exaggerating his conditions, of "milking" his disability. The assistant manager said he would "ride" him until he quit, abused him with profanity, and struck and kicked him on the injured parts of his body. They switched his shift to night without any reason but to induce him to leave the job. The store manager said he thought Haysman was "a joke." Haysman's mental state deteriorated as a result of the mistreatment. He eventually went back on workers' compensation and ultimately obtained a job at a different store.

Robert Kubistal was a seventh grader with an undiagnosed visual impairment.[13] His teacher routinely called him "butthead" and said she would like to take out his eyes and give them to a child who would work harder. His mother complained to Robert's principal and ultimately to the board of education. After the principal assured Robert's mother that the teacher would apologize if necessary, the teacher called Robert up to the front of the class, got down on her knees, and in an exaggerated voice said, "I'm so sorry, Bobby!" She then turned to the class and stuck a finger in her throat to mimic inducing vomiting. At some point the next year, after the visual impairment was diagnosed, Robert was moved to another teacher's room. During that time, the principal came to the classroom and erected an "isolation chamber" for Robert with movable bookcases. Robert sat in the isolation chamber every day for several weeks, including during his lunch period. Robert's mother complained to the teacher, who said the principal was responsible, so she then complained to the principal, who said the teacher was responsible. Robert graduated despite never having been assigned eighth-grade work. At the ceremony, the graduation marshal skipped over Robert's name, looked at Robert's mother, giggled, and finally said, "Oh, Robert Kubistal." As a result of these humiliations, Robert suffered from depression and bed-wetting and lost interest in school.

The stories of Harshbarger and Haysman illustrate stereotypes of two kinds: first, the presumably positive stereotype of the yeoman, eager and able to do any kind of physical work, and second, the negative stereotype of the shirker, who tries to avoid doing a fair share of the labor. The former image is classically male; the latter merges with a common image of feminine dependency, as suggested by the comment to Harshbarger, "Where's your dress?" Simi Linton points out that society tends to ascribe similar characteristics to women and people with disabilities: dependency, emotionality, passivity, the lack of mature judgment.[14] Like women who have attempted to break into jobs that are predominantly male, workers with disabilities who are in ordinary work settings receive the message "You do not belong, and I am using my power to keep you out." Just as sexual harassment is less about sex than about exclusion and dominance,[15] so disability harassment is not so much about disability as about preserving the strength and privileges of those without disabilities.

Robert Kubistal's experience demonstrates an additional stereotype present in Harshbarger's and Haysman's stories. The assumption is that a person who needs accommodations to do a task does not in fact need them but is lazy or unwilling to work. The persistence of Harshbarger and Kubistal, or, for that matter, of Casper, Flowers, and Charlie F. and others, puts the lie to that notion. What is remarkable about all of these cases is that they are the instances where the harassment, at least in the short term, failed in getting the targets of abuse to leave work or school. Their tenacity demonstrates the opposite of Goffman's description of people with disabilities who, being stigmatized, isolate themselves and avoid jobs or other situations where they will experience rejection. But that fact appears not to have mattered to the harassers. The person with the disability who is placed on light duty or needs additional support in learning is a piker, a malingerer.

Lack of daily contact at a level of true equality with persons with disabilities promotes and constantly reinforces stereotypes. Gordon Allport's classic study of prejudice reported that people who have no contact with members of a racial minority or other out-group typically have low opinions about them.[16] Rather than dispel the negative opinions, casual contacts with the minority frequently reinforce them. In their experiences with the minority, people selectively remember what is bad and ignore or forget what is good. Prejudice diminishes, however, when members of the majority and minority work together as equals for some common goal. The rarity of peers with disabilities in public settings locks people without disabilities in the stage of no contact or limited contact, where stereotypes take root and grow.

Stories of Subordination

Stigma and stereotype combine to keep those who appear to be different in a position inferior to others. Some accounts vividly illustrate the verbal and physical brutality that enforces this subordination. Shawn Witte was a ten-year-old with Tourette's syndrome, asthma, attention deficit disorder, an emotional disability, and deformities of the feet and legs.[17] At school, his teacher forced him to eat oatmeal, though his mother had told the teacher that Shawn was allergic to it. The teacher and an aide force-fed Shawn, one of them holding his hands behind his back while the other spooned him oatmeal mixed with his own vomit. The principal was aware of the practice and explained it to Shawn's mother as a form of punishment. To punish Shawn for not running fast enough during an exercise period, the aide choked him, causing an emergency room visit in which the physician diagnosed strangulation. When Shawn made involuntary body movements due to tics, the teacher and aides tackled and sat on him. The staff placed Shawn on a treadmill with weights attached to his ankles in an effort to tire him out and keep him from leaving the classroom. At times, Shawn was punished for failing to perform tasks by being deprived of meals or having water sprayed on his face. The teacher screamed degrading remarks at Shawn. Shawn was also forced to write the sentences "I will not tell my mom" and "I will not tic." He was threatened with physical harm if he ever told his mother about what was happening at school. Derrick Eason, another student at the same school for children with disabilities, endured similar treatment.

Robert Fox was an automobile assembly plant worker who injured his back and returned from disability leave with a medical restriction to light-duty work.[18] Although his immediate supervisor tried to adapt Fox's job duties to meet his medical restrictions, a different supervisor and the foreman blocked these efforts and belittled Fox when he refused to violate his physical restrictions. They placed him at a special work table that was too low for him and exacerbated his back injury. He was blocked from obtaining a promotion, and the supervisor and co-workers subjected Fox and other workers with disabilities who were on light duty to a continual barrage of profane abuse and insults relating to their disabilities. The supervisor told other employees not to talk to Fox and the other workers who were disabled, so the co-workers ostracized them. Fox experienced severe depression, anxiety, and suicidal thoughts as a result of his unfair treatment.

The narratives presented so far all draw from opinions from cases brought to court. In reality, the harassment of people with disabilities is so pervasive that anyone attuned to it observes it everywhere and finds accounts of it in sources meant to be about something else. Philippe Bourgois's remarkable study of the culture of drug sellers in Harlem recounts a conversation between two of the dealers he befriended. Bourgois steered the conversation to their education, and one remarked:

> I never went to school neither. I used to go in for gym, and lunch, and then to play with the girls and shit like that in the afternoon—but I never used to go in the morning.
> No, I'm lying. We used to come to school to fuck Special Ed niggas up— kick their asses. Because they had the retarded here, and the ones that used to walk like this [scraping his toes, inflecting his knees, and pronating his arms to imitate someone with cerebral palsy]. We used to beat the shit out of them. We used to hurt them, because we didn't like them.[19]

After giving several examples of the violence, ranging from beatings to an attempted hanging with a gym rope, Caesar looked up at Bourgois's facial expression and apparently remembered learning that Bourgois's one-year-old son had just been diagnosed with cerebral palsy. Caesar then backpedaled on the story and started describing his beating of one of the children as an initiation to being part of his "posse." But it is quite apparent that the child never became part of the group. The brutality was initiation into the set of those who did not belong. Verbal and physical abuse of children in special education classes by classmates can be witnessed any day in any schoolyard, anywhere, and it has the universal effect of defining who is in the favored group and who is not.

Samuel Bagenstos describes the problem of "impairment-based subordination: Through prejudice, stereotypes, and widespread neglect, society's attitudes and practices attach systemic disadvantage to particular impairments."[20] The impairments themselves do not exclude or disadvantage, but attitudes and practices of the majority subordinate those considered to be outside the norm. Harassment establishes subordination in a very direct way. The person with a disability is verbally or physically abused and can do nothing about it except choose further isolation, which in turn reinforces the subordinate status. Witte's case, viewed in isolation, reads almost like an account of a crime. The reader feels pity for the helpless victim of cruelty. But the abuse is not random or opportunistic. It lights on someone who has already been shunted into an exclusionary setting, and, though obviously self-defeating for its purpose, it has a goal: to change the person with a disability into someone else, to make him eat on command, to make him not tic. The victim's helplessness is not an inherent condition. He has been forced into a position of helplessness, a setting in which the adults have forsaken the role of teacher and assistant and become assailants, and nobody else is around to change the miniature universe the teacher and assistant have created. The identification of Shawn Witte as a victim is harmful in itself. It further reinforces the subordinate status that society assigns to persons with his disability. As Martha Minow writes, assigning victim status "creates a self-fulfilling [prophecy], . . . by suggesting that victims are powerless. . . . It may also lead to a sense of futility and political passivity for just those people."[21]

Subordination in the sense being used here applies to a cohort, a group. Ruth Colker defines antisubordination as the principle that no group should have a lowered status because of its lack of power in society.[22] Bagenstos in turn defines the disability that should give rise to the protections of the Americans with Disabilities Act (ADA) as the set of conditions met with stigma such that the people with those conditions are subordinated.[23] That harassment is commonly a group phenomenon is illustrated by Robert Fox's case. The supervisors and those they egged on pushed him and the other employees with disabilities into a category and subordinated—that is, actively diminished the status of—that group. The category was that of "handicapped MFs" and "911 hospital people."[24]

Of all the stories of subordination here, perhaps Bourgois's story speaks most for itself, in the casualness of the brutality and the persuasiveness with which it shows that disability harassment is the norm, what is expected in ordinary life. The fact that the source for the account is ostensibly about something else (the economic and social role of the drug trade in a community that offers few other opportunities) strengthens the point about the pervasiveness of disability harassment. Hostility directed against people with disabilities is so common that, like the air, we ignore it, and it commonly is ignored by the media, in ordinary conversation, and, as this book seeks to demonstrate, by the instruments of justice. In looking at news about other things, an observer who is aware of how common disability harassment is will find disability harassment appearing time and again. Lennard Davis notes that stories about the 1999 dragging death of an African American man, James Byrd Jr., by a white supremacist barely mentioned the fact that Byrd had a disability.[25] Davis had to conduct extensive research just to learn that his disability was severe arthritis. Attuned to the issue of disability-based harassment, Davis went to the effort to learn that reaction to disability may have played a role in the crime. He describes the pervasiveness of the assumption that violence against a member of a racial minority with a disability is because of race when disability could be the motivation, and he compiles statistics showing that a person with a disability is four times as likely to be the subject of physical assault, robbery, or rape as a member of the general population.[26]

The Law and the Courts

Congress passed the ADA in 1990 to create legal remedies for, among other things, harassment on the basis of disability. The damages and injunctions issued by courts would compensate people for past wrongdoing and keep specific offenders from offending again. Word of damages and attorneys' fees awards would deter future wrongdoing by others. As is more fully explained in later chapters, things have not quite worked out that way.

Of the three individuals selected here to illustrate the operation of stigma, only one, Sandra Flowers, obtained a judicial remedy. Even in her case the appellate court ruled that she presented insufficient evidence of emotional injury to support her $350,000 jury verdict or the $100,000 the judge reduced it to, and the case was sent back for entry of an award of nominal damages.[27] Ricky Casper lost before he got the chance to go to trial. Despite the evidence of the nicknames and jeering questions, the judge ruled that Casper had marshaled insufficient support for a reasonable jury to conclude that he faced "an objectively hostile work environment based on disability."[28] Charlie F. sued for damages for the emotional harm wrought by the elementary school encounter sessions but lost because he had not pursued the case through administrative proceedings designed to evaluate and correct educational programs for children with disabilities.[29]

Of the three cases discussed in connection with stereotypes, Harshbarger lost at the outset when the judge refused to let the case go to trial. The judge determined that he was not protected by the ADA because he was not disabled or regarded as disabled and that he had been subjected merely to isolated comments and incidents that were not severe or pervasive. The opinion asserted that the evidence that any employee on light duty received verbal abuse meant that the abuse was unrelated to disability.[30] The court of appeals, however, concluded that the evidence that Sierra Power regarded Harshbarger as disabled was sufficient to reach a jury, and it sent his disability discrimination claim back for trial, though it held that his harassment claim had not properly been presented to the Equal Employment Opportunity Commission for administrative processing and so could not be pursued.[31] Like Charlie F., Robert Kubistal lost his case because he had not presented it to a hearing officer, even though hearing officers lack the power to order a school district or individuals to pay damages, and even though Robert was no longer receiving educational services from the school district involved in the proceedings.[32]

Of the instances selected to illustrate how harassment relates to subordination, the two that were litigated met with some success. Shawn Witte had a long judicial odyssey, however, losing at first because of the administrative exhaustion defense that was effective in *Charlie F.* and *Kubistal,* but winning reversal from the court of appeals, which sent the case back for trial.[33] The lower court again dismissed the case without trial, holding that the school and its officials were protected by an immunity from suit that generally keeps state agencies from having to pay damages in federal court suits. The court of appeals reversed again, holding that the immunity did not extend to the school district and individual wrongdoers named in the case.[34] Further proceedings are not reported, but the results thus far would be considered a tentative judicial victory. Robert Fox won too, obtaining a jury verdict of $200,000 for emotional injury, though the appellate court overturned an award of $4,000 in unpaid overtime.[35] His case and that of Sandra Flowers are the best-known instances of judicial success in asserting workplace disability harassment claims.

As so many other examples suggest, however, judicial success is by no means typical. The vast majority of disability harassment claims fail, on the ground that the harassment is not sufficiently severe or pervasive to satisfy the judge that the case can go to trial or on the ground that the worker is not disabled enough to gain the protection of the ADA, or on some other basis. This reality and some possible legal responses to it will be taken up in later chapters.

The account of schoolyard harassment from the book about drug dealing in Harlem stands for the thousands of instances in which no one sues and no one even thinks of suing. In general, people do not perceive disability discrimination, much less disability harassment, as something they would go to court over. In a revealing new study, David Engel and

Frank Munger describe the life stories of a set of individuals with serious disabilities and consider the discrimination they experienced.[36] Uniformly, the subjects of the study reject the option of suing over the harms imposed on them by employers and others in a position of authority. Engel and Munger's conclusion from these accounts is not that legal rights are unimportant. The rights contribute to a person's ideas about his or her identity and how he or she deserves to be treated by others. They inform the behavior of friends and colleagues of people with disabilities. Ultimately, they may affect culture, the language and not necessarily conscious actions of those whose decisions constitute social conditions. Even institutions may shift their operation over time in response to widely disseminated ideas about rights. But many people will never assert their legal rights in a court, no matter how badly their rights are violated. Though this does not render the law or legal rights ineffective, it compels attention to the formation of the identity of a person with a disability and the effect of the entirety of the environment, legal, physical, economic, and emotional, in which personalities exist. Legal reform will affect the environment, perhaps even the construction of identities, but other change in the environment, what might be termed social reform, needs attention as well.

2

Harassment, Exclusion,
and Equality

This chapter will establish a frame for analysis of disability harassment, drawing from contemporary works in the field of disability studies. The chapter will develop the minority group model of disability, which stresses the insight that bodily and mental conditions would not necessarily disable, were it not for the human-built environment of physical and attitudinal barriers. The chapter will link harassment to the involuntary segregation and isolation of people with disabilities and the fostering of stereotypes due to that separation. It will trace the attitudes that lead to harassment to sources such as the eugenics movement and popular culture.

The Minority Group Model

The central insight of the disabilities rights movement is that society establishes barriers that disable people who have physical or mental impairments, creating a minority group of individuals excluded from the social mainstream.[1] These barriers may be physical, as with the environment of steps, curbs, narrow halls, hidden obstructions, and inaccessible means of communication. Or they may be attitudinal, as with beliefs that people with disabilities are to be pitied, isolated, ignored, or ridiculed. The result is that people with disabilities do not participate on an equal plane in work, education, or recreational activities. Social action addressed to the barriers frees people with disabilities to take a fuller role in social and economic life.

Disability, then, is not something inherent in the individual but rather a product of the absence of social accommodations.[2] A person who uses a wheelchair for mobility would not be disabled from most activities of ordinary life if curbs, stairs, and narrow halls did not prevent that person from getting from one place to another. That same person is equally disabled, of course, if narrow minds are the barrier: if someone making hiring decisions for a company cannot conceive of a person in a wheelchair performing a job as effectively as someone else, the person in the wheelchair will be disabled from obtaining employment.

The model has applications for people whose disabilities are not related to mobility. A person with limited sight or hearing is disabled by the fact that much of the media and other ordinary communication is inaccessible. A person experiencing chronic fatigue is disabled by expectations of employers that a worker must complete an eight-hour day with only limited breaks in order to make a valuable contribution to the enterprise. Persons with any impairment of mind or body are disabled when others act as though they cannot make decisions or carry on their own affairs. Legal change will force employers, merchants, government agencies, and others to make communications and physical spaces usable by all; over time, attitudes will change as employers and merchants who fear liability change their exclusionary practices and as more people with disabilities enter the public sphere and participate there as equals with those who do not have disabilities.

This model contrasts with a medical model, in which the attention is on the individual with a disability and what is "wrong" with him or her, the defect.[3] Disability is not a dynamic between mental or physical characteristics on one end and social or architectural conditions on the other. Instead, it is a condition of the body or mind of the person with disability, and it must be fixed so that the person can fit into the world of the normal. Approaching disability from a medical point of view confers great power on providers of the medical or other curative services. Persons with disabilities are valued only when they overcome their handicaps. The medical approach tends to reduce the person who is the subject of attention to the sum total of his or her disabilities. It pushes the person with the disability into a separate category from others, and it thus leads to isolation. Observers have rightly credited the development of the minority group model as important progress from custodialism to what Jacobus tenBroek called "integrationism."[4]

The social, or civil rights, or minority group model of disability has generated criticism. Some have argued that the model places too little emphasis on the relationship of individuals to the means of production, arguing that it is futile or simply incorrect to blame an amorphous thing called society for what the critics believe to be the failings of the capitalist production system.[5] Others have complained that the model puts too little emphasis on the role of costs associated with removal of the barriers and integration of individuals with disabilities into society, contending that resources need to be shifted so that people with disabilities do not bear all the cost of the functional limits their impairments may impose.[6] Many others have challenged whether the goal of integration, standing by itself, is sufficient, or even desirable, as the preferred end state after social change has occurred.[7] Nevertheless, the model has the power to illuminate the condition of people with disabilities in a way that the previous models of disability do not. It forms the basis for the analysis of disability harassment in this chapter and in this book as a whole.

Segregation, Isolation, and Harassment

The minority group model observes that attitudes and environments segregate. If a person with a disability cannot surmount a physical or attitudinal barrier, that person is kept apart from the rest of society and reduced to the status of an outsider, if paid attention to at all. It is difficult to overstate the degree to which people with severe disabilities are separated from the world of work, education, and other aspects of daily life that is inhabited by the rest of the population. Work is paramount: the unemployment rate for persons who self-identify as having disabilities but consider themselves able to work and are actively seeking employment is two and one-half times as high as that of the rest of the population.[8] Only 24 percent of working-age individuals with severe mobility impairments are employed. About 32 percent of people with mental retardation, 33 percent of individuals with mental health disabilities, 34 percent of those with severe visual impairments, and 35 percent of persons with severe communication disabilities have jobs.[9] No comprehensive records are kept on the degree to which employment of individuals is segregated or integrated, although it is known that work in segregated settings remains a feature of life for many people with disabilities.[10]

In a society that furnishes the necessities of life only in exchange for labor, separation from the work force has a devastating economic effect, which only adds to separation of people with disabilities in the world of shopping, dining, and recreation. The poverty rate for adults with work disabilities is three times that of the rest of the population. Even those persons with disabilities who work generally work so little or at such low-paying jobs that their poverty rate is three times that of full-time workers who do not have disabilities.[11]

Educational settings also manifest separation of children with disabilities. According to the Department of Education, 80.8 percent of children ages six to eleven, 72.3 percent of children ages twelve to seventeen, and 58.8 percent of children ages eighteen to twenty-one receiving public special education services were educated outside the general education classroom for more than 40 percent of the school day.[12] More than 20 percent of all children with disabilities were in separate environments for over 60 percent of the day. For children with mental retardation, that number climbed to 51 percent who spent 60 percent or more of the day isolated from their nondisabled peers.[13] Many students with disabilities eventually isolate themselves from their classmates more permanently: children with disabilities have dropout rates three times those of other children.[14]

As illustrated below, the separation of persons with disabilities leads to their being viewed as a threatening Other, and harassment is a consequence of that viewpoint. It should not be forgotten, however, that harassment itself leads to further separation. Indeed, as the accounts in chapter 1 illustrated, its purpose frequently is to push those who would break out of segregated settings back into a separate, and subordinate, sphere.

Historical Segregation and Isolation

Theoreticians have stressed a number of historical factors in discussing attitudes that foster isolation and subordination of persons with disabilities. In the nineteenth century, people with disabilities were typically confined in almshouses, eventually in institutions.[15] Alone and ignored, people with disabling conditions experienced life in a Hobbesian state of nature: an existence solitary, poor, nasty, brutish, and short.[16] Legal protections for institutionalized persons with disabilities were long in coming and far from adequate when they arrived. Constitutional doctrine protecting the safety, habilitation, and medical rights of persons with disabilities in institutions developed after those rights had been extended to people in prison; in fact, the reasoning in the seminal case was that persons involuntarily confined without having committed a crime should not be denied protections afforded convicts.[17] The Supreme Court ruled that many basic statutory protections of institutionalized persons with disabilities are unenforceable.[18]

Even those who escaped institutionalization were not necessarily free from legal constraint. Until 1973, Chicago prohibited persons who were "deformed" and "unsightly" from exposing themselves to public view.[19] In many places, the law excluded children with disabilities from public school.[20] One statute imposed criminal penalties on parents if they sent a child with disabilities to school after exclusion.[21] In 1975, when federal legislation finally required states receiving federal educational money to serve all school-aged children with disabilities, 1.75 million children were not receiving any schooling, and an estimated 2.5 million were in programs that did not meet their needs.[22]

Ideas and attitudes characteristic of the eugenics movement were the natural outgrowth of the desire to isolate persons with disabilities and the underlying hostility toward them. Eugenics, the pseudoscience of producing an optimal human population, furnished an ideology that justified the exclusion of the physically and mentally "unfit" from social life through confinement, sterilization, and even outright killing. Courts operating under the influence of this ideology approved the compelled sterilization of individuals on specious assertions that they had a propensity to pass disabilities on to their offspring.[23] Public officials declared that people with disabilities had to be kept from mingling with others.[24] In the 1930s, the German government went even farther and initiated a program of killing individuals with disabilities, something the Nazi government termed euthanasia.[25] In the United States and elsewhere, infants with disabilities were often denied medical treatment in hospitals and left to die[26] or were killed outright.[27] As late as the 1940s, American medical experts defended killing people with disabling conditions, citing benefits to the rest of the population.[28]

Justice Thurgood Marshall exposed the history of legally enforced segregation of people with developmental disabilities in his partial dissent in *City of Cleburne v. Cleburne Living Center.*[29] He began by discussing eugenics and the ideology of segregation:

[T]he mentally retarded have been subject to a "lengthy and tragic history" of segregation and discrimination that can only be called grotesque. During much of the 19th century, mental retardation was viewed as neither curable nor dangerous and the retarded were largely left to their own devices. By the latter part of the century and during the first decades of the new one, however, social views of the retarded underwent a radical transformation. Fueled by the rising tide of Social Darwinism, the "science" of eugenics, and the extreme xenophobia of those years, leading medical authorities and others began to portray the "feeble-minded" as a "menace to society and civilization . . . responsible in a large degree for many, if not all, of our social problems."[30]

This ideology had very real consequences for the individuals with disabilities that the authorities sought to isolate from the general population:

A regime of state-mandated segregation and degradation soon emerged that in its virulence and bigotry rivaled, and indeed paralleled, the worst excesses of Jim Crow. Massive custodial institutions were built to warehouse the retarded for life; the aim was to halt reproduction of the retarded and "nearly extinguish their race." Retarded children were categorically excluded from public schools, based on the false stereotype that all were ineducable and on the purported need to protect nonretarded children from them. State laws deemed the retarded "unfit for citizenship."[31]

Eugenics is neither the sole source nor the sole effect of isolation of and hostility to persons with disabilities. One can trace hostile attitudes toward persons with disabilities to economic practices. The technology of the industrial revolution reinforced the segregation that the era's "the race is to the swift" ideology supported. Industrial production techniques fostered segregation by splitting the tasks involved in production among workers and by eliminating workers who could not keep up with machines or other workers in the same production process. "Industrialization brought policies that segregated disabled people, removing them from their indigenous communities, placing many of them in institutions. . . ."[32]

Current economic conditions do not necessarily help foster integration and replace segregationist attitudes with more progressive ones. Postindustrial techniques have, at best, an equivocal effect. The movement toward high technology in many jobs should make them easier to perform by people with mobility impairments and some other physical disabilities. Some technical advances that enhance communication may diminish barriers to employment for persons with sensory impairments. Nevertheless, the movement toward more technological jobs may further decrease the opportunities available to workers with mental retardation and other developmental disabilities or may result in the shunting of those workers to an ever-greater degree into low-level jobs in maintenance and landscaping. Machines increasingly are doing the repetitive production activities that were once the province of specialized workshops for individuals with developmental disabilities.[33]

Lennard Davis identifies yet another source for the devaluation and isolation of people with disabilities in the emphasis on the normal (as opposed to the ideal) human being that has emerged in the modern era.[34] Using historical and literary sources, he plots the emergence of an obsession with the normal against the prevalence of statistics-based thinking as well as the rise of industrial methods. All bodies are less than ideal, so when premodern-era literature and ideology stressed the ideal, it had less of a devastating effect on those whose bodies or minds were such that they could be considered impaired. But attention to the normal creates an imperative to be normal and a desire to suppress those who cannot come close to the norm.[35] Davis's analysis corresponds to Erving Goffman's observation that persons with disabilities are stigmatized for failure to conform to the standards of "normals":

> By definition, of course, we believe the person with a stigma is not quite human. On this assumption we exercise varieties of discrimination, through which we effectively, if often unthinkingly, reduce his life chances. We construct a stigma-theory, an ideology to explain his inferiority and account for the danger he represents, sometimes rationalizing an animosity based on other differences, such as those of social class. We use specific stigma terms such as cripple, bastard, moron in our daily discourse as a source of metaphor and imagery, typically without giving thought to the original meanings.[36]

Taking a somewhat different approach, one of the founders of the disabilities studies movement, Irving Kenneth Zola, stressed the departure of the disabled mind or body from the ideal, in particular the self-reliant ideal that is so prominent in American ideology.[37] Others have elaborated on this concept, pointing out that the ideal of self-reliance corresponds to a fear of loss of control and autonomy that makes persons without disabilities uncomfortable around persons with disabling conditions.[38] Rosemarie Garland Thomson points to Ralph Waldo Emerson's repeated contrasting of self-reliant men with invalids and the halt and blind.[39]

Thomson details the nineteenth- and early-twentieth-century history of the freak show, which linked disability both to pathology and to "cultural otherness."[40]

The lack of everyday exposure to people with disabilities participating as equals in society strengthens the negative attitudes that led to enforced separation in the first place.[41] Gordon Allport's classic study of the social psychology of prejudice concluded that individuals without contact with members of a racial or other out-group typically hold members of the minority in low esteem.[42] Casual contact may simply reinforce the stereotypes, since members of the majority group unconsciously seek out information that confirms their preexisting views. Nevertheless, prejudice declines substantially when casual contact gives way to closer acquaintance and especially to engagement in activity as equals in pursuit of a common goal.[43] As Martha Field has observed, "One reason many people are so fearful of—even repulsed by—persons with handicaps . . . is that they have never known such persons and have not seen them functioning in the community."[44] Harlan Hahn, a political scientist who is a noted scholar of disability issues, attributes the desire to segregate to the repugnance toward disabled bodies and the fear of someday being disabled.[45] This anxiety flourishes when people without disabilities lack any real experience as equals—as co-workers, classmates, or daily acquaintances—with people who have disabilities.[46] Research confirms that schoolchildren with disabilities, who, as noted below, are pervasively segregated from other children, are vastly lower in social prestige than the other students.[47] Samuel Bagenstos combines the idea that disability is located in the social and physical environment that fails to adapt to persons with impairments with ideas about the subordination that society imposes, and he concludes that the stigma society attaches to disability is disability's defining characteristic.[48]

Legal Challenges to Segregation

As noted in chapter 1, courts have not been aggressive in remedying harassment. Similarly, they have been reluctant to enforce the prointegration mandates of the ADA. In *Caruso v. Blockbuster-Sony Music,* the Third Circuit Court of Appeals required that a lawn area outside a concert arena be made accessible to wheelchair users, citing the obligation to provide public accommodations in the most integrated setting appropriate to the needs of the individual.[49] Other courts, however, have denied demands for integration. *McLaughlin v. Holt Public Schools Board of Education* is one of many cases rejecting the proposition that a child with disabilities should be educated at a school in the child's neighborhood, favoring instead the school system's preference to provide services at a concentrated site with fewer opportunities for mixing with children without disabilities.[50] *Tyler v. Ispat Inland, Inc.* upheld an employer's decision to separate an employee with mental illness from his original worksite and place him in a new location, despite his claim that the separation from the original site segregated him on account of his disability.[51] Nevertheless, the same court held that an employee with mental illness stated an ADA claim when he was transferred to a location in which he had to work alone and was forbidden to speak to anyone.[52]

The Supreme Court's single decision on the integration mandate of the ADA shows some support for the goal, but it also demonstrates caution in pursuing that goal too strenuously. In *Olmstead v. L.C.*, two women with mental retardation and mental illness lived for long periods of time in institutionalized settings despite the conclusion of treating professionals that they could be served in community-based residential programs where they would have more freedom and be more closely integrated into society.[53] The Court upheld a regulation, issued pursuant to authority granted in the ADA, which provides that public entities must administer services and programs in the most integrated setting appropriate to the needs of people with disabilities, finding that "unjustified isolation . . . is properly regarded as discrimination based on disability."[54] The Court, however, also ruled that in implementing the regulation the courts must consider, in view of the resources available to the state, not only the cost of providing community-based care to the individuals making the claim, but also the range of services the state provides to others with mental disabilities and the state's obligation to provide equal services to all.[55] The Court revealed its anxiety over financial problems states may have in maintaining institutions for individuals who require intensive care while paying for community-based placements for others.[56] The Court explicitly approved waiting lists as long as they move "at a reasonable pace."[57] The Court's decision echoed *Brown v. Board of Education II* in its subordination of the integration ideal to the supposed needs of governments engaged in illegal segregation.[58]

The primary federal law addressing education of children with disabilities contains a mandate that children with disabilities be educated with children without disabilities to the maximum extent appropriate and that services be provided to enable that integration to occur. In other writings, I have described the career of the integration requirement as a checkered one. Early judicial decisions established a presumption that a child should be placed in general education but also permitted decision makers to balance against the presumption considerations such as the educational benefits of full-time placement in a regular education class, any effect of having the child with a disability in the mainstream class on the teacher and the other members of the class, and any extraordinary costs of mainstreaming the child.[59] Although some courts have required school districts to be creative in designing programs and furnishing supplemental services to enable children with disabilities to be educated in mainstream settings, the statistics quoted above present a discouraging picture. Moreover, recently some courts and commentators have pushed actively in the other direction. One federal court of appeals has signaled that it will approve as little in the way of integrated services as a public school system wishes to provide so long as the system's choice might be characterized as "not unreasonable" to a hearing officer or court.[60] This effectively nullifies the presumption that integrated settings are to be given the benefit of the doubt. Recently, Ruth Colker has proposed abandoning the presumption in favor of integrated settings altogether. Reasons that she advances for dropping the presumption in favor of mainstream education include the hostility of teachers toward children with disabilities and the harassment that the children experience from their peers, which teachers and others do nothing to stop.[61] One might wish that instead of giving up on the project of integrated education, schools might direct efforts to ending harassment.

Isolation, Harassment, and Popular Culture

It would be comforting to think that the residues of eugenics and other historical bases of fear of persons with disabilities have vanished in the present era and that the passage of laws such as the ADA prove that point, even if the integration mandates of those laws have received uneven enforcement. In fact, as these pages will demonstrate, harassment still exists and continues to be linked to the segregation and isolation of those who have disabling conditions. Aspects of contemporary social life and popular culture continue to reinforce attitudes that permit, even promote, harassment. Architectural, communication, and other barriers in the environment continue to contribute to the separation of people with disabilities.[62] If barriers prevent individuals from riding the bus, entering stores, restaurants, and government buildings, or making use of places of public entertainment, people with impairments will remain invisible, hidden, and a source of fear and unpleasant associations.[63]

Intellectual leaders in universities and the judiciary are hardly immune from exclusionary attitudes. In a speech just a few years ago, the president of Boston University referred to students with learning disabilities as a "plague."[64] In the late 1980s, the judge in the trial of the tort action over birth defects attributed to the drug Bendectin excluded all plaintiffs with visible deformities from the courtroom on the ground that their appearance would improperly influence the jury.[65] The legislative history of the ADA reports an instance in which children with Down's syndrome were kept out of a private zoo on the belief that their appearance would bother the animals.[66] Employers have denied jobs to people with cerebral palsy and arthritis because of the supposed discomfort that co-workers or customers would experience from looking at them.[67] Disability rights activists have felt compelled to array themselves against Peter Singer, the Princeton philosopher who argues that killing of infants with severe disabilities is consistent with principles of morality.[68]

It takes only a few minutes of watching cartoons on television to notice that villains are typically shown as having a physical defect. Movie villains display scars, limps, and hunchbacks, all defects that visually convey evil or moral decay. Conversely, the physical defects of actual persons who have played heroic roles or otherwise served as social pathbreakers often are ignored or downplayed. Until disability activists intervened, the memorial to Franklin Roosevelt was to show him without a wheelchair. John Milton, Alexander Pope, Samuel Johnson, and Henry James all had physical or mental disabilities but are rarely remembered as disabled.[69]

An example of devaluation of people with disabilities in popular culture is the Academy Award–winning movie *Million Dollar Baby*. The bulk of the controversy over the film centered on its apparent endorsement of euthanasia and the predictable cultural divisions over whether euthanasia is ever morally permissible (a dispute that rose to a higher pitch in the subsequent cultural conflict over the termination of life support for Terri Schiavo, a woman in a persistent vegetative state). Among persons attuned to disability issues, however, the question posed by the film was not representative of the ones that typically arise in right-to-die disputes, such as whether a person with unremediable pain and a terminal diagnosis has the right to seek medical assistance to end life or what level of life support should be maintained for a person who has minimal brain activity, needs artificial means to stay alive, cannot now communicate, and has (to a court's satisfaction) indicated at some time in the past a desire not to have life prolonged in the absence of likely restoration to consciousness.[70]

Instead, the moral and political issue raised by *Million Dollar Baby* is whether it should be permissible to end the life of a person who says that she wants her life to end, when the only apparent ground for the decision is ongoing physical disability due to quadriplegia. The film's apparent resolution of the issue is that it is virtuous to take the life of the person with a disability, even though (or perhaps particularly because) the action causes the nondisabled person doing it to disappear into a life of loneliness and hiding from the law. As some writers have noted,[71] the film makes its conclusion easier to accept by systematically equating the disability of Maggie Fitzgerald, the fallen boxer, with illness and death. Attached to machines, the character languishes in bed in a sterile, hospital-like nursing home room doing literally nothing: no television, no music, no visitors save some stereotypically crude, venal family members and the man who ultimately kills her. There, from what seems to be negligent care but is presented as the natural order of things, she develops bedsores and an infection that results in an amputation. She receives no treatment for depression, even after an attempt to end her own life. Indeed, the longer the film goes on, the more she is made to look as though she were already dying. Her life is not worth living because the film portrays it that way.

The assumption that killing a person with a disability is an act of kindness is far easier to make when the person is isolated from ordinary life, confined to a bed in a nursing home with no outside stimulation or even any intrusion at all from the outside world. Physical abuse is a fact of life in institutional settings where persons with disabilities are locked away from society. As noted above, until quite recently persons with developmental disabilities typically lived in isolated, large institutions. Judge Frank Johnson described how in Alabama at one such state school:

[O]ne resident was scalded to death when a fellow resident hosed water from one of the bath facilities on him; another died as a result of the insertion of a running water hose into his rectum by a working resident who was cleaning him; one died when soapy water was forced into his mouth; another died of a self-administered overdose of inadequately stored drugs; and authorities restrained another resident in a straitjacket for *nine years* to prevent him from sucking his hands and fingers.[72]

Numerous other sources make the same connection between separating people with disabilities from society and harming them: "In the hospitals, you get abused."[73] Isolation dehumanizes, and those who are not considered human are apt targets for mistreatment.

Doris Zames Fleisher and Frieda Zames suggest that *Million Dollar Baby* (as well as the 2004 Spanish picture *The Sea Inside,* about the efforts of a writer with quadriplegia to obtain assisted suicide) reflects an unacknowledged impulse "to make them go away."[74] Fleisher and Zames link the perspective of *Million Dollar Baby* to that of the old Chicago ordinance requiring persons with physically unattractive conditions to stay off the streets and with Mary Johnson's description of the resistance to disability rights (led by Clint Eastwood, among others) as part of the reality that many people without disabilities "see people with disabilities as having something wrong with them, needing cure or charitable help, or as sly malcontents."[75] When people with disabilities are relegated to the role of objects rather than subjects, when, to quote activist Stephen Drake, "we have been unable to establish ourselves as the experts on issues affecting our own lives," disability harassment may take its ultimate form: killing.[76]

3

Comparisons to Race and Sex Harassment

This chapter will develop the dominant approach of the courts and some other authorities to disability harassment issues, particularly to disability harassment in the workplace. The conventional approach compares disability harassment to that based on race and sex and argues for liability when a hostile environment exists. The chapter will criticize that way of addressing the problem, particularly its exclusive reliance on the comparison of title VII of the Civil Rights Act to the ADA. The usual application of a test derived from title VII sex and race harassment cases leaves unaddressed tremendous amounts of conduct effectively excluding persons with disabilities from work, social, and educational opportunities. That test demands that harassment be severe or pervasive under unrealistically extreme standards of comparison. Thus conduct continues with impunity even though it has the overwhelming effect of imposing stigma, establishing stereotypes, and enforcing subordination. This chapter will trace the use of title VII standards in employment cases, noting some of the existing criticism of their use in ADA cases. It will also consider the use of a similar standard in education cases. Although in recent years the courts have been more willing to impose liability under a title VII harassment standard in education than in employment disputes, the overall record of the courts is extremely disappointing to anyone who wants to see the pervasive exclusion of persons with disabilities corrected.

Employment

In a series of cases in the 1980s and early 1990s, the Supreme Court established that a hostile work environment could constitute race or sex discrimination under title VII of the Civil Rights Act of 1964.[1] An employer that maintains an environment where workers are subjected to abuse on the basis of race or sex discriminates with regard to the terms and conditions of employment. Unlike "quid pro quo" sexual harassment, in which the employee must submit to sexual demands to maintain employment or obtain promotion, and courts require claimants to show some economic effect from the conduct, an alteration of the conditions of employment is sufficient to establish the hostile-environment claim. The Court stressed that not all conduct that might be described as harassment affects a term or condition of employment: "For sexual harassment to be actionable, it must be sufficiently severe or pervasive 'to alter the conditions of [the victim's] employment and create an abusive working environment.'"[2] Nevertheless, the working conditions need not seriously affect an employee's psychological well-being or lead the employee to suffer injury; "[s]o long as the environment would reasonably be perceived, and is perceived, as hostile or abusive . . . , there is no need for it also to be psychologically injurious."[3]

After passage of the ADA, workers with disabilities began to bring hostile-environment claims premised on the analogy between the ADA and title VII. If a racially or sexually hostile workplace sufficiently altered the terms and conditions of employment as to violate title VII and call for a judicial remedy, then a workplace affected by hostility to persons with disabilities would violate the ADA's prohibition on discrimination with regard to the "terms, conditions, and privileges of employment."[4]

Some lawsuits met with success, notably the case of Neil Haysman described in chapter 1. In *Haysman v. Food Lion, Inc.*, the court found that the facts of the case satisfied the elements of the hostile-environment claim under the ADA.[5] As noted in chapter 1, the plaintiff was a store employee who injured his back and knee on the job; the injury exacerbated a preexisting emotional impairment. He alleged that about ten months after he returned to work in an easier position with a part-time schedule, the store's manager and assistant manager started harassing him. The manager verbally abused him in front of the other employees, accusing him of exaggerating his conditions. The assistant manager said he would "ride" him until he quit,[6] abused him with profanity, and struck and kicked him on the injured parts of his body. His managers switched his shift to night without any good reason.

The court ruled that a jury could reasonably "construe any or all of this behavior as hostile, intimidating or threatening" and that it was "severe and pervasive enough to create an objectively hostile work environment. . . ."[7] The absence of offensive epithets related to disability did not undermine the conclusion that the mistreatment was based on the disability:

> The fact that there are no allegations that Haysman was called slurs such as "cripple" . . . is not dispositive. [A] jury could infer that Food Lion personnel engaged in negative stereotyping of the disabled as people who overstate complaints, do not want to work, and "milk" or "snowball" their employers for benefits. A jury could find that [the manager and assistant manager] acted on this stereotype in deciding to "ride" Haysman until he quit. Based on this possible inference, a reasonable jury could find that Haysman was harassed because of his disability.[8]

The court noted that an employer does not have to keep an employee who is not able to perform the essential functions of the job with reasonable accommodation; nevertheless, if that is the case it should terminate the employee rather than engage in harassment to force a resignation:

> Assuming that Haysman's absences and alleged complaints were the legitimate and direct result of a disability, Food Lion was free to fire Haysman if those problems prevented him from performing (with or without reasonable accommodation) the essential functions of the light duty position. However, if the necessary and foreseeable consequences of Haysman's disabilities did not disqualify him from the job, then Food Lion is not free to harass Haysman in an attempt to get him to quit, solely because of those consequences. If the individual is "qualified" despite his disability and its consequences, then the employer must attempt to accommodate the individual's disability, not harass him because of it.[9]

The *Haysman* court quoted the language the ADA shared with title VII forbidding discrimination in the terms, conditions, or privileges of employment, cited the title VII precedent, concluded that an ADA cause of action existed, and found the claim applicable to the facts alleged.[10] Other district court decisions reached the same conclusion on similar reasoning, permitting disability harassment claims to proceed to trial or entering judgment in the plaintiff's favor.[11] The title VII analogy was the obvious comparison to be made, and courts have drawn it.

A few years passed, but eventually courts of appeals issued similar decisions. *Fox v. General Motors* was described briefly in chapter 1.[12] As noted there, Fox was an automobile assembly plant worker who sustained a series of back injuries and returned from disability leave with a medical restriction to light-duty work. Although his immediate supervisor tried to adapt Fox's job duties to meet his medical restrictions, a different supervisor and the foreman blocked these efforts at accommodation and humiliated Fox when he refused to violate his physical restrictions. They placed him at a special work table that was too low for him and exacerbated his back injury. He was prevented from obtaining a promotion, and the supervisor and co-workers subjected Fox and other workers with disabilities to a continual barrage of profane abuse and insults relating to their disabilities. The supervisor told other employees not to talk to Fox and the other workers who had disabilities, so the co-workers shunned them. Fox introduced expert testimony in support of his claim of emotional damages that included severe depression, anxiety, and suicidal thoughts. The jury returned a verdict of $200,000 compensatory damages against General Motors for Fox's emotional injury and other harms.[13] The court of appeals ruled that a reasonable jury could find the harassment severe or pervasive enough to create a hostile work environment.[14]

The case of Sandra Flowers, also discussed in chapter 1, was followed swiftly by the *Fox* case. In *Flowers v. Southern Regional Physician Services,* the Fifth Circuit Court of Appeals affirmed the entry of judgment on a jury verdict in favor of an employee who had been diagnosed with HIV infection.[15] As chapter 1 explained, after her supervisor found out about the infection, the supervisor stopped going to lunch with her and socializing with her. Instead, the supervisor took to eavesdropping on her. The employer's president refused to shake her hand and avoided her at the office. She was subjected to four drug tests in a week, written up twice and placed on probation, called names, and subjected to other humiliations; eventually, the company fired her.[16] The court of appeals ruled that an ADA cause of action applies when an employee is harassed on the basis of disability. It found the evidence sufficient to support the jury's verdict in favor of the plaintiff.[17]

Both *Fox* and *Flowers* relied explicitly on the comparison to title VII claims for sex and race harassment. *Fox* noted that the ADA bars discrimination regarding terms, conditions, and privileges of employment, just as title VII does; the court stressed that Congress enacted the ADA after the

Supreme Court had held that harassment violates similar language found in title VII.[18] In a similar vein, after citing the statutory language shared by title VII and the ADA and listing the title VII precedent establishing a cause of action for harassment, the *Flowers* court said, "We conclude that the language of Title VII and the ADA dictates a consistent reading of the two statutes."[19] The consistency in purposes and remedial structures of the two statutes reinforced the court's confidence that the ADA provides a damages claim for workplace harassment.[20] In fact, courts have uniformly concluded that the ADA furnishes a cause of action to remedy a work environment that is hostile to persons with disabilities.[21]

The *Fox* and *Flowers* approach has been widely applied. Since those cases came down, a court has upheld a damages judgment for a deaf worker in a case involving name-calling, refusal to communicate, and failure to provide interpreter services as an accommodation.[22] Applying *Fox,* a court denied summary judgment to the employer in the case of a stereo installer with sickle-cell anemia whose supervisor routinely disparaged him, among other things referring to him as "hoppy" and "crip" to his face and before other employees; the worker complained to the personnel manager at least five times, but there was no effective response and ultimately the worker was terminated.[23] Another court denied summary judgment to the employer when the plaintiff, a computer systems administrator who was blind, alleged that the head of the data center, whenever he came in contact with him, would make derogatory comments concerning his blindness, such as "Why don't you have your monitor on?" "[Your] hair is a mess. Didn't you look in the mirror?" and "Can't you look that up faster, what is the problem?"[24] Still another court denied the employer's motion for summary judgment on a hostile-environment claim when the plaintiff, a grinder and tinsmith who had a perceived intellectual disability, alleged that supervisors and co-workers called him names such as "dumb," "stupid," "loser," and worse, with the co-workers adding physical abuse such as striking him with painters' sticks and pipes, knocking him down and kicking him, and taunting him with obscene and humiliating pictures.[25] In the case of a financial analyst with reduced vision, short-term memory loss, and distractibility due to heart failure and a stroke, a court denied the employer's summary judgment motion on the basis of the employee's claims that reasonable-accommodation requests were delayed and denied, training requests were refused without adequate explanation, and various disparaging comments were made by supervisors, such as allegations that the plaintiff was faking the impairment.[26] An additional court denied a motion to dismiss a case in which a painter who experienced smoke-induced asthma attacks claimed a hostile environment when the employer did nothing when co-workers and supervisors smoked near him and when his supervisors responded to his complaints about refusal to enforce the employer's antismoking policies by chastising him, verbally harassing him, and telling him to find another job or retire.[27]

These many courts are quite correct in concluding that the ADA provides an action for the maintenance of an environment that is hostile to people with disabilities. The ADA antidiscrimination provisions were drafted with language similar to the language in title VII that had authoritatively been construed to include hostile-environment causes of action. Nevertheless, whether the contours of the action are precisely the same in the ADA and title VII situations is less clear. Some recent scholarship has questioned the analogy of disability harassment to race and sex harassment and the wholesale importation of title VII's criteria for which cases are covered by the prohibition on discrimination found in the ADA. The argument does not dispute that disability harassment ought to be actionable. Rather, it raises the question of when disability harassment should be actionable and if the standards should be as restrictive as those the courts have developed for title VII cases.

Lisa Eichhorn has observed that the cause of action for disability harassment is not precisely analogous to a Civil Rights Act title VII claim for sex or race harassment.[28] Title VII is premised on formal equality. The employer must treat all races and both sexes equally. The ADA departs significantly from reliance on formal equality ideas, moving toward a more functional equality that requires different treatment for persons whose situations are relevantly different due to the environmental and attitudinal barriers to full integration for people who have disabilities. Eichhorn argues that employers may create hostile environments for purposes of the ADA simply by failing to make needed accommodations, a state of affairs that has no clear analogue in title VII. She further develops a number of more specific considerations in the application of a disability harassment cause of action: (1) the need to recognize that hostile and condescending attitudes toward people with physical and mental conditions may cause an individual to be regarded as a person with a disability, thus placing that person within the protected class; (2) the validity of the observation that refusals of accommodations, particularly when linked with other conduct on the part of the employer, may create a hostile environment; (3) the importance of considering the unique perspective of the individual with a disability in applying the reasonable-person standard for what constitutes harassment; and (4) the need to adapt causation ideas to the reality that disability may be a result of social constructs.

The first insight strengthens the cases of those harassment plaintiffs who have lost because courts did not deem them to be individuals with disabilities under the restrictive definition that courts have given that term.[29] In one notable case, a war veteran with post-traumatic stress disorder was harassed by co-workers who would make loud noises and then laugh when he hid under furniture.[30] The court threw the case out before trial, concluding that the plaintiff's mental condition did not establish him as a person with a disability. The fact of the harassment itself, however, demonstrated that the plaintiff was regarded as a person with a disability, and the court should have recognized this. By contrast, in the case described above regarding the grinder and tinsmith with some diminished mental functioning, the court used the repeated disparaging characterizations of his mental abilities as support for the proposition that he was regarded as disabled.[31] Eichhorn's second insight, about denial of accommodations creating a hostile environment, might seem correct but unnecessary for the success of an ADA claim. After all, denial of a reasonable accommodation is itself a violation of the Act. Nevertheless, there are many cases in which employers refuse to make seemingly reasonable accommodations and the courts find no violation, reasoning that the employers have done enough with the accommodations they have already provided.[32] There may be reason to reexamine those cases as ones in which the gist of the violation is the creation of a workplace setting hostile to the employment of people with disabilities, not simply the denial of reasonable accommodations. The case cited above in which denial of accommodations provided support for the case of the financial analyst with the poststroke visual and mental condition is an example of the approach Eichhorn would support.[33]

The additional insights that a person with a disability has a unique perspective that affects what ought to be considered reasonable reactions to harassment and that social constructs are contributing causes to hostile working conditions relate closely to the observations made in chapter 2 that society imposes isolation and segregation upon people with disabilities. Although persons of nondominant racial groups and women certainly experience isolation and segregation from the mainstream, the degree of separation imposed on persons with disabilities marks a qualitative difference. Persons with disabilities are sent away to separate schools when children and are frequently locked away in institutions when adults. It is not just that they typically have a more limited range of job opportunities than the dominant group or are kept down by glass ceilings. They are not in the workforce at all, and when working they are often in sheltered or other isolated settings. The harassment they face pushes them further into isolation and is bred by the isolation itself in a never-ending cycle. Thus what is severe harassment of a person with disability should be evaluated with a lower threshold than in other cases. In a similar vein, an earlier work by Frank Ravitch proposes asking whether "a reasonable person with the same disability would consider [the abusive conduct] sufficiently severe or pervasive to alter the terms, conditions, or privileges of employment. . . ."[34] Like Eichhorn's ideas, an approach based on this standard would individualize the inquiry and yield liability in a somewhat greater number of cases than is the case under existing standards.

Eichhorn's ideas and these additional questions about the application of title VII standards to disability harassment gain salience from the fact that so many hostile-environment actions brought by persons with disabilities fail. Most often, courts do not consider the mistreatment to which the plaintiffs were subjected to be sufficiently severe or pervasive to satisfy the standards of title VII, and hence of the ADA. In an overwhelming number of instances, courts have granted employers' summary judgment or dismissal motions, usually ruling that the harassment was not sufficiently severe or pervasive under standards established by the title VII sex and race harassment case law.[35]

Silk v. City of Chicago exemplifies the cases in which the plaintiff fails to establish liability.[36] William Silk was a police sergeant who suffered from severe sleep apnea, a disorder in which breathing is interrupted during sleep.[37] Rotating shifts and night work exacerbate the disorder. He requested and obtained an accommodation by which he worked only the day shift.[38] After he had obtained the accommodation, other sergeants and lieutenants in the district openly criticized Silk and treated him with hostility; a sergeant threatened him with injury (an apology followed). Silk's performance ratings declined, though not significantly. He was disciplined for teaching a class one night a week for ninety minutes, on the ground that working anything but a day shift was inconsistent with his disability-related work restrictions. He was denied the opportunity to act as lieutenant when no lieutenant was on duty and was subjected to various other administrative restrictions.

After affirming summary judgment on Silk's claim of retaliation, the court assumed that the ADA encompasses a disability harassment cause of action for a hostile environment. It drew the analogy to title VII but, citing title VII cases, declared that the plaintiff had to demonstrate that the workplace was "permeated with discriminatory conduct—intimidation, ridicule, insult—that is sufficiently severe or pervasive as to alter the conditions of employment."[39] Considering the various items of harassment other than the verbal abuse and physical threats, the court said that the conduct was insignificant or not related to any harassing or retaliatory motivation. Looking at the verbal abuse and physical threats, the court took the position that for each bit of conduct either Silk failed to take advantage of internal procedures to remedy the problems or the problems were in fact remedied, as with the apology for the threat by the other sergeant Evaluating the conduct as a whole, the court concluded that Silk could still do his job "without impediment" and that the workplace was not permeated with discrimination.[40] Hence summary judgment was affirmed.

Other cases include one in which a supervisor called a physically impaired worker on light duty "lazy," "crippled," and "worthless" in front of other workers, and the worker with a disability was asked by co-workers "Where is your dress?";[41] in which co-workers, with the supervisors' knowledge, routinely ridiculed and made fun of the speech of an employee with a severe developmental speech disorder;[42] in which a worker with mild mental retardation was referred to as "Rick Retardo" and taunted as ignorant;[43] and in which the supervisor of an employee with a jaw joint disorder who was recovering from multiple surgeries excluded her from business meetings, transferred work away from her, and refused to acknowledge her presence when she was with him.[44] In still another case, a worker with a metal plate in his head lost his harassment case despite being branded with the name "platehead" after improper disclosure of the information.[45] The courts require that the hostile environment be so severe or pervasive that the terms of employment are altered; then they go on to require discrimination that permeates the workplace. Some plaintiffs succeed in getting their harassment claims to trial, but they are the exceptions, not the rule.

It is not that *Silk* and the cases like it misapplied the title VII harassment standard, that the harassment in fact would have been deemed severe or pervasive if the same conduct had been visited on a member of a racial minority group or a woman on account of that person's status. The interpretation of the harassment standard in *Silk* is not out of line with the courts' decisions in the title VII sex and race harassment cases from which the standard is drawn. For example, in *Johnson v. Cambridge Industries,* a race harassment case, the court granted summary judgment for the defendant even though the plaintiff, an African American, established that two co-workers referred to him with a racial epithet (although one of the two was disciplined and the other left the employer for independent reasons); that a supervisor threatened him with firing; that he was ordered to get back to work while still on break; and that he was assigned heavier tasks than white employees were.[46] The court relied on the *Silk* case for the proposition that the incidents had to be sufficiently severe to alter the terms and conditions of employment and found that they fell "well below the threshold of what the law regards as hostile environment harassment."[47]

Johnson is typical. Large numbers of title VII race and sex harassment claims founder on the severe-or-pervasive standard.[48] The conventional interpretation of the law is that harassment is actionable conduct only when it works an alteration in the terms or conditions of employment. The conventional interpretation of an alteration in the terms and conditions of employment is that it occurs only when the harassing conduct is exceedingly pervasive or severe. By establishing this conventional approach, the Supreme Court has set a high bar—in most cases an impossibly high bar—for the definition of a hostile environment, and lower courts have, if anything, elevated it still further.[49] The Court's statement that a hostile-environment claim exists "[w]hen the workplace is permeated with discriminatory intimidation, ridicule, and insult"[50] is almost universally taken, not as a description of what may constitute harassment, but as the minimum standard, effectively the floor, for a determination that actionable harassment occurred.[51] It might be possible to rewrite the hostile-environment standard for disability cases to make it more sensitive to the precise condition of the person with a disability asserting the claim.[52] Nevertheless, the title VII analogy creates inherent limits on which claims will succeed.

Education

Title VII is applicable only to employment, so courts acting outside that field are less prone to look to title VII as a source of analogies. Nevertheless, courts dealing with cases in which plaintiffs allege disability harassment in education have recognized a hostile-environment cause of action, drawing comparison to cases alleging discrimination on the basis of race or sex in federally assisted educational activities under title VI of the Civil Rights Act (which forbids discrimination on the basis of race and national origin by federal grantees) and on the basis of sex in federally assisted education under title IX of the Education Amendments of 1972 (which forbids sex discrimination by entities receiving federal education money). Those laws have been authoritatively construed to create causes of action for the imposition of a racially or sexually hostile environment. Courts have responded to claims of disability harassment under the ADA or section 504 of the Rehabilitation Act by asking whether they are comparable to the sex and race claims that have received judicial relief.

A leading example is *Guckenberger v. Boston University*.[53] In that case, students at the university sued the school and three of its administrators, alleging that policies for providing learning disabilities accommodations violated the ADA and that the policies, together with other actions by the university president, created a hostile learning environment. The policies included a requirement that all testing in the documentation of the learning disability be not more than three years old and be performed by a licensed physician or psychologist; new procedures for handling accommodations requests that included personal decision making by the university president; and a ban on course substitutions for mathematics and foreign languages. The president's conduct included denying twenty-six of twenty-seven student requests for accommodation during one school year, as well as making two major speeches and various media comments in which he referred to students with disabilities as a "plague" and the sign of "a silent genetic catastrophe." His assistant referred to students with learning disabilities as "draft dodgers."[54]

The court upheld claims for disability discrimination based on some of the policies,[55] but it dismissed the claim that the actions of the university and its administrators constituted disability harassment by creating a hostile educational environment. The court focused on the university president's speeches and declared, "Although these comments, viewed objectively, may certainly be offensive to learning-disabled students . . . , they are not physically threatening or humiliating" and were not of the kind courts in employment cases had found sufficient "to establish severe and pervasive harassment that alters a plaintiff's working conditions."[56] Notably, the court transmuted the "severe *or* pervasive" requirement to "severe *and* pervasive." It conceded that a lower standard than that for the workplace might properly apply to educational settings, but it concluded without further discussion that any such standard was not met. The court further said that imposing liability for a university president's speeches would "have serious First Amendment implications," though it did not develop the point beyond citing another case involving speeches of a Boston University president and a Red Scare–era Supreme Court case refusing to penalize a university professor who was a socialist.[57] Additional higher education cases have failed because of failure to meet the title VII severe-or-pervasive standard.[58]

Nevertheless, some ADA hostile educational environment actions have achieved success, notably some cases brought by elementary and secondary school children with disabilities that have managed to surmount the various procedural hurdles; these will be discussed in chapter 5. One case in which a federal court of appeals upheld a hostile-environment claim is *M.P. v. Independent School District No. 721,* involving an eighth grader with schizophrenia who experienced relentless harassment by peers after the school district's health paraprofessional disclosed his condition to the school community.[59] The child's mother repeatedly called to complain to the school social worker and the principal about the disclosure and subsequent abuse, but no action was taken from January until the end of the following summer, when the child was placed in an out-of-district school. According to the judicial opinion, the child, given the pseudonym M.P.,

> . . . was called "druggie," "fag," "psycho," "weirdo, " "mental kid," "special," "squealer," and "idiot," among other names. Students also shoved M.P.'s head into the drinking fountain, picked him up by the throat, slammed him into lockers, threw him to the floor, shoved, scratched, spat on, and cut him. M.P. never had experienced this treatment by classmates before [the] disclosure of his medical information.[60]

The stigma of a mental health disability was thus so extreme that it led to oppressive and violent actions that the school did nothing to remedy. In fact, the school abetted in the effort at exclusion by taking no steps to stop the harassment and agreeing only to exclude the child from the school community. The alternatives it offered M.P. during the meeting that took place at the end of the summer included having M.P. arrive late for school and leave early, attend school only half the day, or attend an alternative learning center for children with emotional disorders. The court overturned a district court decision granting summary judgment in favor of the school district, holding that the school district could be found to have violated section 504. The court applied a standard that requires "bad faith or gross misjudgment" to support a claim for damages under section 504. It found that the standard could be met on the basis of the repeated failure to return phone calls from the mother regarding her son's safety, the ultimate response of the district to propose shortening M.P.'s school day or send him to another school, and the failure to honor a promise to cover the cost of transportation to the new school district. Whether the original disclosure of information was actionable "is irrelevant if it can be shown that the District acted in bad faith or with gross misjudgment when it failed to take appropriate action to protect M.P.'s academic and safety interests after the disclosure, pursuant to the Rehabilitation Act."[61]

In two additional recent cases, courts found that students could proceed with section 504 and ADA claims based on hostile educational environments. In *K.M. v. Hyde Park Central School District*,[62] the court denied a motion for summary judgment in favor of the school district when a child of normal intelligence who had pervasive developmental disorder and dyslexia put forward evidence that during his seventh- and eighth-grade school years he was repeatedly "called 'stupid,' 'idiot,' 'retard,' and other disability-related insulting names and subjected to physical aggression and intimidation by other students at school and on the school bus. The court summarized the allegations concerning the child, identified as "D.G.":

(1) D.G. was "thrown to the ground," "body slammed" and taunted by several students during lunch one day . . . until an aide intervened and took D.G. to the school nurse; (2) D.G. was physically beaten by two boys—held down and hit on the head and back with his own binder—between classes in his special education teacher's resource room . . . ; (3) D.G. was subjected to "disability-related slurs," and his school books were thrown into the garbage in the cafeteria on five to eight separate occasions . . . resulting in his special education teacher's offering to eat

lunch with D.G. in a separate room for the remainder of the . . . school year; (4) an unidentified student called D.G. a "retard" and started a fist fight on an afternoon bus ride . . . ; (5) an unidentified student took D.G.'s planner . . . ; (6) two students repeatedly taunted and hit D.G. on an afternoon bus ride . . . , after which D.G. returned home upset, "locked himself in the bathroom, cried, and yelled 'I can't stand this anymore,'" and then bolted from the house.[63]

According to the parent's evidence, she or D.G. reported the incidents and the school district did not take any effective action to stop the harassment, apart from ultimately telling her to keep D.G. out of school. D.G. developed depression and suicidal ideation.

The court held that the school district and its administrators would be liable under section 504 and the ADA if they were deliberately indifferent to "pervasive, severe disability-based harassment that effectively deprived a disabled student of access to the school's resources and opportunities . . . ," a standard that these facts would meet.[64] The court made a special point that the social isolation created by the harassment and the school administrators' failure to stop it is precisely what the ADA targets. Citing the Supreme Court's decision in a case finding unjustified institutionalization of persons with disabilities to be a violation of the ADA, the court said that simply being forced to eat lunch alone for fear of one's safety deprives a student of "an integral part of the public school experience."[65] The court further found that a school administrator could not claim immunity from personal liability on the ground that the rights of the child were not clearly established; the court found the relevant right under the ADA to be well established on the basis of the Supreme Court's declaration that a similar right exists for students to protection from peer sex harassment.

Scruggs v. Meriden Board of Education denied a motion to dismiss a claim against a school district based on the district's failure to respond when a middle school student with a learning disability was bullied as a result of his disability.[66] He was "punched, kicked, had desks slammed into him, and had his hair pulled so violently that his head snapped back."[67] After he missed thirty-seven days of school in sixth grade, he was placed in class with, and seated just in front of, a student who had assaulted the child's mother the year before. The bullying and harassment led to still more absenteeism. The child ultimately committed suicide. The court held that the allegations about the school district's acts and omissions were sufficient to constitute bad faith or gross misjudgment and created "an abusive educational environment" in violation of section 504 and the ADA.[68] An earlier successful case is the Fourth Circuit Court of Appeals' 1999 decision *Baird v. Rose,* in which the court overturned dismissal of the ADA claim brought by a child with depression who was humiliated in class by a teacher who removed her from a musical performance and then blamed her in front of the class for causing other students to be dropped from the performance on the basis of an attendance policy that the teacher had wanted to apply to her alone.[69]

The elementary and secondary cases draw support from two Supreme Court decisions in sex harassment claims brought by children in public schools. In the well-known 1998 case *Gebser v. Lago Vista Independent School District,* the Court ruled that a school system will be liable in damages for the known acts of sexual harassment of a student by a teacher if the district manifests deliberate indifference to the activity.[70] The following year, the Court held in *Davis v. Monroe County Board of Education* that a school district will be liable if it is deliberately indifferent to known acts of peer sexual harassment.[71] Deliberate indifference will be found when the school's actions or omissions in response to the harassment are clearly unreasonable in light of known circumstances.[72] The statute under which these cases were decided, title IX of the Education Amendments of 1972, carries wording that bars sex discrimination that is exactly parallel to the wording of section 504 barring disability discrimination. Hence it is no surprise that courts would be likely to find disability harassment actionable under circumstances similar to those identified as actionable in cases of sex discrimination under title IX.[73] More importantly, the activity of the Court in upholding a federal remedy for both teacher and peer sex harassment in elementary and secondary settings sends a signal that harassment of public school students should be taken seriously. Perhaps that lesson has begun to carry over into the context of harassment of students with disabilities.

If it is correct that the recent trend in the case law is more favorably disposed to claims of disability harassment under the ADA and section 504 brought by public school children than to claims either of university students or of individuals in the workforce, there may be reasons beyond the prominence of the two Supreme Court school sex harassment cases. In line with the ideas developed in chapters 1 and 2, perhaps the courts are more willing to accept the idea that children with disabilities belong in school, that it is part of the natural order of things for them to be there and that exclusion from the grade school or high school environment is illegitimate. Acceptance of that idea stops when the environment is higher education or the workplace, where people with disabilities have not broken through the barrier and for which judges, like others, are victims of the stereotype that people with disabilities, particularly those with mental disabilities, simply do not belong.

This distinction may say something about the influence of law over time. Congress established the guarantee for appropriate education of elementary and secondary school children with disabilities in 1975, and the law applies to all children with disabilities, not merely those who meet a test of "qualified person with a disability." The public schools have to serve every child who asks for services. Although legal obligations to serve persons with disabilities have applied to higher education since the 1970s, the "qualified" screen applies, and a person does not obtain appropriate higher educational services simply by showing up. In the first higher education case the Supreme Court decided, it declared that a qualified person "is one who is able to meet all of a[n educational] program's requirements in spite of his handicap." In private employment, the legal protections date only from the 1990s, and the idea of obtaining a position as a matter of right is wholly foreign. It is conceivable that attitudes toward persons with disabilities in higher education and at work will change over time, but it seems likely that more than law will be needed.

The higher level of judicial protection from harassment for elementary and secondary school children than for adults in school or work may also be due to a somewhat less benign set of attitudes toward persons with disabilities. Children with disabilities, particularly younger children, may inspire sympathy as victims who need the courts to protect them because they cannot help themselves. Of course, children and adults use the courts system as part of the means to protect themselves and their interests; they ask not for sympathy but for justice.[74] Nevertheless, though the poster-child image reinforces stereotypes of helplessness, it is likely to work in favor of some younger disability harassment claimants when they seek judicial relief.

There are many elementary and secondary school harassment cases for which the courts have denied that the conduct could be found to be a violation of section 504 and the ADA. For example, in *Biggs v. Board of Education,* the court refused to permit the claim of a child with epilepsy to go to trial when the student alleged that during seventh grade she had repeatedly been taunted on the basis of her history of seizures and her physical appearance.[75] Her classmates called her "ugly dog," "seizure girl," and other names, and told her, "Go have a seizure, ugly dog."[76] Because the school district made some response, meeting with the students accused of the harassment and notifying their parents, the court found that the deliberate indifference standard could not be met, despite the absence of any indication whether the students were subject to disciplinary sanctions beyond the meetings and despite the plaintiff's allegations that the harassment continued until the point where she withdrew from school. In *Waechter v. School District No. 14–030,* a recess supervisor forced a child that the school knew had a heart defect to run a 350-yard sprint as a punishment for misbehavior in class. The child died from cardiac arrest.[77] The court dismissed a section 504 damages claim, declaring relief unavailable. There also are a number of cases that failed at the trial level and succeeded only because the plaintiffs lodged an appeal.[78]

Moreover, as will be developed in chapter 6, large numbers of elementary and secondary school harassment cases are dismissed for reasons other than the restrictive attitudes of the courts with regard to what harassing conduct constitutes a violation of the ADA and section 504. For example, many cases lose on grounds of failure to exhaust administrative remedies under the special education laws, even when no one is raising a claim under the special education laws. The situation is sometimes eased by the fact that there may also be additional avenues of relief, such as those under the Individuals with Disabilities Education Act (IDEA) and the Constitution, that may help stop harassment.[79] The point remains, however, that under current interpretations the ADA or section 504 claim for hostile environment is frequently inadequate to deal with the harassment that children with disabilities must face at school, even though the courts appear somewhat more willing to accept the reality of hostile environments in elementary and secondary school than in universities or workplaces. The inadequacy of current legal doctrine in all these various settings highlights the need for a new approach.

4

A New Approach to Legal Claims for Harassment in the Workplace and Other Settings

Although courts have failed to notice it, there is an antiharassment provision in the ADA that title VII lacks. The ADA includes language comparable to that of title VII banning discrimination, and it contains a title VII–style ban against retaliation for opposing an unlawful practice and for making a charge, testifying, assisting, or participating in an investigation, proceeding, or hearing. But the ADA also includes this provision, section 12203(b) of title 42: "It shall be unlawful to coerce, intimidate, threaten, or interfere with any individual in the exercise or enjoyment of, or on account of his or her having exercised or enjoyed, or on account of his or her having aided or encouraged any other individual in the exercise or enjoyment of, any right granted or protected by this chapter."[1] Courts evaluating harassment claims have ignored this language. They have asserted instead that the ADA, like title VII, lacks any explicit prohibition on harassment and that the prohibition must be found, if anywhere, in the banning of discrimination in the terms, conditions, and privileges of employment. The courts are correct for title VII. They are wrong with regard to the ADA.

The analogy to what constitutes hostile-environment discrimination under title VII should not control the interpretation of section 12203(b). Interference, coercion, and intimidation can take place when there is no discrimination as defined by title VII. The conduct forbidden by section 12203(b) is not the alteration of terms and conditions of employment. Instead, it is interference with doing one's job, coercion against showing up, intimidation from acting the same as any employee who has the same right to be in the workplace as anyone. In *Harris v. Forklift Systems, Inc.*, the

Supreme Court established that the purpose of the title VII test of severity or pervasiveness is to screen out conduct that fails to alter the terms and conditions of employment.[2] *Faragher v. City of Boca Raton* stated the point directly: "[S]imple teasing . . . offhand comments, and isolated incidents (unless extremely serious) will not amount to discriminatory changes in the 'terms and conditions of employment.' . . . We have made it clear that conduct must be extreme to amount to a change in the terms and conditions of employment."[3] By contrast, coercion, intimidation, threats, and interference are not necessarily considered subsets of discrimination and do not always imply a change in the terms or conditions of employment. If they did, a separate provision listing them would be unnecessary. They are more akin to retaliation, which itself is different from discrimination if discrimination is defined as an alteration of terms or conditions of employment based on the status of race, sex, or disability.

Even so, the provision banning coercion, intimidation, threats, and interference does not duplicate the ban on retaliation. The coercion, intimidation, threats, and interference provision follows the ADA's ban on retaliation, found in section 12203(a), which reads: "No person shall discriminate against any individual because such individual has opposed any act or practice made unlawful by this chapter or because such individual made a charge, testified, assisted, or participated in any manner in an investigation, proceeding, or hearing under this chapter." The existence of a separate provision prohibiting interference, coercion, and intimidation demonstrates that Congress meant to do more than create a second, redundant ban on retaliation. The ordinary rule of statutory construction is that courts must read statutes so that each term has a meaning and no portion is superfluous.[4] Frequently, courts have lumped subsections (a) and (b) together, ignoring the difference in language and coverage.[5] But retaliation differs from coercion, intimidation, threats, and interference. To the extent that retaliation comes into play at all with regard to section 12203(b), it is retaliation for exercising any rights at all under the ADA. Those rights include taking a job on a nondiscriminatory basis, coming to work, and participating in the daily activities of the workplace, precisely what harassment penalizes.

In fact, verbal abuse and physical harassment are highly effective tools of coercion and intimidation against individuals with disabilities who dare to integrate the workplace. The threats of violence, actual hostility, lowered performance ratings, denied supervisory opportunities, and petty humiliations visited on the police officer in the *Silk* case interfered with his right to work subject to a reasonable accommodation, and they had a coercive effect of pushing him off the police force.[6] A threat of violence is of course a "threat" and meets a dictionary definition of intimidation.[7] Similarly, in other cases that were dismissed for failure to meet the severity-or-pervasiveness screen, supervisory conduct such as calling a worker with a physical disability "lazy," "crippled," and "worthless" in front of other workers,[8] allowing co-workers to engage in daily ridicule of an employee with a severe speech disorder,[9] and excluding a worker who was recovering from medical treatment for her disability from business meetings, transferring work away from her, and refusing to acknowledge her presence[10] all interfered with the exercise of the right to participate in the workforce while having a disability. The conduct intimidated the employees from obtaining accommodations and working while accommodated. The supervisors, acting as agents of the employers, coerced the employees to leave their jobs and in most instances were effective in doing so.

Two components of section 12203(b) distinguish it from the (a) provision, which is identical with antiretaliation language found in title VII: the (b) provision forbids a broader range of conduct than the retaliation section does, and it covers a wider range of motivations than retaliation for opposition to discrimination and participation in proceedings. These two distinctions from the retaliation provision in turn establish a basis for distinguishing interference, coercion, and intimidation from the discrimination in terms or conditions of employment—that is, severe or pervasive hostile-environment harassment—that title VII forbids.

Liability under section 12203(a), the retaliation provision, hinges on the plaintiff's having opposed an act or practice that violates the ADA or having made a charge, testified, or participated in an investigation, hearing, or proceeding. Liability under section 12203(b) requires only that the plaintiff exercise or enjoy, or aid or encourage any other individual to exercise or enjoy, any right granted or protected by the ADA. Those rights, such as taking a job on a equal basis, working every day the same way that others work, and participating as an equal in the workplace, are what subsection (b) protects.[11] Co-worker and supervisor conduct that harasses—under a common sense, not a Supreme Court definition of that word—interferes with those rights. It coerces workers with disabilities to give up their entitlements under the ADA and go home. In other words, a worker exercises ADA rights at work simply by being there and undergoes coercion and intimidation if harassed while doing so.

It is the right of being there that is the most important right the ADA establishes. The second of the nine findings in the preamble to the ADA states that "historically, society has tended to isolate and segregate individuals with disabilities, and, despite some improvements, such forms of discrimination against individuals with disabilities continue to be a severe and pervasive problem."[12] The isolation, the segregation, the invisibility of people with disabilities kept hidden in institutions all manifest and continually reinforce the attitudes of hostility and fear that motivate discrimination. The ADA's goal is to promote integration and to dash attitudes of hostility and fear against the reality of day-to-day contact.[13] Left unregulated, however, that contact will inevitably lead some individuals to react negatively, to abuse, threaten, ridicule and coerce, until the discomforting presence of someone who is different goes away. Liability under section 12203(b) gives employers an incentive to prevent precisely that occurrence.

These considerations reinforce the point that the title VII test, with its severe-or-pervasive standard, is out of place when assessing liability under subsection (b). Even the retaliation that is actionable under section 12203(a) need not meet a severe-or-pervasive standard. Thus courts have allowed retaliation claims to proceed when the plaintiffs have alleged such things as lateral transfers without reduction in pay or status.[14] They have refused to dismiss retaliation claims while at the same time holding that the employers' conduct does not constitute a severe or pervasive hostile environment.[15] If there is no ground to adopt a severe-or-pervasive screen for retaliation claims, there is still less for section 12203(b) claims, which do not even require a showing of discrimination, however that term may be defined. Unlike the retaliation provision, which says that "[n]o person shall discriminate" by retaliating, section 12203(b) does not even mention discrimination but instead directly forbids coercion, intimidation, threats, and interference. Thus by the statute's own terms the coercion, intimidation, threats, or interference need not rise to the level of discrimination. Section 12203(b) does not require even an adverse employment action within the meaning of the constructions of section 12203(a), much less a severe or pervasive hostile environment.

Courts have engaged in an overly facile use of the title VII analogy to dismiss cases that fail to meet the severe-or-pervasive screen, even though the statute is different. The point is not alteration of the terms and conditions of employment (which is what title VII by its terms requires) but simply intimidation, coercion, and interference with the exercise of protected rights. Courts have entirely missed the distinction between the ADA and title VII. For example, one district court said in dismissing a harassment claim, "The ADA's language does not explicitly prohibit harassment or a hostile work environment, but instead prohibits discrimination in the 'terms, conditions, or privileges of employment.'"[16] The statement is true for title VII but ignores ADA section 12203(b).

Applying the Interference, Coercion, or Intimidation Standard

Section 12203(b) should serve as the standard for evaluating ADA workplace harassment claims that do not rise to the standard of severity or pervasiveness set in the title VII race and sex cases and applied in cases like *Fox* and *Flowers*.[17] Section 12203(b) has a discernable meaning other than the discrimination by severe or pervasive harassment of title VII; moreover, proper interpretation of the section 12203(b) standard carries implications about who may sue for violations, who may be sued, what remedies exist, and what defenses may apply. To the extent that the meaning of section 12203(b)'s language may be unclear, existing case law interpretations, interpretations of similar language in other contexts, historical interpretations, and regulatory interpretations all provide useful guidance and lend support to the position advanced here.

Existing interpretations of section 12203(b) are somewhat sparse. Cases do, however, establish that the provision covers conduct different from that covered by the retaliation provision and different from what title VII proscribes regarding race and sex discrimination.[18]

Brown v. City of Tucson ruled that the plaintiff, a police detective with a psychiatric impairment, failed in her section 12203(a) claim of retaliation when she failed to put forward evidence rebutting the police department's evidence that it had investigated and suspended her because she had falsified a report to cover up the fact that she had failed to submit a form in a timely fashion.[19] It nevertheless reversed a grant of summary judgment on her section 12203(b) cause of action, holding that the claim differed from one of retaliation. The court ruled that specific conduct by a supervisor demanding that the plaintiff stop taking medications that made her unable to perform nighttime duties and that she agree to accept nighttime assignments or face demotion or forced retirement, when viewed along with allegations the supervisor made unauthorized inquiries about the nature of the plaintiff's disability, constituted violations of section 12203(b) when she suffered harm from the threat.[20]

Although the court recognized that the section 12203(b) claim bore resemblance to a hostile-environment claim of the sort recognized in the *Fox* and *Flowers* cases, it ruled that because the section 12203(b) claim did not derive from the general prohibition in discrimination found in title I of the ADA it was not to be measured by the same standards the courts employed in cases that have insisted on a showing of a severe or pervasive hostile environment. "We . . . note that [title I]'s prohibition of employment discrimination against the disabled would appear to lend support to Brown's argument that [section 12203(b)] of the ADA gives rise to something other than a Title VII-style 'hostile environment' claim."[21] Instead of looking for pervasive discrimination, the court zeroed in on specific allegations of threats and other conduct barred by section 12203(b).

Other cases reinforce the distinctions from section 12203(a) and the title VII–standard harassment cases emphasized in *Brown*. In *Lovejoy-Wilson v. NOCO Motor Fuel, Inc.*, the Second Circuit Court of Appeals reversed a grant of summary judgment in favor of the defendant on a section 12203(b) claim.[22] The plaintiff, whose epilepsy prevented her from driving, asked for promotion to assistant manager at a convenience store but was rejected because she lacked a driver's license and could not drive to the bank to deposit the store's receipts. After she wrote a letter proposing several accommodations that would enable her to get to the bank without needing to drive, the company president wrote back accusing her of "slanderous" allegations and saying, "If you continue this behavior, we will have no choice but to address your behavior through legal channels. This is NOCO's final position on this matter and [we] will not be entertaining further communication on this matter."[23] The court ruled that a jury could reasonably conclude that the employer's statements "served to 'intimidate' or 'threaten' her in the assertion of her right to make complaints or file charges under the ADA."[24] The protected activity was a request for accommodation rather than the simple assertion of the right to show up at work. Nevertheless, and of greatest significance for the point being made here, the court permitted a claim that did not fit neatly into the section 12203(a) box of retaliation for opposing unlawful conduct, and the court did not require an environment permeated with discrimination before granting relief.

Along similar lines, another court upheld a section 12203(b) claim of a worker with epilepsy whose supervisors granted her the accommodation of a late arrival time but then failed to notify other supervisors of the accommodation, subjected her to negative and sarcastic comments about the accommodation, and held the accommodation against her in performance reviews.[25] Still another court ruled that an employer violated section 12203(b) by imposing increased supervision and unfounded criticism on a worker after she requested an accommodation.[26] Yet another court, after ruling that the harassment alleged was insufficient to meet standards of severity and pervasiveness for an ADA title I claim, considered separately a claim that the worker was nonetheless subjected to actionable intimidation and threats under section 12203(b). The court, however, dismissed the claim on the ground that it was not raised in a timely fashion.[27]

In one of the earliest section 12203(b) decisions, *Doe v. Kohn Nast & Graf*, the court found that an attorney infected with HIV stated a cause of action under section 12203(b) when he claimed that the law firm that employed him had asked him to leave because it had discovered that he planned to file a lawsuit accusing the firm of refusing to renew his contract on the basis of his HIV-positive status.[28] The court looked simply for allegations of coercion and intimidation, and it found them. The court did not look for a pervasively hostile environment or any hostile environment at all. In another case, the court held that the form of retaliation actionable under section 12203(a) need not rise to extreme hardship but could be simply the changing of the employee's shift to one less desirable to the employee. The court commented that on remand the district court should consider additional allegations of unfavorable treatment under the standard of section 12203(b), criticizing any use of an extreme hardship test there as well and commenting that section 12203(b) "arguably sweeps more broadly than 42 USC § 12203(a)."[29]

None of these cases upholds a section 12203(b) claim for coercion, threats, intimidation, and interference on the basis solely of the plaintiff's assertion of the right to show up for work. But it is only a slight extension of the existing case law to recognize that the "any right granted or protected by this part" means not just the rights to make an accommodation request, continue to receive accommodations, or plan a lawsuit but also the right to come to work and perform the job on an equal basis with employees who do not have disabilities. The extension gains further support from the reality that retaliation for requesting an accommodation is already actionable under section 12203(a), so subsection (b) must cover something more.[30] Section 12203(b) does not require a plaintiff to show termination or other ultimate adverse employment action. Courts in the existing section 12203(b) cases have recognized that hostility, negative and sarcastic comments, and unfavorable remarks on performance reviews (even without direct consequences for pay or promotions) meet the definition of coercion, intimidation, threats, and interference. Not one of the cases discussed above required a severe or pervasive hostile environment to establish liability under section 12203(b).

Sources other than the existing case law under section 12203(b) also give guidance on its meaning. Cases interpreting identical language found in other statutes are instructive. The language in section 12203(b) appears in other statutes, including the Fair Housing Act and laws governing labor organizing.[31] In those contexts, the courts have read the protected-activity term of the statutes broadly and have refused to require anything resembling an environment permeated with discrimination.

Courts construing the identical language in the Fair Housing Act have found liability based on any conduct that impairs the exercise of rights protected by the statute.[32] In *Sofarelli v. Pinellas County,* the Eleventh Circuit Court of Appeals found a violation of the coercion provision when neighbors of a person proposing to move a house to a neighborhood left the owner a single threatening note and engaged in one incident of shouting obscenities and spitting at him.[33] *United States v. Pospisil,* a district court decision, rejected an interpretation of the Fair Housing Act analogue to section 12203(b) that would have restricted it to discriminatory conduct in violation of other Fair Housing Act sections and granted summary judgment in favor of the plaintiffs and against defendants who burned a cross on the lawn of a person of nonwhite appearance.[34] The Seventh Circuit Court of Appeals in *Halprin v. Prairie Homes of Dearborn Park* reversed the dismissal of a claim for violation of the Fair Housing Act's "coerce, intimidate, threaten, or interfere" section when the plaintiff alleged that the defendants had marked their home with graffiti, vandalized the property, and harassed them in other ways because they were Jewish.[35] Notably, all these cases are ones where the essential right that the plaintiffs asserted was the simple right of being there, not any request for accommodation or any assertion of legal rights beyond the right to be present and not undergo harassment for being present.

The National Labor Relations Act (NLRA) makes it illegal "to interfere with, restrain, or coerce employees in the exercise of the rights" to organize, choose bargaining representatives, and engage in other concerted activity.[36] One court summarized the NLRA's provisions:

> Section 8(a)(1) of the NLRA prohibits employers from interfering with, restraining, or coercing employees in the exercise of rights guaranteed them by § 7 of the NLRA. See 29 U.S.C. §158(a)(1) (1998). Section 7 of the NLRA guarantees employees "the right to self-organization, to form, join, or assist labor organizations . . . and to engage in other concerted activities for the purpose of collective bargaining or other mutual aid or protection." 29 U.S.C. § 157 (1998). Courts may find a violation of § 8(a)(1) even where the evidence does not show that employees were actually intimidated or coerced by an employer's conduct. . . . Rather, the evidence must demonstrate that, taken from the point of view of the employees, the reasonable tendency of the employer's conduct or statements is "coercive in effect."[37]

A court is to consider the power imbalance between employer and employee in evaluating language thought to contain a threat or other effort at coercion and "must take into account the economic dependence of the employees on their employers, and the necessary tendency of the former, because of that relationship, to pick up intended implications of the latter that might be more readily dismissed by a more disinterested ear."[38] The Railway Labor Act has a provision similar to that in the NLRA.[39] Courts have found that conduct such as a single instance of threatening to sue an employee for defamation[40] and threatening to terminate employees[41] or shut down facilities[42] violates the coercion standard when done to keep employees from asserting rights to unionize.

The legislative history of section 12203(b) combines with the interpretations of like language in other laws to support the interpretation that it reaches conduct not considered discrimination by title VII and similar statutes. As far as it can be traced, section 12203(b)'s language originated in the National Industrial Recovery Act (NIRA) provision protecting collective bargaining rights, which required every code of fair competition to guarantee that "employees shall have the right to organize and bargain collectively through representatives of their own choosing, and shall be free from the interference, restraint, or coercion of employers, or their agents, in the designation of such representatives, or in self-organization or in other concerted activities for the purpose of collective bargaining or other mutual aid or protection."[43]

Congress used the same language in the other statutes discussed above, the NLRA and Railway Labor Act, the Fair Housing Act, and ultimately the ADA. There is no specific provision in the ADA legislative history that gives more background to the decision to adopt the language or the decision to adopt it as a distinct subsection apart from the retaliation provision. The NIRA's terms embrace both retaliation and other more subtle means of discouraging the free choice of representatives, unionization, and other collective activity.[44] The NIRA is quite unrelated to title VII, which Congress passed thirty-one years later and did not incorporate into the nation's labor-organizing laws.

Regulatory provisions also support the conclusion that section 12203(b) reaches harassment that does not meet title VII's discrimination test. The EEOC's regulations interpreting title I of the ADA repeat the language of section 12203(b) but add the term "harass" to the list of forbidden conduct: "[I]t is unlawful to . . . coerce, intimidate, threaten, *harass,* or interfere with any individual in the exercise or enjoyment of . . . any right granted or protected in this part."[45] Although in the past the Supreme Court has behaved erratically in following the EEOC's regulations interpreting the ADA,[46] in at least some cases regarding employment matters the deference has been strong. In its most recent decision on the validity of an EEOC regulatory interpretation of the ADA, the Supreme Court afforded deference to a regulation inserting a new term in the statute, holding that a regulation establishing a defense based on danger to a worker's own health fits within permissible rule making when the statute provides a defense based only on danger to others.[47] The insertion of the term "harass" in the coercion regulation, which covers conduct so closely akin to the statutorily listed conduct as to be arguably within its range, is far easier to accept than a regulation that adds a term that appears quite conspicuously to have been omitted, such as the "to self" term in the danger defense.

Of course, the insertion of harassment in the regulation may be thought simply to incorporate the title VII meaning of unlawful harassment, in which instance the regulation adds nothing to what has already been established by *Fox, Flowers,* and the rest of the current ADA case law: disability harassment is forbidden if the same conduct would be forbidden by title VII with regard to race or sex.[48] The placement of "harassment" in the regulation suggests a different meaning for the term, however, one that matches the commonsense meaning of "harassment" rather than a meaning that requires pervasive discrimination. When a word is included in a list of other words, it gains meaning from the context. The list "Treason, Bribery, or other high Crimes and Misdemeanors"[49] gives meaning to the term "Misdemeanors" and excludes misdemeanors such as spitting on the street.[50] The regulation covers harassment that fits in with and occupies the edges of coercion, intimidation, threatening, and interfering. When a person with disabilities is harassed for the high crime of coming to work, the person has a cause of action. The environment need not be permeated with discrimination for that sort of harassment to occur. It need only meet the dictionary definition of "harassment": "to annoy or vex"[51] or "to disturb persistently; torment."[52]

The existing case law under section 12203(b), the judicial applications of the language in other contexts, the history of the language's use, and the regulatory interpretation of section 12203(b) imply both positive and negative conclusions about the scope of liability conferred. Harassment of an employee with disabilities for working coerces, intimidates, interferes with, and frequently threatens an individual for exercising the ADA-protected right to equal employment. Punishing workers with disabilities and pushing them out of their jobs by shunning them, giving them nicknames like "Rick Retardo," or constantly making fun of their speech or other physical or mental limits is no less offensive to section 12203(b) than is criticizing someone for making a request for accommodation. Rights protected under the ADA include the right of simple enjoyment of one's status, just like the right to live in a white neighborhood if one is of nonwhite appearance or the right to be a member of a labor union if one is a nonsupervisory worker. These rights of status are what the ADA and the other laws protect, just as they protect rights to use the legal system. And defendants infringe these rights when they coerce, intimidate, threaten, or interfere, not merely when they create a subjectively and objectively hostile environment that meets the extreme standards of discrimination under title VII.

This does not mean that every comment or bit of insensitive conduct will trigger liability, however. Some cases that have failed under a title VII–derived standard would fail under section 12203(b) as well. For example, in *Keever v. City of Middletown*, a police officer who had suffered several injuries on the job had disagreements with his supervisors over his performance and use of sick leave time.[53] The court held that what it called mere "conversations" about those issues did not create an objectively hostile work environment.[54] Communication about legitimate work issues does not constitute coercion, intimidation, threats, or interference. Justified criticism and stronger responses to employees' tardiness,[55] absenteeism,[56] slow work pace,[57] or otherwise inadequate job performance do not violate section 12203(b). It is only when disability-related conduct becomes coercive, intimidating, threatening, or interfering, when it constitutes harassment (under a commonsense, not a title VII, definition), that it violates the statute. Because courts rejecting hostile-environment cases under the severe-or-pervasive standard frequently give only the sketchiest description of the facts, it is difficult to tell how many of the cases that failed under the title VII standard would come out differently under section 12203(b).

Even with regard to claims that meet the section 12203(b) standard, an additional consideration that will necessarily keep case filings within bounds is the amount of the damages in proportion to the cost and effort of litigation. If the harassment does not force the employee out of the job or inflict serious distress, if it cannot be proven willful on the part of the employer, the damages will diminish accordingly. At some point, the damages will not be worth pursuing and the claim will fall out of the system. Litigation costs act as a screen for legal claims, in the disability discrimination field as in other areas.[58]

Who May Sue and Who May Be Sued

The general antidiscrimination provisions of the ADA, which support disability harassment claims under the theories applied by *Fox* and *Flowers,* give protection only to persons with disabilities. Individuals may not assert claims under the *Fox* and *Flowers* formulas unless they satisfy the statutory test for having a disability. That test is not always easy to meet. Though Congress drafted the definition broadly to include persons with a record of an impairment and persons regarded as having an impairment, the Supreme Court has read it narrowly to exclude persons for whom medical appliances, medication, or the body's own process mitigate the disabling effects of their conditions.[59] A vast number of ADA claims fail because of the courts' conclusions that the individual does not have a disability under the meaning of the statute, applying the Supreme

Court's approach to mitigating measures or the courts' own attitudes about who is disabled. Cases include those brought by persons with multiple sclerosis,[60] post-traumatic stress disorder,[61] and breast cancer requiring significant reconstructive surgery.[62]

In contrast, a person who is asserting a claim under the coercion section need not be a person with a disability. The statute says "any individual," not an individual with a disability.[63] A person need not have a disability to sue under the retaliation provision of the ADA, whose language, like that of the coercion provision, does not specify that the victim be a "person with disabilities."[64] As a practical matter, of course, it is people with disabilities, and most likely people with severe disabilities, who will sue for harassment under section 12203(b). Unless the person has an impairment, is perceived to have an impairment, or has a record of an impairment, employers or co-workers are not likely to harass him or her on that basis. The section 12203(b) claimant has the very real advantage, however, of not having to prove disability—under whatever standards the court is using de jour—in order to get into court to present the claim that harassment occurred because he or she exercised rights to work on an equal basis with others.

The question of who may be sued—that is, who is liable under section 12203(b)—embraces the question of what conduct by supervisors and by a plaintiff's co-workers leads to employer liability and when individual harasser liability may exist. Under current sex and race harassment law, conduct by supervisors that results in tangible employment action imposes liability on the employer. However, the 1998 Supreme Court cases *Burlington Industries, Inc. v. Ellerth*[65] and *Faragher v. City of Boca Raton*[66] held that if the supervisory harassment does not result in tangible employment action, the employer may escape liability if it proves that it exercised reasonable care to prevent and correct promptly any harassing behavior and that the employee unreasonably failed to take advantage of preventive or corrective opportunities. Tangible employment action includes discharge, denial of a raise, demotion, and undesirable reassignment but does not necessarily encompass the humiliation and ostracism that affect many who are harassed.[67]

The *Ellerth-Faragher* affirmative defense is an elaborate gloss on title VII's element of liability that the employer has committed the discriminatory conduct. An employer acts through its agents, but the agents are not necessarily always acting on behalf of the employer. The defense allows the employer to escape liability for the harm its agents have done, but only in situations in which no tangible employment action occurred and only in situations when, in the view of the Supreme Court, assigning liability would unfairly penalize a diligent company or unfairly compensate a employee who failed to help him- or herself.[68] In various cases, courts have explicitly applied *Ellerth* and *Faragher* to the disability harassment cause of action under the general antidiscrimination provision of the ADA, causing the plaintiffs to lose their claims.[69]

As emphasized above, section 12203(b) is not part of the ADA's prohibition on discrimination. Although the liability developed in *Fox* and *Flowers,* which flows from the ban on discrimination, may be subject to the analogous title VII affirmative defense, the liability under section 12203(b) should not be. An entity can coerce, intimidate, or threaten without "discriminating" as that latter term has come to be defined under title VII and its Supreme Court interpretation. The requirement of corporate negligence and an absence of contributory employee negligence may inhere in the idea of discrimination by a corporate entity, but the specific conduct prohibited by section 12203(b) has a much more immediate and direct meaning. No permutations of the language are needed to ascribe this narrowly defined conduct to the entity whose supervisors conduct it or tolerate it. No affirmative defense exists in the context of labor organizing or other fields in which section 12203(b)'s language is found, and the Supreme Court has obviously had ample time to develop such a defense had it thought that the defense was needed to effectuate congressional intent.

The language of section 12203 does not restrict liability to employers or other covered entities under the ADA; accordingly, a claim may be made against an individual such as a co-worker or supervisor who personally coerces, intimidates, threatens, or interferes. Section 12203(b) simply states, "It shall be unlawful to coerce, intimidate, threaten, or interfere. . . ."[70] The retaliation provision, section 12203(a), is similarly broad, saying, "No person shall discriminate" against an individual who has exercised rights in proceedings. Courts generally have upheld individual liability under section 12203.[71] Several courts deciding cases under section 12203 have ruled that individuals are not liable despite the section's language, however.[72] Some of those courts appear to be reasoning in a purely reflexive way that the ADA was supposed to impose liability only on the covered entities specified in each of titles I, II, and III. They ignore the specific language found in section 12203, which is part of title

V, as emphasized in *LaManque v. Massachusetts Department of Employment and Training,* where the court upheld individual liability:

> The interference provision of Title V proscribes interference with, coercion and intimidation of, and threats to any individual exercising, or aiding another in exercising, rights under the ADA; and it appears to make it unlawful for *anyone* to engage in the proscribed practices, beginning as it does with the words of general application: "It shall be unlawful . . ." 42 U.S.C. 12203(b).[73]

A few courts considering the matter a little more carefully argue that section 12203(c) incorporates by reference the remedies and procedures of titles I (employment), II (public services), and III (privately operated public accommodations) for violations of section 12203 in those respective areas and that since individual damages liability does not exist for violations of those titles, it cannot exist for violations of section 12203.[74] This approach renders meaningless the language in section 12203 that extends its duties to everyone rather than just to covered entities. Moreover, it disregards the interpretation of section 12203 found in the regulations that Congress had the Department of Justice write to implement the statute in state and local government cases.[75] These regulations are entitled to deference from courts, and they provide explicitly that section 12203 embraces violations by individuals.[76]

Remedies

Most courts considering claims under section 12203 for either retaliation or coercion have not questioned the proposition that the claims carry the same range of remedies that other ADA claims do.[77] As noted above, subsection 12203(c) specifies that remedies listed elsewhere in the statute for title I, title II, and title III are available to persons aggrieved by violations of the coercion and retaliation provision that fall within those respective subject areas.[78] Thus, for employment cases, the remedies include back pay, injunctive relief, and compensatory and punitive damages up to the limits provided in the Civil Rights Act of 1991.[79] For state and local government cases, which may include employment disputes, the remedies applicable to section 504 apply, which include injunctions and unlimited compensatory damages.[80] In *Ostrach v. Regents of the University of Cal-*

ifornia, an employment action under the ADA's retaliation provision, section 12203(a), the court pointed out that section 12203(c) incorporates the remedies provisions of titles I, II, and III, which in turn incorporate 1964 Civil Rights Act remedies provisions that are then expanded by section 1981a, the Civil Rights Act of 1991, to include compensatory and punitive damages, subject to the limits established by that latter statute.[81] The Civil Rights Act of 1991 makes direct reference to title I rather than to section 12203, which is found in title V. Nevertheless, the incorporation-by-reference pathway leads in a straight line from ADA title V's section 12203 to ADA titles I and II to the Civil Rights Act of 1964 to the Civil Rights Act of 1991, placing section 12203 squarely within section 1981a with regard to employment cases. The conclusion that damages lie at the end of this chain is buttressed by the principle that courts construing the remedial provisions of federal statutes should assume the existence of the full range of remedies, including damages relief.[82]

There are cases holding that no compensatory or punitive damages liability exists for employment cases under section 12203.[83] The most prominent of these is the Seventh Circuit Court of Appeals decision *Kramer v. Banc of America Securities,* which contends that the incorporation by reference applies only to the violations listed in the cross-referenced statutes, not to the violation whose remedy section 12203(c) specifies and that is the subject of the cross-referencing.[84] This reasoning is not persuasive, however. The cross-referenced statute can hardly be expected to contain language directly covering the statute doing the cross-referencing. The whole point of incorporating another law by reference is that the incorporated law does not include the conduct covered by the law and does not itself refer to the provision that is doing the cross-referencing.

The recent decision *Edwards v. Brookhaven Science Associates* considered the argument that compensatory damages should not be awarded in an ADA employment case claiming retaliation.[85] It traces the statutory chain and finds that the omission of a direct reference to section 12203 is irrelevant. Its analysis is worth quoting at length:

> In the Court's view, the omission § 12203 in § 1981[a] is of no consequence when § 1981[a] is read in conjunction with the relevant provisions of the ADA. . . . [T]he retaliation provision of the ADA contains no remedy of its own. Rather, it is clear that the "remedies and proce-

dures . . . available to aggrieved persons" for violations of § 12203 are the *same* as the "remedies and procedures available under" Title I of the ADA. . . . Considering that the remedies available for retaliation under the ADA are commensurate with those available under Title I, it was unnecessary for Congress to separately mention retaliation in § 1981[a]. Thus, it is fair to assume that the expansive effect of § 1981[a] applies equally to claims under Title I as it does to retaliation claims by virtue of the fact that the remedies available for retaliation claims incorporate, and are coextensive with, the remedies available under Title I.[86]

Even beyond the reasoning in cases such as *Ostrach* and *Edwards*, there exists the irrefutable point that barring a damages remedy for retaliation would eliminate the most sensible relief for violations of a law such as section 12203. In fact, it would deprive a plaintiff of any redress in the common situation in which the employee does not want or is not entitled to equitable relief, as when the employee has promptly obtained a similar-paying job elsewhere following a retaliatory discharge. No one would sensibly ascribe an intention to Congress to specifically bar retaliatory conduct and then take away the prohibition by eliminating the remedy. The inconsistency with title VII cases should also be noted. As admitted even by one judge who ruled that an ADA damages remedy for retaliation did not exist, "[T]he court can discern no logic in a rule that precludes an award of compensatory and punitive damages in an ADA retaliation case when such damages are available in Title VII retaliation cases."[87] Under the most fundamental principles of statutory interpretation, absurd results are to be avoided.[88] Accordingly, cases such as *Ostrach* and *Edwards* have far the better of the remedies argument, and damages should be available for violations of section 12203 in employment.

In public services cases, including those concerning state and local government employment, the remedies for violations of section 12203 are those of the Rehabilitation Act, which incorporates the remedies of title VI of the Civil Rights Act, which in turn has been construed so as to be closely in alignment with title IX of the Education Amendments. Recently, the Supreme Court upheld a compensatory damages claim under title IX against a covered entity for retaliation, so the damages remedy should be equally available in state and local government employment cases for retaliation or coercion under section 12203.[89]

Application beyond the Workplace

Section 12203 is found in title V of the ADA, the general provisions title, and so is not limited in its application to employment-related cases. In fact, the remedies provision, section 12203(c), adopts the remedies of whatever title is applicable to the situation—workplace under title I, state and local government under title II, privately owned public accommodations under title III—for violations of 12203(a) or (b). In many situations outside employment, persons subjected to harassment have found themselves thrown out of court because the harassment was deemed insufficiently severe or pervasive. These cases include a higher education case that would be subject to title III of the Act where the president of the university referred to students with learning disabilities as a "plague" and made it difficult for them to obtain accommodations.[90]

5

Liability for Harassment
in the Public Schools

This chapter will consider harassment in elementary and secondary schools. The chapter will describe how courts have approached legal challenges to harassment using statutes such as the ADA, section 504 of the Rehabilitation Act of 1973, and the Fourteenth Amendment to the United States Constitution, as well as IDEA. It will begin with several recurring fact patterns, then discuss the legal claims in turn. When courts take seriously the harassment that occurs in schools, they have no shortage of legal grounds on which to offer relief. As often as not, however, the courts do not take the claims seriously and overlook the clear legal authority, or they invent defenses to block claims against schools and others. All claims but those under IDEA will be discussed here; causes of action under that law and all relevant defenses will be covered in the following chapter.

The Facts of School Harassment

The cases dealing with allegations of disability harassment in the schools fall into several categories: first, outright physical mistreatment and verbal abuse of highly vulnerable children by school personnel; second, conduct by teachers that treats children with disabilities unfairly and actively encourages fellow students to join in the ridicule; and third, failure to provide protection against known risks of physical or psychological harm by other students, often including the risk of physical assault. Each category contains cases that fail and cases that succeed in establishing a claim for relief. This pattern itself supports an inference that courts do not fully appreciate the gravity of the conduct and its character as a form of disability discrimination.

Cases in the first category include the *Witte* case, discussed in chapter 1, in which a ten-year-old with multiple disabilities placed at a specialized public school was force-fed food to which he was allergic, choked, physically abused in other ways, and made to write "I will not tell my mom" and "I will not tic."[1] They also include *Franklin v. Frid,* in which a child with severe cerebral palsy was "intentionally humiliated and tormented" by his public school aide, who poked, hit, and slapped him, routinely yelled at him, and called him degrading names.[2] The aide's supervisors did nothing to stop the abuse, even after a psychological evaluation of the child concluded that it was probable he had been repeatedly assaulted. In *Covington v. Knox County School System,* a child with multiple mental and emotional disabilities attended a public school's adaptive education center, where he routinely was locked in a "vault-like" time-out room for hours at a time without supervision.[3] The room was four-by-six feet, dark, and unheated, with a concrete floor but no furniture and no ventilation. There was one small, reinforced window five feet above the floor. At least once he was made to disrobe before being locked in the room. At least once he was in the room so long he had to relieve himself on the floor.

Cases in the second category include *Kubistal*[4] and *Charlie F.,*[5] both discussed in chapter 1. Kubistal was the child with a visual impairment whom the teacher routinely called demeaning names, subjected to a mocking apology in front of the class, and placed in an isolation chamber of movable bookcases for the entire school day. Charlie F. was the child with attention deficit disorder and panic attacks whose teacher subjected him to the sessions at which she encouraged them to humiliate him. Another case in which the teacher harassed the child and encouraged peers to do the same is *Baird v. Rose,* in which a high school girl, Kristen Baird, was diagnosed with severe depression and placed on a program of counseling and medication after a suicide attempt.[6] Her mother informed a counselor at the school about the diagnosis, and the counselor informed Kristen's teachers. The next day, the teacher in Kristen's musical performance class announced to the class that Kristen would not be permitted to participate in the next performance and assigned her role to another student. After Kristen's mother complained, the teacher told her that it was her belief that individuals with depression could not be counted on to meet their responsibilities.

When the mother submitted letters from a doctor and psychologist stating that Kristen was able to participate and would suffer harm from exclusion, the teacher decided to exclude her on the ground of several absences from class. The principal informed the teacher that if she were to take that action, she had to exclude all students who exceeded the number of absences set in the teacher's previously unenforced absences policy. Later, in Kristen's presence, the teacher announced to the class that, against her will, she was being forced to exclude three other students from part of the performance. The teacher "then asked the class members if they understood why she was being forced to adhere to the strict attendance policy, and other students commented that someone was taking advantage of the lax enforcement of the attendance policy."[7] Kristen left class crying uncontrollably and shaking, and required tranquilization by a doctor. She ultimately was kept from participating in many practice sessions and in all but a small part of the performance. The effects of the humiliation continued, including sleeplessness, fear of humiliation, symptoms of physical illness, and academic decline.

The third category of cases, those concerning failure to supervise students who present a known danger to students with disabilities, includes numerous cases arising from incidents of sexual assault by other students.[8] *Sutton v. Utah School for the Deaf and Blind* is typical.[9] James Sutton had severe cerebral palsy and was mentally retarded, totally blind, and unable to speak. At age fourteen he functioned at the level of a three- to five-year old. He was a day student at a state school. One day, he communicated to his mother through sign language that a very large boy who was not in his class had touched him in his genital area while he was in the bathroom at school. James's mother immediately notified the school superintendent, the principal, and the teacher. She met with them the next morning and was assured that the incident could not have occurred because students never went to the bathroom without adult supervision. A week later, a teacher's aide escorted James to the door of the bathroom but left to answer the telephone. After the call, she returned and discovered that the same student James had previously described was sexually attacking him. Following the occurrence, James suffered from uncontrollable bursts of rage, nightmares, compulsive behavior, and other signs of acute mental distress.

Other cases in this category involve violent peer-on-peer harassment that the school district knows about but fails to stop. *Shore Regional High School Board of Education v. P.S.* concerned a child with a perceptual impairment and other disabilities who was viewed by classmates as effeminate and who endured relentless harassment that included name-calling, having rocks thrown at him, being hit with a padlock during gym class, and being shunned at lunch and in other settings.[10] The student attempted suicide and was eventually placed in home schooling, after which the child's parents placed him at a school in a neighboring school district, resisting his home school district's plan to place him in a high school with the bullies who had previously harassed him. *M.P. v. Independent School District No. 721* was the case of a child whose classmates, after the school district improperly disclosed his diagnosis of schizophrenia, routinely called him abusive names, shoved his head into a drinking fountain, "picked him up by his throat, slammed him into lockers, threw him to the floor, shoved, scratched," spat at, "and cut him."[11]

Two very recent cases further exemplify peer harassment of an all-too-typical kind. Daniel Scruggs was a middle school student with a learning disability.[12] Bullying caused him to miss thirty-seven days of class in the sixth grade after his special education services were terminated. In the seventh grade, one of the students who was harassing him was seated behind Daniel, though his mother complained and though the student had assaulted Daniel's mother herself the previous year when she had worked at the school as a paraprofessional. Assaults continued through that school year, including specific incidents in which Daniel was "punched, kicked, had desks slammed into him, and had his hair pulled so violently that his head snapped back."[13] An assessment of Daniel's learning and social skills was agreed upon but never scheduled because he committed suicide. A child identified as D.G., who had pervasive developmental disorder and dyslexia, with normal intelligence, was a middle school student who endured continual disability-related name-calling, physical aggression, and intimidation by his peers, both at school and on the school bus.[14] In the fall of seventh grade, he was thrown to the ground, body-slammed, and taunted by several students during lunch one day until an aide intervened. He was held down and beaten on the back and head with his class binder between classes in the special education resource room during March of that year. On five to eight occasions his school books were thrown into the garbage in the cafeteria; he ate lunch with his special education teacher for the rest of the year. The next fall, a student called him a "retard" and started a fistfight on the bus, another student took his planner, and other students repeatedly taunted and hit him.[15] He experienced suicidal ideation, vomiting brought on by stress, anger, and clinical depression. He left school in November and did not return for the remainder of the school year.

The results are mixed in suits over harassment that falls into the first category, physical abuse by teachers and other school personnel. In the *Witte* case regarding the force-feeding, near-strangulation, and other mistreatment, the trial court dismissed the case but the court of appeals reversed and reinstated it. In *Franklin v. Frid*, the case of the violently abusive aide, the court dismissed the claim for failure to exhaust administrative remedies, even though damages are unavailable in the administrative process and the parent had withdrawn the child from that school system and enrolled him elsewhere. In *Covington*, the case regarding the timeout vault, the trial court also dismissed on exhaustion grounds, but the court of appeals reversed. With regard to category two cases, those in which teachers verbally harass and encourage peers to join in, judicial reception again is mixed. In *Kubistal* and *Charlie F.*, the courts dismissed the claims for failure to exhaust administrative remedies. In *Baird v. Rose*, the musical performance case, the court of appeals reversed the district court's judgment of dismissal. Ordinary peer abuse cases found in category three have a similar checkered pattern of results. In *Sutton*, the appellate court reversed the trial court's dismissal for failure to state a claim. In *Shore Regional*, the lower court overturned an administrative decision in favor of the child and his family that had permitted the parent to claim funding for the placement at the out-of-district high school, where, free of his tormenters, the child thrived. It took an appeal to reverse that decision and reinstate the administrative ruling in the child's favor. Cases claiming damages for peer-on-peer harassment usually hinge on whether responsible school district personnel were deliberately indifferent to student misconduct that deprived the child of equal educational opportunities on the ground of disability. In *M.P.*, the court of appeals overturned a grant of summary judgment against the child and his parents with respect to his disability discrimination claim. In the cases brought over the peer harassment of Daniel Scruggs and D.G., the lower courts permitted disability discrimination claims to proceed, denying a motion for judgment on the pleadings in the first and denying a motion for summary judgment in the second. It is easy to find other teacher and peer-on-peer harassment cases that are unsuccessful.[16]

The fact that all but two of the cases described lost on at least one level and that many more cases also fail indicates that courts largely refuse to view disability harassment and official toleration of disability harassment as violations of the law. Instead, the incidents are viewed as aspects of disputes over levels of special education services to be resolved by an administrative process or as unfortunate life experiences that simply must be borne in silence. To use the phrase made popular with respect to sexual harassment accusations in the Clarence Thomas confirmation hearings, the judges "just don't get it." Nevertheless, as will be explained below, the better reasoned of the judicial decisions demonstrate that valid legal claims exist to remedy disability harassment at school. The problem is getting the courts to follow the law.

Completely apart from the court cases, observations from daily life show that disability harassment occurs constantly at school as well as outside the schoolhouse gates, that its effects are harmful and severe, and that nothing is done to stop it. Flannery O'Connor once said, "Anybody who has survived his childhood has enough information about life to last him the rest of his days."[17] Anyone who survived childhood in a public school in which special education students attend with other students knows that the children who are different are subjected to verbal abuse and physical intimidation every day. The word "retard" has become a common insult on and off the playground. Students with disabilities, particularly those with mental retardation and mental illness and those with disfigurements, are frequently objects of ridicule and mistreatment.[18]

Harassment reinforces hierarchies of prestige and peer acceptance within the school setting.[19] If a harasser can taunt or physically intimidate a child with impunity, it reinforces a sense of power and diminishes both the perceived and real power of the child who is harassed. In any context, school or work, harassment frequently establishes who is in the accepted group and who is in the out-group. Vicki Schultz has observed how even sexual harassment is often not at all sexual.[20] It consists instead of constant reinforcement of the message that the woman does not belong in the position she occupies. Similarly, disability harassment constantly reinforces the message that the child with disabilities does not belong and that nothing he or she does can change that reality. The negative attitudes that the children encounter at school are likely to follow them the rest of their lives, harming them in the workplace and other settings. In these settings as well, they will suffer harassment from peers and supervisors because of mental and physical differences.[21]

Children cannot avoid reacting to harassment. Many children who are teased and bullied by peers or teachers resist going to school and even develop physical symptoms such as headaches and abdominal pain to support their pleas to stay home. Not surprisingly, children with disabilities have dropout rates three times those of other children. That fact alone has severe consequences: the unemployment rate for students with disabilities who drop out of high school is 40 percent higher than the rate for students with disabilities who graduate.[22]

What avenues of redress exist for children who are subjected to disability harassment at school? The relevant sources of legal protection include section 504 of the Rehabilitation Act and title II of the ADA, ADA section 12203(b), IDEA, and the United States Constitution.[23]

Discrimination under the Rehabilitation Act and the Americans with Disabilities Act

Disability harassment of the type just described treats people with disabilities unequally and unfairly; it is thus disability discrimination. The relevant disability discrimination statutes are section 504 of the Rehabilitation Act of 1973 and title II of the ADA of 1990. These laws forbid discrimination on the basis of disability in, respectively, federally funded activities and activities of state and local government. Both statutes, as well as their regulatory interpretations, bar disability harassment.

Section 504 provides that no otherwise qualified individual with a disability shall, "solely by reason of his or her disability, be excluded from participation in, be denied the benefits of, or be subjected to discrimination under any program or activity receiving Federal financial assistance."[24] Public schools and state educational agencies receive federal financial assistance, so the law covers them. Students receive the protection of the law if they meet a disability standard of having a physical or mental impairment that substantially limits one or more of the person's major life activities, have a record of such an impairment, or are regarded as having such an impairment.[25] Regulations promulgated under section 504 further define the discrimination prohibited by the Act, barring conduct that denies a person with a disability the opportunity to benefit from services that are not equal to those provided others and that are not as effective as those provided to others.[26]

Disability harassment violates section 504 and its regulations. Being subjected to abuse either at the hands of school personnel or at the hands of peers with the knowledge of school personnel makes the public school experience decidedly unequal to the experience of others. Harassment excludes students with disabilities from the educational environment provided to students without disabilities and discourages students with disabilities from continuing their education beyond the minimum period required by law. Title II of the ADA recapitulates the section 504 prohibition against discrimination by public entities, and the definition of banned conduct in the ADA regulations echoes that found in the section 504 regulations.[27] Although there are some technical distinctions between the two laws, the only difference for purposes of the current discussion is that title II extends section 504 coverage to any public educational agency that somehow does not receive federal money.[28]

Baird v. Rose, the case about the child with depression and her exclusion from the musical performance class, sustained a claim for damages under title II of the ADA for harassment by a teacher.[29] The court stated that to establish an ADA claim, three elements must be shown: that the person has a disability, is otherwise qualified for the benefit at issue, and was excluded from the benefit due to discrimination on the basis of the disability. The court said there could be no dispute that the plaintiff adequately alleged she had a disability and was otherwise qualified to participate in the class. On the issue of whether discrimination was on the basis of the student's depression, the court ruled that plaintiffs had made sufficient allegations to support a conclusion that the charge of absenteeism was a pretext and further held that the disability discrimination did not need to be the sole cause of the adverse action but only a motivating factor. Applied to other cases of harassment, *Baird* stands for the proposition that if a child is treated in such a way that she is excluded from an academic activity—or by extension, deprived of equal enjoyment of the activity—and disability is a motivating factor, a title II ADA action exists to recover damages for all the losses, including humiliation, that the child suffers. Other appellate court cases also sustain claims under title II and section 504 for harassment of students with disabilities. In *Witte v. Clark County School District,* the case concerning force-feeding and other physical and psychological abuse by the teacher and aide, the court overturned a dismissal of claims under Rehabilitation Act section 504 and title II of the ADA.[30] Although most of its discussion centered on administrative exhaustion under the special education laws, the court effectively approved a cause of action for disability harassment under the two statutes.

As chapter 3 described, courts have unanimously agreed that title I of the ADA establishes a damages claim for a hostile work environment. Drawing analogies to hostile-environment sexual harassment cases, courts have applied a test that focuses on whether the harassment is sufficiently severe or pervasive to alter the conditions of the plaintiff's employment and to create an abusive working environment. With regard to intent, they have required that the defendant knew or should have known of the harassment and failed to take prompt, effective remedial action. Two appellate decisions from 2001 upheld jury decisions finding liability in ADA title I hostile-environment cases. In *Flowers v. Southern Regional Physician Services,* the Fifth Circuit Court of Appeals affirmed judgment on a jury verdict in favor of an employee who had been diagnosed with HIV infection, whose bosses shunned, humiliated, and ultimately terminated her.[31] Two weeks after *Flowers* came down, the Fourth Circuit also affirmed a judgment in favor of an employee in a disability harassment case. The plaintiff in *Fox. v. General Motors Corp.* returned from disability leave with a light-duty work restriction, but a supervisor and foreman humiliated him when he refused to do tasks beyond his restrictions, placing him at a low work table that exacerbated his back injury, verbally harassing him, and blocking his efforts to obtain a promotion.[32] The court ruled that a reasonable jury could find the harassment severe or pervasive enough to create a hostile work environment and affirmed a verdict of $200,000 compensatory damages for emotional injury and other harms. As chapter 3 indicated, the basis for the ADA title I hostile–work environment cases was an analogy to race and sex harassment that courts had found to violate title VII of the Civil Rights Act. of 1964. The strengths and weaknesses of the analogy are discussed in chapters 3 and 4.

A disability harassment claim under title II of the ADA and section 504 of the Rehabilitation Act rests not just on the comparison to ADA title I claims for disability harassment in the workplace but also on an analogy to sex harassment claims that the Supreme Court has found to be actionable under title IX of the Education Amendments of 1972. Title IX, section 504, and title VI of the Civil Rights Act of 1964 share similar language barring discrimination in some or all federally funded activities on the basis, respectively, of sex, disability, and race or national origin.[33] *Gebser v. Lago Vista Independent School District* held in 1998 that a school district is liable in damages under title IX for known acts of sexual harassment of a student by a teacher if the district is deliberately indifferent to the activity.[34] The next year, *Davis v. Monroe County Board of Education* held that a school district is liable if it is deliberately indifferent to known acts of peer harassment.[35] The Court said that the conduct must be sufficiently severe, pervasive, and objectively offensive that it denies the victim student equal access to education. Deliberate indifference occurs whenever the school's actions or inactions in response to the harassment are clearly unreasonable in light of known circumstances.[36] Applied to disability harassment in the public schools, the lesson of *Gebser* and *Davis* is that districts face liability under section 504, and thus under title II of the ADA, for activity both by employees and by student peers, if the conduct is sufficiently severe and the district meets an intent standard, for instance, deliberate indifference to known conduct. A single incident will support a hostile-environment sex harassment claim under title IX if the incident is severe enough,[37] and a similar rule should apply by analogy in disability harassment cases.

One noteworthy decision relying on the analogy to *Davis* and *Gebser* is *K.M. v. Hyde Park Central School District,* the case regarding the child D.G. who was taunted and physically attacked by other students on the bus, in the lunchroom, and in the classroom and who left school in November of his eighth-grade year.[38] The court quoted *Davis* at length and noted that *Davis* placed special stress on the power disparity between the classmates who keep female students from making use of educational resources and the female students who are harmed. The *K.M.* decision pointed out that the child with a developmental impairment "was not on equal footing to defend himself against harassment from his more able peers, leaving him vulnerable to abuse that the District should have anticipated and worked harder to prevent."[39] The court also called attention to the integration strain of the ADA, stating that unnecessary social isolation violates the Act and stressing that the harassment caused the child to relinquish participation in community life, most obviously by driving him out of the school lunchroom.

Damages are the proper remedy for intentional conduct that violates section 504 of the Rehabilitation Act or title II of the ADA. Most authorities, however, have rejected the idea of section 504 or title II damages liability against individuals, arguing that the laws create duties, respectively, for units of state and local government themselves and for recipients of federal funds—that is, agencies and other impersonal entities.[40] Hence the bulk of the damages case law bears on the liability of school districts for harassment of students with disabilities by school officials or the students' peers. Although damages are plainly available against school districts or other public educational agencies for the harassment, the challenge lies in proving intent on the part of the public agency as a predicate for damages relief. Once that challenge is met, damages are an appropriate form of relief on the basis of considerations of policy as well as statutory interpretation.

As mentioned above, section 504 and ADA title II follow the same wording as title VI of the Civil Rights Act of 1964 and title IX of the Education Amendments of 1972 in prohibiting discrimination and providing remedies to its victims. When confronting actions for damages liability under title VI and its parallel statutes, the courts have generally required a showing of intent, just as the Supreme Court required a showing of intent for damages liability under the Equal Protection Clause of the Constitution.[41] In *Consolidated Rail Corp. v. Darrone,* the Supreme Court held that the Rehabilitation Act permits monetary claims, but courts elaborating on that rule have insisted on a showing of intentional discrimination before compensatory damages may be awarded.[42] As with municipal liability for equal-protection and other constitutional violations, the liability of a corporate entity for an intentional violation of section 504 or the ADA requires a determination of the intent of a constructive being that has no single "mind." In *Monell v. Department of Social Services,* the Supreme Court stressed that municipal liability under federal law for violations of the Constitution would not attach simply because an employee had committed the violation in the course of employment.[43] Instead, the unlawful conduct of the municipality had to be pursuant to policy or custom, though the Court later ruled that a single decision of an authoritative officer could satisfy the test, as could inadequate training or supervision, if the conduct met a standard of "deliberate indifference."[44]

In the context of section 504 and ADA title II liability for damages on the part of a school district, the dominant test for intent, and thus for damages liability, is the requirement of bad faith or gross misjudgment, though there is no reason to believe that the test is an exclusive one.[45] What constitutes bad faith or gross misjudgment differs greatly from court to court. For example, in *Sellers v. School Board,* the court affirmed the dismissal of a claim for damages, reasoning that the long-term failure to identify a child's learning disabilities and the consequent failure to provide special education services that the child needed did not amount to bad faith or gross misjudgment.[46] By contrast, in *McKellar v. Commonwealth of Pennsylvania Department of Education,* the court found that the bad-faith-or-gross-misjudgment standard could be met when the district failed to provide an appropriate education over a period of time and repeatedly ignored a child's written education programs.[47] In *M.P.,* the case of the child routinely beaten by peers after the school disclosed his diagnosis of schizophrenia, the court applied the bad-faith-or-gross-misjudgment standard to uphold his claim for damages under section 504. The court noted that the child's section 504 accommodations plan was never updated after the disclosure, though it plainly should have been. It ruled that a finding of bad faith or gross misjudgment was a permissible inference:

> Although M.P. may not have complained to the faculty about the harassment he suffered, his mother called school administrators on a weekly basis to discuss the harassment. One could therefore find that the District acted in bad faith or with gross misjudgment on the basis of its failure to return M.P.'s mother's repeated phone calls regarding the safety of her son, the school administrators' proposals to either drastically alter M.P.'s school day or send him to an alternative school for behaviorally troubled students, and the District's assurance that it could cover the costs of M.P.'s transportation to the Northfield School District, and rescission of that offer once M.P. had enrolled in Northfield.[48]

In the context of sexual harassment in the public schools, the Supreme Court applied the deliberate indifference standard without reference to any bad-faith-or-gross-misjudgment test. In *Davis v. Monroe County Board of Education,* the decision permitting damages liability against a school district for sexual harassment by a student's peers, the Court applied a standard for liability requiring that the responsible school official or officials be deliberately indifferent to known behavior serious enough to have a systemic effect of denying the victim equal access to an educational program or activity. The Court said that the standard is met and a suit for damages is appropriate when school officials know that a child in the victim's school is engaging in sexually assaultive behavior but fail to do anything to stop it, and the child then sexually assaults the victim.[49] *Davis* involved liability under title IX of the Education Amendments of 1972, but because of the nearly identical wording of title IX and section 504, the decision suggests that assaults motivated by a child's disability will produce damages liability under section 504 or the ADA if the deliberate indifference standard is met, just as title IX imposes liability if the standard is met regarding assaults related to a child's sex. The Court had previously applied a similar standard to teacher sexual harassment of students.[50]

All the various tests that courts have used in the section 504 cases and analogous situations are simply efforts to construct the intentions of an artificial, corporate body. In the context of disability harassment, damages should be available under section 504 and title II against a school district upon a direct-evidence or inferential showing of intent on the part of that entity. Plaintiffs should be able to demonstrate intent by policy or custom, by a decision of an authoritative official to do or fail to do something, by inadequate training that amounts to deliberate indifference, by an official's deliberate indifference to known acts of harassment, by bad-faith conduct of officials, or by the officials' gross misjudgment. The *M.P.* court recognized this point when it declared, after the passage quoted above, "Whether [the employee] acted with deliberate indifference to the confidentiality of M.P.'s disability [by disclosing it] is irrelevant if it can be shown that the District acted in bad faith or with gross misjudgment when it failed to take appropriate action to protect M.P.'s academic and safety interest after the disclosure. . . ."[51]

Apart from questions about what statutes and precedents require as a predicate for damages relief, the question remains whether damages are a sensible remedy for disability harassment. They are. Disability harassment's nearest analogy among common-law causes of action is the intentional infliction of emotional distress.[52] Indeed, many cases of disability harassment that proceed on federal statutory causes of action include pendent state law claims for intentional infliction of emotional distress. Courts imposing damages remedies in intentional-infliction cases have recognized that monetary compensation is the only viable way to respond to the indignity and humiliation imposed on the victim of outrageous treatment. Moreover, it is the only sensible way, short of criminal sanctions, to deter potential defendants from engaging in behavior that oversteps the bounds of civil society.

Compensatory services are, in a word, undercompensatory. They do nothing to pay for the humiliation that the child has suffered and do little to deter school districts from engaging in similar conduct. Moreover, in the all-too-frequent situation in which a family, seeing no way out, moves away from the district, there is no longer any connection with the school that is supposed to provide the compensatory services. If the child remains in the district, compensatory education prolongs a relationship between the child and the school without necessarily changing the character of the relationship. As a remedy, it is reminiscent of Albert Alschuler's account of the first time Bernard Goetz was robbed: the mugger, savvy to the system, tried to use a mediation process to derail the criminal justice proceedings.[53] Compensatory education may be a good remedy in situations in which solutions can be mediated between a school district acting in good faith and a child whose parents want to maintain a long-term relationship with that school. It is no remedy for a child who has been "mugged"—physically or mentally assaulted—by the school district, its employees, or students.

Tuition reimbursement, though it may be an appropriate part of monetary relief in some cases, is similarly inadequate as a remedy standing by itself. Relatively few parents incur tuition bills as a direct result of harassment. Typically, they incur tuition costs because the particular mix of services the child needs is not available in the educational program the school district offers, so the parents contract for education at a specialized private school. In some instances, parents remove their child from public school and pay tuition elsewhere to get the child away from abuse by peers or teachers. Even in that situation, however, tuition reimbursement is undercompensatory. It makes up for the out-of-pocket costs caused by the defendants' conduct but does nothing to remedy the humiliation and loss of self-esteem the child suffers.

Moreover, the deterrent and symbolic effects of damages awards matter.[54] Although school district administrators may not pay awards out of their own pockets, the school superintendent will certainly be in an awkward position trying to explain a large damages award to the school board, which makes decisions about the superintendent's contract and salary. If disability harassment is ever to be stopped, the threat of damages will be an important reason for the change. In addition, damages awards have an important symbolic role in expressing social disapproval. Social disapproval of disability harassment is crucial to taking harassment seriously and stopping it.

Violation of ADA Section 12203(b)

Chapter 4 of this book noted that the ADA has a provision barring intimidation, coercion, threats, and interference with ADA rights and argued that the provision establishes a claim for workplace harassment that discourages individuals from exercising the right to obtain and work at a job and to demand and receive accommodations, even when the harassment does not amount to a severe or pervasive hostile environment that violates the antidiscrimination provisions of title I. The same provision, 42 U.S.C. § 12203(b), applies to the exercise of rights under title II, such as the right of a person with a disability to enroll in and attend public school and to demand and receive accommodations there; one of the title II regulations specifically recapitulates the language of the statute.[55] Physical or verbal abuse that children with disabilities sustain simply because they are on public school grounds is conduct that intimidates and interferes with people who are exercising rights to participate in a public educational program. The remedies provision for violations of this provision incorporates the same remedies that are available generally in title II cases, specifically damages (with no set limits) and any other appropriate relief, such as injunctions. As noted in chapter 4, though liability under some other provisions of the ADA extends only to covered entities rather than persons, individual personal liability exists in claims for coercion.[56]

Constitutional Violations

Constitutional claims over disability harassment sound in equal protection and due process, rights guaranteed by the first section of the Fourteenth Amendment. The initial question in determining whether a given form of discrimination violates equal protection is what standard of review to apply. Violations are far more readily found if an elevated standard, either intermediate scrutiny or strict scrutiny, applies to the practice being challenged. The Supreme Court has asserted that it applies a rational-basis test in evaluating claims of discrimination based on mental retardation, although many commentators believe that the leading case, *City of Cleburne v. Cleburne Living Center, Inc.,* in fact applies a higher standard of review.[57]

In *Cleburne,* the Court ruled that a municipality violated equal protection by not permitting a group home to be established for persons with mental retardation. The Court swept aside asserted justifications for application of the zoning ordinance barring the proposed use of the land, including congestion in the neighborhood, overcrowding of the home, fire hazards, and other safety concerns. Though the Court accurately noted that these justifications had not been used to zone out other comparable uses of the land, such as nursing homes or fraternities, the Court appeared to be ignoring a key aspect of rational-basis review: that when the rational-basis test applies, the government simply needs to have a rational connection between the chosen category and the legitimate goal, not to pursue the goal consistently across all categories. Under the rational-basis test, the government does not violate equal protection when it approaches a problem piecemeal or along lines of least political resistance for what it is doing.[58] Thus *Cleburne* in its language might be a rational-basis case, but implicitly it sets a higher standard.

In a later case, *Heller v. Doe,* the Supreme Court applied an ordinary rational-basis test to sustain a statute that imposed a clear-and-convincing-evidence standard of proof and provided party status for relatives in proceedings for civil commitment of persons with mental retardation.[59] The state's law established that persons subject to proceedings for civil commitment on the basis of mental illness had to be shown to meet the test for commitment by a reasonable-doubt standard, and it denied relatives the status of parties in those cases. More recently, in *Board of Trustees of the University of Alabama v. Garrett,* the Court denied that *Cleburne* established anything higher than a rational-basis standard for the disability classification it considered.[60] The Court used that conclusion to support the position that the portion of the ADA permitting damages claims against state governments in employment cases for failure to accommodate workers violates the Eleventh Amendment, which prevents courts from allowing damages relief against states unless the damages are ordered pursuant to a law that is a proper exercise of the power Congress has to enforce the Fourteenth Amendment. The Court reasoned that Congress lacks the power under the Fourteenth Amendment to provide damages remedies against states for violating any prohibition that is not proportional to and congruent with what the Fourteenth Amendment forbids. If the Fourteenth Amendment prohibits only irrational discrimination against persons with disabilities, failure to provide what the Court called "special accommodations" does not violate the Amendment, for the Court considered it "entirely rational, and therefore constitutional, for a state employer to conserve scarce financial resources by hiring employees who are able to use existing facilities . . . . "[61] Thus the Court again affirmed the use of a rational-basis test for disability classifications under the Equal Protection Clause.

Heller and *Garrett* might lead to the conclusion that the Court has once and for all rejected elevated scrutiny for government activity that disadvantages persons on the basis of disability. This conclusion, however, may be premature. The *Garrett* case was a five-to-four decision, with a strenuous dissent arguing for a broader view of *Cleburne* in which state decision making based on negative attitudes and stereotypes violates equal protection. Two justices who made up part of the five-member majority steered clear of the controversy over *Cleburne*'s meaning and read the conduct that title I of the ADA sought to correct with regard to state employers more as "failure of a State to revise policies now seen as incorrect under a new understanding of proper policy" than anything that would violate the Constitution, seemingly under any test, rational basis or elevated scrutiny.[62] *Heller* itself was an unusual case in that the parties challenging the statute never properly presented the contention that elevated scrutiny ought to apply.[63] It is at least arguable that the distinctions drawn between people with mental retardation and those with mental illness would pass an intermediate scrutiny test, had *Heller* employed one. A substantial relation between the distinctions and important governmental goals does not appear that difficult to demonstrate, for the long-term nature of mental retardation and the relative ease of showing its existence compared to mental illness, combined with the relative intrusiveness of forced psychiatric treatment compared with forced commitment for mental retardation, all support the idea of less stringent safeguards for individuals with mental retardation.

In other words, the Court might still be on a road to elevated scrutiny for disability categories, or at least some disability categories in some instances. History suggests that an erratic pattern of decisions, combined with protests by the Court that it is applying a rational-basis test, may lead to an eventual use of intermediate scrutiny. The Court's modern decisions on sex discrimination initially used a rational-basis test, then in one instance applied a strict-scrutiny test, then settled down into an intermediate test, though the content of the test remains a subject of debate.[64] The characteristics of long-term, severe disability (its permanence and the stigma that attaches to it, for example) support the application of some form of elevated scrutiny, as Justice Marshall's opinion in *Cleburne* convincingly demonstrated.[65] Applying intermediate scrutiny to disability harassment yields the unavoidable conclusion that the harassing conduct violates equal protection. The government singles out an individual for ridicule or physical intimidation or other harm simply because that person is different and vulnerable. There is no substantial relationship to any important goal that the government is actually pursuing.

The argument that official harassment or tolerance of harassment violates equal protection does not, however, require applying intermediate scrutiny. The rational-basis test demands that the government classification be rationally related to a legitimate governmental end. In cases of harassment in the public schools, a governmental entity singles out children with disabilities for mistreatment. No legitimate governmental end is served. Indulging popular prejudices is not a legitimate governmental goal, nor is the "bare . . . desire to harm a politically unpopular group."[66] As James Leonard has pointed out, the Court's condemnation of the antigay initiative in *Romer v. Evans* in 1996 shows that disadvantaging unpopular groups for the simple sake of so doing continues to be a clear violation of equal protection.[67] Disadvantaging for the sake of doing so is precisely what harassment does. *Garrett* further reinforces the conclusion that government-sponsored or tolerated harassment violates equal protection by reaffirming *Cleburne*'s central holding that irrational conduct motivated by negative attitudes against people with disabilities is indeed a Fourteenth Amendment violation. The concurring opinion of Justice Kennedy took special pains to distinguish what the Court said did not constitute a clear violation of the Constitution from conduct based on "malicious ill will," which does.[68] In its two most recent decisions regarding the ADA and its role as a proper measure to enforce the Fourteenth Amendment, the Court approved the use of damages claims under title II against states for failure to accommodate in cases regarding access to courtrooms and regarding prison conditions that violate the prohibition on cruel and unusual punishment. Thus, without elevating the standard of review for disability classifications, the Court has affirmed that failure to accommodate may be irrational discrimination in violation of the Equal Protection Clause.[69]

Courts are beginning to recognize that disability harassment in the schools constitutes a violation of equal protection. In *Smith v. Maine School Administrative District No. 6*, the plaintiff, a student with mental retardation and other disabilities, alleged that the assistant principal had excluded her from a school dance because of her disabilities; that room was not made for her to sit with the rest of the school chorus during a performance until her father intervened; and that at the instruction of the chorus director, a fellow student directed her to stop singing too loudly during the performance.[70] The incidents resulted in students ridiculing and shunning the plaintiff. The court found that the allegations gave rise to an inference of discriminatory intent and that if a rational-basis test were applied to the way in which the defendants treated the plaintiff on the basis of her disability, the allegations were sufficient to support the conclusion that the defendants violated equal protection.

Damages are an appropriate remedy for equal-protection violations. In general, proof of equal protection and other constitutional violations brought under the Civil Rights Act of 1871, 42 U.S.C. § 1983, gives rise to the full range of remedial options, including compensatory and punitive damages.[71]

Due process claims include both substantive and procedural due process. Abuse of power by individuals with governmental authority over persons subject to them violates the aspect of the Due Process Clause identified as substantive due process. Governmental creation of a danger to an individual may support liability for the resulting harm. For example, in *Armijo v. Wagon Mound Public Schools*, the Tenth Circuit upheld a substantive due process claim based on a child's suicide when school officials were on notice of a child's suicidal propensities but suspended him and drove him home, where they knew he had access to firearms, without determining whether an adult was present there.[72] Liability for violations of substantive due process may also be premised on the existence of a special relationship between the school officials and the victim, such as when the child is in the school's custody. For example, in another Tenth Circuit case, *Sutton v. Utah State School for the Deaf and Blind*, the court held that the plaintiff stated a substantive due process claim against the principal of a state school in his individual capacity when the principal failed to adopt or implement a policy or training program to prevent sexual assaults on a child with disabilities after the principal was placed on notice of a previous assault on the same victim by the same offender.[73]

On analogy to these cases, substantive due process liability exists for disability harassment at least in instances in which serious mental or physical harm is visited on a child with disabilities in school and the school, as in *Armijo*, is aware of the dangers and places the child in a dangerous position, such as an unsupervised classroom or playground, without taking precautions to prevent abuse on account of the child's difference. Similarly, substantive due process liability exists when, as in *Sutton*, the child is in a custodial relationship, the school officials are on notice of the danger to the child, and they take no precautions to prevent harassment.

What about procedural due process? Disability harassment, even in ordinary, rather than more extreme, cases constitutes a procedural due process violation. Procedural due process applies when government makes an individualized determination that deprives a person of life, liberty, or property. The Supreme Court has found that suspending a child for a disciplinary infraction violates procedural due process if the child does not receive some kind of hearing before the punishment.[74] Harassment by teachers, principals, and others with governmental authority over a child deprives the child of a liberty and property interest in receiving educational services. When a teacher ridicules a child or physically abuses her, the teacher is singling the child out for mistreatment without affording the child any fair opportunity to contest whether the harm is merited. In one of the two cases that led to congressional passage of the law that is now IDEA, a court found a violation of procedural due process in the conduct of District of Columbia schools in excluding children from regular classes, without a hearing or other procedures, on the grounds that they had behavior problems, mental retardation, emotional disturbance, or hyperactivity.[75] If exclusion from school on these bases requires a hearing, so too does singling out a child for harassment on the same basis, official action that interferes with the child's enjoyment of the right to attend school and profit from it.

Damages are an appropriate remedy for violations of due process.[76] Even when the denial of due process causes no discernable harm, the plaintiff is entitled to a remedy of nominal damages.[77]

6

New Approaches to Liability for Harassment in the Public Schools

The previous chapter outlined a number of remedies for disability harassment in the public schools that have exceedingly strong support in existing case law. When courts reject the arguments for those remedies, the obstacle appears to be the courts' failure to address the facts as a serious problem and apply widely accepted legal principles. This chapter will address some legal approaches with regard to harassment in the schools that have somewhat less support in existing case law. These include claims for damages for harassment brought under the special education law—that is, IDEA—and responses to the defenses that often have defeated damages claims under section 504, the ADA, the Constitution, and other sources of law. The chapter will focus on the most important of these defenses, the failure to administratively exhaust a potential claim under IDEA as a barrier to damages claims brought under other laws. It will present arguments for the existence of a damages claim for violations of IDEA and will contend that the legal principle of mandatory exhaustion of administrative remedies has no place in barring cases brought under other statutory or constitutional provisions for damages in school harassment cases. It will further argue that government officials' immunity should not be an obstacle to damages suits against them.

Claims under the Individuals with Disabilities Education Act

IDEA guarantees children with disabilities a free, appropriate public education. Accordingly, the claims and remedies under the statute merit discussion in the context of legal claims for disability harassment.

Education in a setting rife with harassment is hardly conducive to learning and is antithetical to "appropriate education" for children with disabilities. Nevertheless, when the drafters of what was to become IDEA conceived of how it would operate, they predominantly had in mind situations in which children with disabilities were getting inadequate or improper services. This preoccupation led the Supreme Court to comment that through the Act "Congress sought primarily to make public education available to handicapped children" and that Congress relied on the observance of statutory procedures by schools and parents to achieve the correct type and level of services for eligible children.[1] The kind of dispute that would be resolved by following procedures for meetings, written plans, and administrative hearings would be like those found in the Supreme Court's special education docket early in the history of the statute: a dispute over whether a sign-language interpreter had to be provided to a deaf child with excellent lipreading abilities, or a demand that a school district provide catheterization at school for a child who could not urinate normally.[2] Problems such as harassment of children with disabilities subvert the appropriate education guaranteed by the Act, but the Act's focus is on getting the appropriate services in the first place, not on the proper remedies to impose when peers or teachers engage in discrimination and effectively undermine the program. Indicative of the congressional preoccupation with getting the services to the children rather than providing against intentional interference with use of the services was the failure to enact an antiretaliation provision in IDEA, even though Congress was familiar with such provisions and had inserted them in the Civil Rights Act of 1964 and other civil rights laws.[3]

Moreover, only children who meet the definition of children with disabilities under IDEA are able to obtain the protections of that law. Many children have physical or mental impairments, but they do not need to receive special education in order to learn, so they are not covered under the terms of the Act. For example, a child who needs a wheelchair for mobility would meet the ADA's definition of a person with disabilities, but if she does not need special education, she is outside the coverage of IDEA. Similarly, children with mental conditions that limit major life activities unrelated to learning or with borderline effects on learning may not qualify for the Act's protection. These children may be entitled to services or to program modifications pursuant to section 504 or the ADA, but they would not be able to make a claim under IDEA for harassment by teachers or peers or for any other conduct.[4]

The emphasis in the Act on educational and related services and the gaps in the coverage of the Act make it a less than ideal avenue for relief in harassment cases. This is not to say that a school district's maintenance of an environment in which harassment occurs does not violate IDEA. If the environment renders the education inappropriate for an eligible child's needs, the district has violated IDEA, so, typically, harassment will violate the Act. An example of a successful claim brought under the special education law is *Shore Regional High School Board of Education v. P.S.*, discussed in the last chapter, the case of the boy with multiple disabilities who was called names, pelted with rocks, on one occasion hit with a padlock, and otherwise harassed by his peers.[5] The school did not respond effectively, so the parents enrolled him in a school in a neighboring district, incurring out-of-district tuition. Although the lower court rejected the claim, the court of appeals reinstated an administrative decision awarding tuition reimbursement to the parents on the ground that the original school district failed to offer an appropriate education and the school the parents chose did. Reimbursement of tuition is an established form of relief under IDEA, as are compensatory services.[6]

Although maintaining an environment in which harassment takes place violates IDEA, it will be a rare instance in which tuition reimbursement or compensatory services will be an adequate remedy. Even in *Shore Regional,* no compensation was provided for the child's humiliation, pain and suffering, or physical invasion. The tuition award provided little deterrence for future toleration of harassing conduct. The consensus of decisions is that the statute itself does not permit administrative hearing officers to award damages other than tuition reimbursement, such as compensation for humiliation, pain and suffering, or physical invasion; several circuit courts have generalized the point to forbid damages claims in court actions under IDEA.[7] Tuition reimbursement and compensatory education are no more than second-best remedies for the pain and humiliation that harassment inflicts.

A number of courts, however, have permitted courts to award damages for at least some classes of IDEA violations, not directly under the statute itself but under 42 U.S.C. § 1983, which permits individuals to sue when their federal statutory rights have been infringed by people acting with government authority.[8] In *W.B. v. Matula,* for example, the Third Circuit ruled that the plaintiffs could assert a claim for a violation of IDEA under section 1983 when a school district took most of a child's first-grade year to find that he was eligible for services under section 504 due to attention deficit hyperactivity disorder, used most of his second-grade year to determine that he was neurologically impaired and eligible for services under IDEA, and then spent all of the following year resisting an independent evaluation—which ultimately found that the child had Tourette's syndrome and a severe obsessive-compulsive disorder in addition to hyperactivity.[9] A hearing officer finally resolved the dispute over the services, ordering the child placed in a private school with additional therapy sessions, but the decision did not occur until the beginning of the following school year. The court noted that section 1983 exists to provide a means of redress for violations of federal law by governmental agents. The court acknowledged that section 1983 will not furnish a remedy if Congress intended to foreclose its use by adopting a comprehensive statutory enforcement plan inconsistent with section 1983. But with regard to the statute that is now IDEA, Congress overruled a Supreme Court decision, *Smith v. Robinson,* which had found the section 1983 avenue to be closed off under that theory.[10] In the Handicapped Children's Protection Act of 1986 (HCPA), Congress intended to overrule *Smith* and to restore the availability of section 1983 in special education cases. As the *W.B.* court stated: "In enacting [the HCPA], Congress specifically intended that [IDEA] violations could be redressed by § 504 and § 1983 actions . . . ."[11] Section 1983 actions carry the full range of available civil remedies, including compensatory damages.[12] The *W.B.* court found no obstacle to the award of damages pursuant to section 1983 for IDEA violations, though it cautioned that other remedies may be more suitable under the facts of a given case.

In *Padilla v. School District No. 1,* the Tenth Circuit Court of Appeals took a view contrary to that of the Third Circuit.[13] *Padilla* involved a child with severe disabilities who sued her previous school district, alleging that the district had ignored the written program it had created for her services and had failed to provide her with behavioral programming, augmentative communication, and tube-feeding services. District personnel also repeatedly placed her in a windowless closet, restrained her in a stroller, and left her without supervision. During one of those incidents, she tipped over and suffered a skull fracture, which exacerbated her seizure disorder. Her injuries kept her from school the rest of the semester, but the district did not provide her with the homebound services to which she was entitled. Although the court permitted a claim for damages to proceed under the ADA, it required the dismissal of a section 1983 claim premised on violations of IDEA. It held that although Congress overruled *Smith v. Robinson* in the HCPA, the overruling was intended to restore only the ability to make section 1983 claims for constitutional violations, not the ability to make section 1983 claims for violations of statutes, including IDEA. For support, the court noted two occasions on which the Supreme Court after passage of the HCPA cited *Smith* in discussing the availability of section 1983 in contexts other than the special education law. The *Padilla* court thought the citations indicated that some portion of the holding remained valid.[14]

Padilla's approach to this issue is misguided. The HCPA's legislative history makes clear that Congress intended to maintain means of enforcing IDEA other than the section 1415 process.[15] The HCPA established that, contrary to what the Supreme Court held in *Smith,* section 1415 is not an exclusive remedy. Once the assumption that section 1415 is exclusive is done away with, ordinary principles regarding the scope of section 1983 dictate that it is available to remedy violations of IDEA.[16] The fact that the Supreme Court cited *Smith* in other contexts does not indicate any conscious effort by the Court to maintain an implied holding about the preemptive effect of IDEA in the teeth of congressional action to the contrary. Given that the Supreme Court has decided only a dozen cases under the special education statute in the thirty years the law has been in existence, it is imputing to the Court a phenomenal degree of knowledge of the intricacies of the statute to conclude that the Court meant to recognize the preservation of an implied holding about preemption of section 1983 IDEA claims by twice referring to *Smith* in cases having to do with different laws.[17] At the most, the citations indicate only the continued use of the same methods that *Smith* used in determining when section 1983 has been preempted when Congress has said nothing explicit about preemption one way or the other.[18] The majority of the courts of appeals that have ruled on the question have found that section 1983 provides a private action for IDEA violations, at least in some circumstances.[19]

Harassment is a violation of IDEA for which the section 1983 remedial avenue seems the most logical. If section 1983 is a vehicle for remedying statutory torts, harassing conduct that violates the federal special education statute falls within the center of that purpose. Unlike some statutes whose private enforcement would be inconsistent with federal policies, IDEA's basic purpose was to give parents a means by which they personally could enforce federal special education law.[20] Moreover, as noted above with regard to the ADA and section 504 claims, damages are the most sensible remedy for harassment. Accordingly, a remedial vehicle that provides damages relief merits consideration, if only because of that fact. If the section 1983 claim is available for outrageous conduct such as harassment, the ordinary action under IDEA can be reserved for placement disputes or other cases in which prospective relief, tuition reimbursement, or compensatory services are the most sensible remedies.

The discussion of disability harassment claims suggests that the conduct creates damage liability under any number of theories. Although some courts succeed in misunderstanding the nature of the remedy and dismiss valid cases on that basis, the greater number of cases are dismissed on the ground of various defenses to liability. These defenses include failure to exhaust administrative remedies; the application of official immunity; and the application of Eleventh Amendment immunity of state governmental agencies. Many courts, however, misapply these defenses in dismissing harassment actions.

The Defense of Failure to Exhaust Administrative Remedies

The exhaustion requirement poses the single greatest obstacle to damages claims for disability harassment. Some courts recognize exceptions to exhaustion for these cases and properly treat the claims as discrimination cases. Other courts do not appreciate the significance of the discrimination at work and apply the exhaustion defense without serious consideration of the nature of the claim.

To bring a civil action under 20 U.S.C. § 1415 for violations of IDEA, the plaintiff must be a "party aggrieved by the findings and decision" of the hearing procedure created by the statute.[21] This restriction on who can sue operates as an administrative exhaustion requirement, keeping anyone who has not pursued the hearings procedure from filing an action under section 1415. The HCPA, which overruled *Smith v. Robinson* and permitted section 504, section 1983, and, once the ADA was passed, title II actions, spelled out the rule by providing that "before the filing of a civil action under such laws seeking relief that is also available under [section 1415], the procedures [for administrative hearings and appeals] shall be exhausted to the same extent as would be required had the action been brought under this subchapter."[22] Although Congress intended the exhaustion requirement to be flexible so that meritorious cases would get a judicial hearing, many courts have applied the rule woodenly, barring cases even when the plaintiffs present persuasive reasons for excusing ex-haustion.[23]

In a number of cases involving disability harassment or closely analo-gous situations, courts have dismissed cases for lack of administrative ex-haustion. The most prominent of these may be *Charlie F. v. Board of Ed-ucation*, the case about the fourth-grade encounter sessions in which stu-dents were encouraged to vent their rage at a child with a variety of disabling conditions.[24] The court ruled that the case had to be dismissed on exhaustion grounds, even though the child was no longer in the school system, was not suing under IDEA, and was asking only damages as a remedy. It declared that the portion of the exhaustion requirement refer-ring to relief available means relief for events or conditions at issue in the suit, not relief preferred by the plaintiff. The court concluded that some useful forms of relief that were not asked for, such as compensatory edu-cation or services, would be available from the administrative process even though damages were not.

The court's reasoning that the usefulness of any potential relief in an IDEA proceeding triggers the duty to exhaust is impossible to square with the language of the HCPA. The HCPA phrase "seeking relief that is also available under this subchapter" refers to the civil action filed by the plaintiff, not a hypothetical action that the plaintiff could have brought.[25] The court neatly read the word "seeking" out of the statute. Moreover, the court's argument about the usefulness of alternate relief is weakened by the fact that the child was no longer in the district at the time of the suit and is then toppled by the reality that compensatory services will never make a victim whole for humiliation and intimidation. If they did, courts would award services in intentional tort cases, not damages. The nature of the harm caused by harassment and its inability to be made whole by measures such as orders for services or tuition reimbursement distinguishes harassment cases from cases having to do with educational methodology or levels of educational services, in which a damages claim might be pled simply to circumvent the administrative process.[26]

Courts have frequently excused exhaustion in cases involving ADA or section 504 claims, as well as cases in which violations of IDEA are as-serted through either section 1983 or the statute itself. Many of these cases use reasoning that casts doubt on that employed in *Charlie F*. A leading case is *W.B. v. Matula*, discussed above in connection with section 1983 claims to enforce IDEA.[27] The plaintiffs alleged protracted delays in the evaluation of and delivery of services to a child who was eventually diagnosed with neurological impairments and other disabilities. The court noted that the mere assertion of a section 1983 claim does not excuse exhaustion, but it stressed that the plaintiffs in the case were seeking damages and that damages were not available in an IDEA administrative proceeding. Accordingly, following the statement in the HCPA legislative history that "'[e]xhaustion of administrative remedies would . . . be excused where . . . resort to those proceedings would be futile,'" the court ruled that exhaustion was not required.[28] The court also pointed out that evidentiary matters concerning evaluation, classification, and placement were no longer in dispute and thus there was no justification for exhaustion for developing a record on those issues.

Harassment cases present an even stronger basis for excusing exhaustion than does a delay and neglect case such as *W.B.* For one thing, the harassment cases are likely not to include an IDEA claim at all but instead usually are framed in terms of violations of section 504, the ADA, and the Constitution. Any IDEA claims will be, like those in *W.B.*, section 1983 damages claims for violations of the statute. Even more than a dispute over failure to evaluate and provide services to a child, matters of deliberate harassment go beyond the core concerns of IDEA and its main goal of promptly getting adequate services to children. As a second reason to excuse exhaustion, the propriety of damages relief for harassment is far clearer than it is for delays. Compensatory services may be a sufficient remedy for delays in some cases. Thus, even if one were to work the kind of changes in the text of section 1415(*l*) that the *Charlie F.* court did and ignore the drafters' stress on the relief actually sought in the case, exhaustion should be excused because the proper relief in a harassment case—damages—is not available from the IDEA administrative process.

An approach similar to that of *W.B.* was adopted in *Covington v. Knox County School System*, the case in which a child was routinely locked in a darkened, vaultlike time-out room. The court declared that in a case in which the child's "injuries are wholly in the past, and therefore money damages are the only remedy that can make him whole[,] proceeding through the state's administrative process would be futile and is not required before the plaintiff can file suit in federal court."[29] The court upheld a claim for violation of substantive due process.

In the years since the *Charlie F.* decision, most courts excusing exhaustion in harassment cases have distinguished the case rather than confronting it head on. Thus in *Witte v. Clark County School District*, the case in which a student was force-fed, choked, and otherwise abused, the court said that the situation was different from *Charlie F.* in that the parties in *Charlie F.* did not ultimately agree on a different placement, whereas in *Witte* the new placement came about during informal administrative procedures.[30] The court also distinguished *Charlie F.* on the ground that damages there were considered a substitute for remedial services, whereas in *Witte*, "Plaintiff expressly eschews any claim for monetary damages to provide, or to be measured by the cost of, remedial services. Rather, the claim for damages is retrospective only."[31] Finally, the court considered a case involving primarily physical abuse to be distinguishable from one involving primarily verbal abuse. The court permitted the section 504 and ADA claims to stand, even though the plaintiffs had not exhausted. In *Padilla v. School District No. 1*, the case of the child kept in a stroller in a closet, the court also distinguished *Charlie F.*, reading the case as a requirement that when "the IDEA's ability to remedy a particular injury is unclear, exhaustion should be required in order to give educational agencies an initial opportunity to ascertain and alleviate the alleged problem."[32] The court said that damages for the fractured skull and other injuries the child sustained were not redressable through the IDEA administrative process and permitted an ADA damages claim to proceed.

The fact that these decisions distinguished *Charlie F.*, rather than flatly disagreeing with it, does not lend support to the *Charlie F.* approach and its judicial rewriting of section 1415(*l*). In reality, the first two distinctions relied on in the *Witte* decision are thin; they depend entirely on how the plaintiff chose to characterize the dispute with the school district and the relief being sought. The third distinction, also relied on in *Padilla*, that the injuries were physically as well as verbally inflicted, is dubious in that Charlie also suffered physical attacks from his classmates and the plaintiffs in both *Witte* and *Padilla* also suffered abuse other than physical assaults. Moreover, the courts never explained why psychological abuse is any less a matter for the judicial system, as opposed to the administrative system, than physical abuse is. Effectively, the courts have limited the application of *Charlie F.* in their circuits in cases involving disability harassment. Even in the Seventh Circuit, *Charlie F.* has somewhat limited application. For example, the court reversed a dismissal for failure to exhaust in a case in which a child with muscular dystrophy sued for damages when a physical education teacher ignored the restrictions on activity in his individualized education program and forced him to run laps and do push-ups, causing him serious muscle and kidney damage.[33] The court cited *Padilla* and *Witte* and said that the injuries could not be addressed by the administrative procedures. The same logic applies to *Charlie F.* itself.

Although some commentators have argued that considerations of policy support an exhaustion rule for damages cases, as if policy considerations could permit courts to disregard the language and intent of section 1415(*l*), the case for the exhaustion rule in the harassment context is exceedingly weak. The policies behind administrative exhaustion include making maximum use of the policy-making authority and expertise of administrators and achieving economy in provision of procedural mechanisms to challenge government decisions.[34] The connection between exhaustion and those policies is highly attenuated in educational harassment damages cases. First, the due process hearing officer is required to be independent of the school system and the state educational agency and so is in no position to be developing policy for those entities.[35] Second, the due process hearing officer need have no particular training or credentials and thus will not necessarily have any expertise to apply.[36] Third, assuming hearing officers lack the power to order awards of damages, it is not clear that hearing officers confronting damages-only claims will even hold a hearing on the issues relevant to the damages claim.[37] And if they do, it is highly likely that the parties will take the case to court and retry it before a jury, the factfinder in a section 504 or ADA damages case, eliminating any administrative or judicial economy advantages of exhaustion.

Moreover, Congress did not approach exhaustion in special education cases purely as a policy matter. Congress understood that practical considerations about the utility of the administrative process should control, and it recognized the probable weaknesses in the IDEA due process scheme. Section 1415(*l*) excuses exhaustion when the claim is brought under something other than the IDEA cause of action and the relief sought is not available under IDEA. The language of § 1415(*l*) prevails over any administrative law policy that might call for its judicial rewriting.

When courts assimilate disability harassment into disputes over services and methodology and apply an exhaustion requirement intended for those cases, they fail to treat with necessary seriousness the real injuries that harassment inflicts. These real injuries are best addressed by court actions for damages, and, under the language of the special education law as well as the evidence of the intentions of its drafters, exhaustion of administrative remedies should not be required.

The Official Immunity Defense

Official immunity may also bar some disability harassment claims against individual teachers or school administrators. Public-official defendants may claim immunity from section 1983 claims for violation of the Constitution if their conduct was not contrary to established law a reasonable person would have known of at the time the conduct occurred.[38] In several cases, courts have immunized public school teachers and administrators from liability for violating the Constitution by engaging in conduct that some might consider analogous to engaging in or tolerating disability harassment. Harassment, however, is behavior that is contrary to established law, so it should not be protected by official immunity against constitutional claims.

Courts have immunized defendants from damages liability in cases alleging violations of substantive due process by improperly using a body-wrapping technique on a child with severe mental retardation, by failing to prevent a child in a state residential school for the deaf from being sexually assaulted by an older classmate, and by confining a young man with mild mental retardation and behavior problems in a state institution where his liberty was unjustifiably restricted and he was sexually abused by an employee.[39] Without agreeing that the courts properly applied qualified immunity in each of these situations, it is easy to conclude that perpetrating or condoning disability harassment is a different case, one to which qualified immunity does not apply. In none of the three cases that applied qualified immunity did the individual defendants act out of malice or hostility toward people with disabilities. In each case the court stressed that the defendants did not depart significantly from professional standards without just cause, did not engage in deliberate indifference to the known needs of the plaintiffs, or did not fail to protect an individual for whom the duty to protect was clearly established.[40] Actions undertaken out of malice or hostility, or inactions that constitute deliberate indifference, form the foundation of claims for disability harassment. Malicious conduct and deliberate indifference to known harassment engaged in by others are violations of established rights of which any teacher or school official should be aware.[41]

In a number of cases closely analogous to disability harassment situations, courts have rejected defenses based on qualified immunity. *Armijo v. Wagon Mound Public Schools* is the case discussed in chapter 5 involving the child who, though he had told a school aide his suicidal thoughts, was suspended by the principal and driven home by a counselor without notice to his parents, and who killed himself when he arrived there.[42] In that case, the court of appeals ruled that the principal and guidance counselor had increased the danger to the child in violation of the child's established rights, and it rejected the official immunity defense. In situations in which teachers or administrators know of dangers of peer harassment but place the children with disabilities in unsupervised situations with students who are prone to harm them because of their disabling conditions, the school personnel knowingly place the children in danger in violation of established rights.

In other situations, such as protracted delays in provision of services and failure to provide required procedures, courts have found that defendants have violated established rights and forfeited official immunity.[43] Harassing children or permitting the harassment to take place would appear to be a clearer violation of rights of which the administrators should have been aware than the omissions that cost defendants their immunity in those cases.

Municipal corporations such as school districts do not enjoy the protection of official immunity. The courts have reasoned that leaving an injured plaintiff without a remedy in order to induce persons to undertake public service is an appropriate trade-off for immunity from personal, not entity liability.[44] Hence school districts may not claim immunity from liability for disability harassment.

Eleventh Amendment Immunity

Some entities engaged in public schooling are agencies of state government rather than agencies of local government. These state agencies may be state schools for children who are blind or deaf or schools on the site of state institutions for children with developmental disabilities or mental illness. State defendants in these settings may attempt to claim Eleventh Amendment immunity against causes of action for damages for harassment if the cases are brought in federal court. The Eleventh Amendment barrier to retrospective monetary remedies is a serious obstacle to enforcement of the right to be free from harassment in settings operated by the state, one that would apply with regard to state (but not individual) liability even in cases of blatant or acknowledged violations of the law.[45]

The Eleventh Amendment's text appears merely to limit the provision in Article III of the Constitution authorizing jurisdiction in the federal courts when a citizen of one state sues a citizen of another. The Amendment bars foreigners and citizens of other states from suing a state in a federal court, and it originated in the controversy that followed a Supreme Court case upholding the ability of out-of-state or foreign holders of state obligations to collect against a state government by suing in federal court. Under the Supreme Court's case law since 1890, however, the Amendment has come to represent a broad immunity from private suit in federal court that may be asserted by state agency defendants. The immunity extends to suits by citizens of the state being sued, and it extends to actions when there is federal question or another basis for jurisdiction in the federal courts, not just when diversity of state citizenship is the reason the case is there.[46]

Two doctrines are available to escape the operation of the immunity as a barrier to damages claims against state entities for harassment in the school setting. One is the recognized authority of Congress to abrogate the immunity; the other is the states' own power to waive the immunity. In *Fitzpatrick v. Bitzer*, the Court held that Congress has the authority to abrogate Eleventh Amendment immunity if it imposes liability on states using its power under section 5 of the Fourteenth Amendment, the amendment's enforcement provision.[47] Congress intended to act pursuant to its section 5 authority to enforce the Equal Protection Clause when it made the ADA and section 504 damages remedies apply to the states.[48]

These congressional intentions may not matter to the courts, however. The Supreme Court has placed limits on what Congress may do under its section 5 powers, finding in several cases that congressional enactments proscribed conduct too far afield from what the Court had established were actual violations of the Fourteenth Amendment. In each of those cases, *City of Boerne v. Flores* (concerning the Religious Freedom Restoration Act),[49] *Florida Prepaid Postsecondary Education Expense Board v. College Savings Bank* (Patent Remedy Act),[50] *United States v. Morrison* (Violence Against Women Act),[51] and *Kimel v. Florida Board of Regents* (Age Discrimination in Employment Act),[52] the Court found that the statutes imposed duties that were not congruent with and proportional to the constitutional violations they sought to remedy, so the Court held the statutes not to be proper exercises of section 5 authority.

One case concerning the ADA is part of this line of authority. In *Board of Trustees of the University of Alabama v. Garrett*, the Supreme Court ruled that title I of the ADA did not validly abrogate state immunity from suit for damages.[53] An employee brought an action against the trustees of a state university for damages for disability discrimination under titles I and II of the ADA and section 504. Alabama argued that the ADA and section 504 exceeded the section 5 power because the ambit of those statutes lacks a congruence with and proportionality to the violations of the Fourteenth Amendment that they seek to remedy. The court of appeals, however, found for the employee. It relied on an earlier holding, which concluded that in enacting the ADA Congress had acted on the basis of ample evidence of purposeful unequal treatment of people with disabilities by state and local government and thus that the congressional response was within its powers under section 5. The court of appeals in *Garrett* extended that holding to section 504, basing its decision on similar evidence showing that Congress sought to remedy and prevent violations of equal protection by passing that statute.[54]

The Supreme Court reversed. It restricted its decision to employment claims against states under title I of the ADA, however, reserving the question whether employees may sue their state employers for damages under title II.[55] The Court reasoned that Fourteenth Amendment claims of disability discrimination are evaluated under the standard of whether the conduct passes a rational-basis test. If the government's classification is a rational means to reach a legitimate governmental end, there is no Fourteenth Amendment violation. "States are not required by the Fourteenth Amendment to make special accommodations for the disabled, so long as their actions towards such individuals are rational."[56] The Court agreed that Congress may act in a prophylactic way, outlawing a broader range of conduct than the Fourteenth Amendment violation, if there is enough evidence of a pattern of violations and the congressional response is proportional to and congruent with the violations. But the Court found that there was no congressional identification of a pattern of unconstitutional employment discrimination against people with disabilities by the states and that the provisions of the statute were not proportional to and congruent with the actual violations of the Fourteenth Amendment. Therefore Congress was not acting validly in its capacity to enforce the Fourteenth Amendment when it abrogated states' Eleventh Amendment immunity in title I employment cases.[57]

In *Tennessee v. Lane*, the Court distinguished *Garrett* and adopted a different approach for an ADA title II case regarding access to public courtroom facilities.[58] On one occasion, Lane had to crawl up the courthouse steps because the facility made no accommodations for his use of wheelchair; on another he was arrested and jailed after refusing to crawl or be carried up the steps. He sued for damages under title II. The Court emphasized that title II was enacted against a backdrop of pervasive unequal treatment of persons with disabilities in the administration of state services and programs, including systematic deprivation of fundamental rights. Moreover, whatever level of equal-protection scrutiny is applied to failure to accommodate in general, failure to provide judicial access may be subject to elevated scrutiny. Thus the provision of a damages remedy for states' failure to provide accessible courtroom facilities is a response proportional to the deprivation of constitutional rights. *Lane* has a close bearing on disability harassment in the schools. The claim is one exclusively under title II, which unlike title I was a congressional response to a recognized history of pervasive discrimination against persons with disabilities in the provision of services, contrasted with the absence of a record of pervasive state discrimination in the administration of employment opportunities. And the claim is for denial of access to education on account of failure to stop harassment. When an insular minority is denied access to a meaningful education, heightened scrutiny applies, and a mere rational basis will not suffice to sustain a classification against an equal-protection challenge.[59] Accordingly, when the state is responsible for harassment that singles out someone with a disability, and the result is a deprivation of access to an education that confers a meaningful benefit, the equal-protection violation may be remedied with damages under title II.

Even *Garrett*'s reliance on the reasonable-accommodation obligation of title I and its discussion of title I's prohibition of practices with disparate impacts raise the negative inference that when state conduct amounts to a constitutional violation, Congress may provide a cause of action that abrogates state immunity. In other words, when title II of the ADA provides a remedy for government mistreatment that is motivated by hostility against people with disabilities or by fear and stereotypes that meet constitutional standards of intentionality, it is a congressional enforcement measure that is proportional to, and congruent with, the prohibition in the Constitution. Disability harassment is precisely the kind of intentional conduct motivated by hostility or the desire to subordinate that exceeds the standard established in *Cleburne* for an equal-protection violation.

To make the comparison to *Cleburne* more precise, not only do the state officials deny the permit to the group home, but they then humiliate or abuse the would-be residents or they are deliberately indifferent when those under their control do so. No matter whether *Cleburne* is viewed as a rational-basis case or something more, it established that the Equal Protection Clause forbids conduct that lacks any sensible justification and that works harm on a defined class of people with disabilities. There is no justification for harassment under any constitutional standard. *Garrett* does not bar a damages remedy under the ADA in that case, one far different under the Court's analysis[60] from a reasonable-accommodation-in-employment claim.[61]

The Supreme Court's most recent case on title II and the Eleventh Amendment confirms the conclusion that ADA title II provides a means to assert damages claims against states for intentional harassment that violates the Equal Protection Clause. In *United States v. Georgia*, the Supreme Court ruled unanimously that a state prisoner whose conditions of confinement allegedly violated both title II of the ADA and the Eighth Amendment's prohibition on cruel and unusual punishment could rely on title II's abrogation of Eleventh Amendment immunity in suing for damages. "[I]nsofar as Title II creates a private cause of action for damages against the States for conduct that actually violates the Fourteenth Amendment, Title II validly abrogates state sovereign immunity."[62] Because state violations of the Eighth Amendment deprive victims of due process guaranteed by the Fourteenth Amendment, they violate that latter provision. The general point is that the ADA's abrogation of Eleventh Amendment immunity is fully effective for conduct that actually violates the Fourteenth Amendment. That conduct includes state-sanctioned disability harassment.

Harassment claims may be brought under section 504 and IDEA as well as the ADA. Both section 504 and IDEA are exercises of Fourteenth Amendment enforcement authority, but states might raise the same question they have raised regarding the ADA about whether the statutes exceed that power.[63] For the same reasons that the ADA is within Congress's Fourteenth Amendment power, at least with regard to disability harassment claims against states, so too section 504 and IDEA are proper uses of the authority. Even if the Supreme Court were ultimately to disagree with those arguments, however, section 504 and IDEA would still be constitutionally proper exercises of congressional power under the Spending Clause. The spending for which the two statutes provide is for the general welfare, and the conditions that they impose are not coercive; a state may decline the money if it wishes. In the last seventy years, the Court has not found a single federal statute unconstitutional on the ground that it exceeded the scope of Spending Clause authority.[64]

The successful defense of the statutes as exercises of spending power has consequences for the Eleventh Amendment immunity analysis regarding waiver. State governments may waive the immunity. Acceptance of federal funds after Congress enacted a clear abrogation of immunity in section 504 and IDEA is a waiver of Eleventh Amendment immunity. The state knowingly relinquishes immunity from suit in federal court for damages in exchange for the federal money that is provided subject to the relinquishment.[65]

7

Common-Law Remedies
for Disability Harassment

This chapter will develop still another legal approach to remedying disability harassment, one that has received some attention from courts and commentators but has proven only intermittently effective in deterring the harassers or compensating those harmed by the misconduct. The approach focuses on common-law remedies, those unwritten principles of tort law that permit courts to enter civil judgments—comprising damages and possibly other relief—in favor of persons wrongfully harmed by others. This chapter will discuss the current use of common-law remedies in disability harassment cases, outline the possible legal claims, note some relevant considerations regarding the scope of disability harassment tort law, and suggest new interpretations of the law that would make the common law a more effective means of challenging wrongful activity against persons with disabilities.[1]

Current Use of Intentional-Infliction-of-
Emotional-Distress Cause of Action: Work

Common-law actions served as instructive precedent when courts first upheld statutory claims for sexual and racial harassment, but commentators described the nonstatutory tort as an inadequate response to the problem.[2] Common-law liability, which can be obtained upon the establishment of elements different from those that pertain to title VII or other statutory provisions, and which is subject to different defenses, may also prove in the end inadequate as a remedy for disability harassment. Nevertheless, it holds potential and needs further exploration. At present, plaintiffs most often join common-law claims with statutory disability harassment claims rather than bringing them as freestanding lawsuits. Nevertheless, there is no barrier to bringing such a claim on its own, and that course of action may be the only option in some cases because of problems with statutes of limitations, exhaustion, or other barriers to assertion of statutory causes of action.[3]

Even when joined to a statutory claim against an employer, a tort action may provide additional avenues of liability by permitting liability against a greater range of defendants than the ADA covers. For example, a common-law tort claim may lie against an individual co-worker or supervisor even when it does not lie against the employer. Similarly, it may apply when the plaintiff is an independent contractor of the defendant rather than an employee. Unlike damages under the employment provisions of the ADA, intentional-infliction damages are generally not subject to statutory caps. In some jurisdictions, the claim supports an award of punitive damages. Thus common-law remedies properly play a role in the response to disability harassment. Moreover, with some modest reform of the law, the remedies might be a good deal more effective.[4]

Intentional infliction of severe emotional distress is the most obvious common-law tort cause of action in cases of disability harassment. To establish liability for intentional infliction, the plaintiff must show that the defendant, by extreme and outrageous conduct, intentionally or recklessly caused the plaintiff severe emotional distress. The *Restatement Second of Torts*, which summarizes the general state of the law as of the mid-1960s, states: "Generally, the case is one in which the recitation of the facts to an average member of the community would arouse his resentment against the actor, and lead him to exclaim, 'Outrageous!'"[5] The "liability clearly does not extend to mere insults, indignities, threats, annoyances, petty oppressions, or other trivialities."[6]

The tort of intentional infliction of severe emotional distress is of recent origin. In one of the earliest cases recognizing the cause of action, the California Supreme Court gave a remedy to a businessman who had been coerced into signing a garbage collection contract by threats that were not sufficiently imminent to satisfy the standards of a cause of action for assault. Other cases have recognized the existence of the tort when plaintiffs experienced serious emotional harm when they were subjected to continual verbal abuse and abusive and threatening conduct by debt collectors and job supervisors. A few courts have expressed the importance of being cautious in extending liability, but the tort is recognized by all states.[7]

Harassing conduct relating to an individual's disability is clearly included in the tort, as long as the conduct and the harm reach the requisite level of outrageousness and severity. The *Restatement* points out that "[t]he extreme and outrageous character of the conduct may arise from the actor's knowledge that the other is peculiarly susceptible to emotional distress, by reason of some physical or mental condition or peculiarity."[8] One of the illustrations in the *Restatement* provides that liability exists for pulling a prank on a gullible person who is "eccentric and mentally deficient."[9] A leading authority stresses that a characteristic of the tort is the misuse of power: "[T]he defendant uses the inequality [of position] to inflict emotional harm without regard for the plaintiff's interests."[10] In an illustration of this principle, a court found that an intentional-infliction action lay against a police officer who belittled a victim's report of sexual assault.[11] As noted in chapters 1 and 2, the isolation experienced by persons with disabilities in the workplace and in school places them in a subordinate position, one in which others have effective power over them and frequently use it to marginalize them. The school situation is illustrative: Not only are schoolchildren with disabilities subordinate to teachers, principals, and other school personnel, but they also lack power and prestige in the social hierarchy of students. In fact, students with disabilities have the lowest social status of all children in school. They are uniquely vulnerable to abuse from other students with greater social prestige, which abuse in turn reinforces their inferior position.[12] It is particularly fitting that they should receive the benefit of a tort law cause of action whose special purpose is to protect against the abuse of power. Similar dynamics apply in the workplace and other settings, again making the invocation of the intentional-infliction tort appropriate.

In a number of cases involving employment of people with disabilities, courts have ruled that the allegations about conduct of employers or co-workers satisfied the criteria for intentional infliction of emotional distress and so have denied motions for dismissal or summary judgment. Some cases involve patterns of offensive behavior comparable to those found in the cases upholding statutory claims for hostile-environment disability harassment.

For example, in *Martinez v. Monaco/Viola, Inc.*, the plaintiff, a salesman, alleged that he had one of the best sales records in the company. When he missed six days of work due to bronchitis, one of the principals of the company called the plaintiff's doctor and learned that he had AIDS.[13] The principal told the plaintiff to resign, but he refused, and from then on neither of the two principals of the company spoke with him. A month and a half after the initial confrontation, the plaintiff was told he would no longer receive a salary, only a commission. He tried to meet with the two principals to learn how the compensation arrangement would work, but when he attended the meeting he was fired. When he refused to sign a release of liability, he was told that he would not be paid the salary and commissions due him. Applying Illinois law, the court found that the conduct could support liability for intentional infliction of emotional distress, and it denied a motion to dismiss.[14]

In a somewhat similar case, *Dutson v. Farmers Insurance Exchange,* an independent-contractor insurance salesman with hemophilia and HIV infection was "vilified and humiliated before colleagues and co-workers, his business was under constant scrutiny for no good cause, and his agency activities were flagged in such a way that administrators and officers would ridicule him to clients and in-house personnel at will."[15] Ultimately, he was forced to resign in a meeting that took place shortly after he had undergone major surgery. At the meeting, representatives of the defendants threatened to ruin his credit record, cause him to be prosecuted without any cause, ruin his reputation, and keep him from ever working again in the insurance industry. The court ruled that if a jury accepted this account of the facts, there would be a valid claim for intentional infliction of emotional distress.[16]

In yet another case, *Metzgar v. Lehigh Valley Housing Authority,* a court denied a motion to dismiss a claim for intentional infliction of emotional distress against a public agency employer, its executive director, its deputy executive director, and a supervisor when the supervisor engaged in a campaign of harassment of a worker with cerebral palsy and the directors did not address the problem after receiving notice of it.[17] The supervisor denied various accommodations requests and made verbal attacks, calling the plaintiff stupid and a cripple and making callous remarks about her disability, denigrating her abilities, berating her, cursing at her, and mocking her condition in the presence of other employees. In addition, according to the allegations of the complaint:

[The supervisor] further harassed Plaintiff in the following ways: falsely telling Plaintiff that a male had telephoned the office to say that he intended to visit her home on Christmas eve to "play games" with her; making false and defamatory remarks about her to other employees; falsely telling her clients that she was no longer employed by the Lehigh

Valley Housing Authority when she was merely on sick leave; demanding that she meet her at the office on Plaintiff's day off, conducting conferences in overheated rooms; leaving messages in places where Plaintiff would not see them and then yelling at her for not responding to them; and leaving threatening messages on her voice mail.[18]

Ultimately, the plaintiff resigned. The court ruled that she did not need to allege anything more in the way of physical injury or harm in order to sustain a claim for emotional infliction of emotional distress than the statement in the complaint that the conduct forced her to take sick leave.[19]

Some cases that may not meet one or another requirement for an ADA or other statutory harassment claim may succeed under the criteria for outrage. One such troublesome requirement for statutory claims is that the harassment be related directly to the disability. In the case of *Robel v. Roundup Corp.*, Robel, who worked in a delicatessen, fell and was injured while on the job; she filed a workers' compensation claim.[20] On returning to work, she obtained a light-duty assignment. The work consisted of a four-hour shift standing at a display counter outside the deli area offering samples of food items to customers. Several co-workers at the deli promptly began laughing at her and reenacting the slip and fall, calling her "bitch" and "cunt" while doing so.[21] They told customers she had lied about her back injury and was being punished by being assigned to give out free samples. An assistant manager joined in making fun of Robel, laughing, pointing, and staring at her. Robel complained to her union representative, who went to the store director; the store director, in turn, met with the employees and told them that further harassment would result in their termination. Three days later, the same employees resumed the conduct, laughing at Robel and loudly telling each other not to harass her. The conduct continued for the next week, with the assistant manager again participating. Eventually, Robel obtained a two-week release from work from her doctor. When she gave the note to the assistant manager, the assistant manager told the other employees, "Can you believe it, Linda's gonna sit on her big ass and get paid."[22] Robel complained again to her union representative, and one deli employee was fired, but Robel never returned to her job.

After holding a three-day nonjury trial, a judge awarded Robel nearly $52,000 in damages. The Washington Court of Appeals reversed the decision, but the Supreme Court of Washington reinstated it, upholding Robel's claims under the Washington disability discrimination law, the workers' compensation law (for discrimination in retaliation for filing a claim), and the common-law obligation not to intentionally inflict emotional distress.[23] On the intentional-infliction issue, the court characterized the conduct as that which a trial judge or jury could consider to be beyond all possible bounds of decency, atrocious, and utterly intolerable. It noted the power dynamics of the workplace and said that the abuse of power was evident. In upholding the company's liability for its employees' conduct, the court stressed that the activity took place at the workplace on working hours while the workers performed the duties they were hired to perform. It distinguished the situation of sex discrimination cases in which harassing employees acted for their own sexual gratification.[24]

The majority in *Robel* also believed that the facts satisfied all of the elements needed to sustain an action under the state disability discrimination statute. The dissenter, however, stressed that hostility between one of the co-workers and Robel preexisted Robel's injury. Thus, according to the dissent, the element that the harassment needed to be because of disability was not met. The dissenter insisted that the statutory requirement was that the harassment must not simply be related to the disability but must be motivated by the disability. Apparently, if a personal dispute motivated the harasser, and the harasser seized on the fact of the disability in order to torment the plaintiff, that would not be enough to satisfy the statute. The majority, of course, did not adopt that view. The point, however, is that the precise causation of the conduct does not matter for the intentional-infliction cause of action. If the conduct is sufficiently outrageous, no specifically disability-related motivation need be shown. *Robel* itself shows how the distinction could matter. Given the isolation and subordination that those with disabilities encounter, harassment that might have some other underlying cause—interpersonal conflict, predisposition to evil, whatever—is likely to focus upon the disability. This harassment is just as harmful to the victim and just as likely to reinforce isolation as harassment motivated solely by the fact of the disability itself. Whatever the requirements of relief might be under disability discrimination statutes, under intentional-infliction law, harassment that is outrageous simply because it focuses on the disability of the plaintiff will support a claim for relief. The dissenter did not dispute that the conduct was sufficiently outside the bounds of civilized society to sustain the intentional-infliction claim but nevertheless argued that the employer should not have been found liable for intentional infliction of emotional distress based on the employees' conduct.[25] That topic will be discussed further below.

Intentional infliction may also succeed as an avenue for relief when the ADA claim would fail because the plaintiff is not a person with a disability within the coverage of the Act. For example, various courts have found that persons with diabetes, even diabetes severe enough to cause the person to be insulin dependent, are not disabled for purposes of the Act.[26] Disability status as such does not matter for the intentional-infliction claim. In one case applying New Jersey law, the court denied a motion to dismiss a claim for intentional infliction of emotional distress when the plaintiff, a waitress with type-I insulin-dependent diabetes, was initially denied breaks in which to monitor and control her blood sugar.[27] Then, after she suffered a diabetic emergency on the job, she was ridiculed for taking the breaks, reprimanded for not monitoring customer payments during her breaks, reassigned to a less profitable part of the restaurant, written up for being late, informed that she would be fired for being late or calling in sick, and ultimately fired when she did arrive late one day. She brought no claim under the ADA. She did sue under the New Jersey Law Against Discrimination for disability discrimination, but the court did not reach that claim, so the question of her status as a person with a disability was never discussed. The intentional-infliction claim hinged on the question whether the employer's conduct was sufficiently outrageous to give rise to liability under intentional-infliction principles. The court ruled that it was.[28] As pointed out in previous chapters, the narrow reading of the term in the ADA defining a person with a disability excludes from its coverage many persons who most need the Act's protection. Samuel Bagenstos has noted that the definition of "individual with a disability" employed by the Supreme Court fails to match the range of conditions that occasion stigma.[29] Stigma both leads to and is the product of harassment. Common-law claims provide a means to escape the restrictive definition imposed by the Court.

As noted in previous chapters, while many statutory disability harassment cases fail on the ground that disability did not motivate the conduct or that the plaintiff is not considered disabled, by far the largest number fail on the ground that the harassment is insufficient to constitute a change in the conditions or terms of employment. Courts have stated that the workplace must be "permeated with discriminatory conduct—intimidation, ridicule, insult—that is sufficiently severe or pervasive to alter the conditions of [the plaintiff's] employment."[30] Although earlier chapters of this book propose an interpretation of the ADA that may return the definition of outlawed harassment to reality, the question for this chapter is whether the common-law claim of intentional infliction of emotional distress might furnish a remedy for cases that would fail if the severe-or-pervasive test were employed. The answer is maybe.

There appear to be some cases that would have difficulty under the severe-or-pervasive test that nevertheless succeed under intentional-infliction standards. Some cases in which courts have upheld intentional-infliction claims involve little more than the bare fact of termination from employment on account of a disabling condition, something that might not sustain a disability harassment case if the severe-or-pervasive standard borrowed from title VII were applied. For example, in *Soodman v. Wildman, Harrold, Allen & Dixon,* a law firm discharged an secretary while she was on medical leave for a high-risk pregnancy, the high risk being the result of a physical impairment, an incompetent uterus.[31] The firm underwent a retrenchment and laid her off; she presented evidence that the firm chose her for the reduction in force at least in part because she was on leave with her medical condition. She ultimately gave birth prematurely, and the baby died eleven days later. A doctor stated that stress could have contributed to the premature delivery.

The court denied summary judgment on the intentional-infliction claim and said she could proceed to trial. It did not require a showing of offensive language or demeaning comments directed toward the plaintiff or any pattern of abusive conduct: "Although it is . . . undisputed that Wildman, at all times, treated Soodman in a cordial and professional manner, on this record it cannot be said that no reasonable jury could find that Wildman's actions were sufficiently outrageous or that Wildman knew that severe emotional distress was substantially certain to result from its actions."[32] The court pointed out that the evidence supported an inference that the defendant knew the plaintiff was particularly susceptible to stress due to her medical condition and that the stress could itself interfere with her ability to carry the unborn child to term.

Soodman is not an isolated case; some additional precedent supports liability for intentional infliction of emotional distress based on discharge alone, and that line of authority seems generally inconsistent with the near-unattainable title VII-style liability standard for harassment liability.[33] Although success is rare on intentional-infliction claims based solely on the fact of termination, the manner of termination may support such a case. In *Archer v. Farmer Bros. Co.,* a Colorado decision, the court upheld a jury verdict for a total of $35,499 compensatory and $30,500 punitive damages in an intentional-infliction case when the employer fired Archer, an employee of twenty-two years, barely five days after he had apparently suffered a heart attack.[34] The company had two employees visit Archer while he was lying partly unclothed in bed, and they abruptly told him his employment was terminated. The appellate court ruled that this conduct could be considered intentional infliction of emotional distress, even though it noted that the trial court had dismissed the ADA and Colorado Anti-Discrimination Act claims and that the jury had found for the employer on the Age Discrimination in Employment Act claim. *Moysis v. DTG Datanet* affirmed a verdict for a worker who had sustained a brain injury in a case in which his employer led him to believe that he could return to work, knew that he strongly desired to return to work, but then fired him just one week after a meeting to discuss returning to work.[35] The court emphasized those circumstances in finding that the conduct could be considered outrageous and further stressed that the company's officials lied about the reasons for termination, damaging the worker's self-confidence.

In still other intentional-infliction cases, there was outrageous conduct beyond the simple fact of firing or even the manner of firing, but the plaintiff was nevertheless unsuccessful or might well have been unsuccessful on an ADA or other statutory harassment claim due to the severe-or-pervasive requirement. For example, *Pudim v. Colella,* a federal case applying Connecticut law, did not discuss any ADA claim, but in that case the court denied a motion to dismiss an intentional-infliction-of-emotional-distress cause of action where the employer required that a teacher on sick leave write daily lesson plans and reflections on the lessons in handwritten form despite knowledge that she had a disability of the hand that made it impossible for her to do the tasks that way.[36]

Education, Public Services, and Public Accommodations

The exaggerated character of the harassment usually required for liability under the ADA affects nonemployment disability harassment cases. Statutory hostile-environment claims regarding education, public services, and public accommodations have to contend with the severe-or-pervasive discrimination obstacle. For example, the court found conditions not to be actionable in the case alleging that Boston University created a hostile learning environment when the school adopted onerous requirements for students to obtain learning disabilities accommodations and when President Westling, who personally reviewed the accommodation requests, made speeches referring to students with learning disabilities as a plague.[37] Stating that the learning environment had not been shown to be permeated with discriminatory intimidation, ridicule, and insult, the court denied the claim. It said that even if the ADA hostile-environment standard in educational settings is less rigorous than the title VII severe-or-pervasive requirement, the standard was not met. The court in that case also rejected a common-law claim for intentional infliction of emotional distress, relying on the conclusion that the conduct was not extreme and outrageous enough. The court, however, did uphold a common-law claim for breach of contract for the university's failure to provide the accommodations promised by its promotional materials that induced the students to enroll there.

The leading education case upholding a claim of intentional infliction of emotional distress on account of disability harassment is one in which the court also upheld a claim against the school under the ADA. In *Baird v. Rose*, discussed in chapter 5 in connection with ADA claims for hostile educational environments, the Fourth Circuit Court of Appeals considered the case of a child with depression who was humiliated in class by a teacher who removed her from a musical performance and then blamed her in front of the class for causing other students to be dropped from the performance on the basis of an attendance policy that the teacher had wanted to apply to the plaintiff alone.[38] In a brief discussion of the student's intentional-infliction claim under Virginia law, the court commented that the intentionality of the conduct, its causation of the distress, and the severity of the distress were more than adequately alleged. The court then ruled that the conduct could be considered sufficiently outrageous and intolerable, particularly in light of the defendants' position of power and authority and knowledge of the student's susceptibility to the distress imposed.

In another case involving a student with depression, a court applying Illinois law refused to dismiss a claim for intentional infliction of emotional distress asserted by a student who contended that his private high school and several people associated with it impeded his athletic career.[39] The high school authorities allegedly called him a drug dealer, refused to allow him to play basketball, and undermined his academic work, trying to provoke a mental breakdown that eventually occurred. The court found that the conduct alleged went beyond merely rude or inconsiderate behavior and could be considered outrageous in light of the student's youth and the defendants' knowledge of his depression. The case did not consider an ADA or section 504 claim, so it is hard to tell if the court would have deemed the conduct sufficiently severe or pervasive to support a statutory cause of action.

Disability harassment can also occur in nonemployment, nonschool situations, such as harassment of customers in stores or clients of public agencies. In a number of cases, courts have upheld disability harassment-related liability for intentional infliction of emotional distress in settings other than the workplace, based on either a single incident or a pattern of conduct. One example is the denial of a motion to dismiss a claim based on a doctor's refusal to treat a patient with HIV infection on account of her condition. The court upheld the claim on the basis of the simple fact of failure to treat a patient at a clinic after the doctor learned of the infection: "Given the sensitive nature of her claim, it cannot be said as a matter of law that she would be unable to prove facts consistent with her present allegations that would meet [the stringent] standards [of Illinois law for intentional infliction of emotional distress]."[40] Another court denied a motion to dismiss a suit for intentional infliction when the allegation was that a disability insurer discontinued benefits under the policy of a customer who had a brain tumor, accusing him of malingering and unethically trying to continue to receive payments under the policy.[41] The court ruled that although the simple breach of the insurance policy's terms would support nothing more than a contract claim, making the accusation of malingering and unethical conduct against someone with a brain tumor could give rise to a claim for intentional infliction of emotional distress.

In still another case, *Williams v. Tri-County Metropolitan Transportation District,* a bus passenger who used a service dog alleged that the driver loudly questioned her right to bring the dog onto the bus, refused to look at papers authorizing use of the dog, wrongly insisted that the dog had to have a photo identification card, then asked why the passenger needed the dog, said that she did not look disabled but was trying to take advantage of a reduced fare, and finally ordered the passenger off the bus at her destination, loudly stating that he, the driver, did not have to have any dog on the bus if he did not want to have it there.[42] The trial court dismissed the case, but an Oregon appellate court overturned the decision and sent the case back for trial. In upholding the intentional-infliction claim, the court noted that the public obligations of a transit provider and the public nature of the alleged conduct supported the imposition of liability, but it placed greatest stress on the fact that the harassment was in connection with the status of disability. As the court observed, "[I]nsults or harassment directed to individuals on the basis of historically disfavored personal characteristics more readily transgress contemporary social bounds than do other forms of antagonistic behavior."[43] The court found this conclusion supported by the existence of hate-crime and public accommodations laws; it noted that Oregon civil rights laws clearly extend their protections to persons with disabilities. "That extensive legal framework amply reflects our social sensitivity to the distinct injuries that accrue from attitudes and behavior that single out disabled persons."[44]

The education cases, in which the courts appear generally to be applying similarly difficult standards for statutory claims and intentional infliction, may give little reason to believe that common law can provide an effective remedy when the ADA and section 504 do not. Nevertheless, intentional infliction may be an effective avenue of relief in education when the disability status of the plaintiff or the relation of the harassment to the disability is in question. Interestingly, the other nonemployment cases just described suggest the application of a more realistic standard for harassment that ought to be actionable. Several show the courts' willingness to impose liability on the basis of single incidents; all recognize the powerlessness of people with disabilities in many social situations and provide remedies for abuse of power by those who have it.

Failure to Meet Courts' Standards for Outrageous Conduct

Like statutory disability harassment claims, many, many employment, education, and other kinds of intentional-infliction cases fail, and those that fail greatly outnumber those that succeed on motions to dismiss or motions for summary judgment or at trial.[45] Unsuccessful cases usually fail on the ground that the conduct alleged is not outrageous enough to support judicial relief. Often, however, it is difficult to find anything that separates the factual patterns in the losing cases from those in the rarer victories. For example, courts have granted motions to dismiss or motions for summary judgment against a worker who alleged that he was subjected to barrages of insults and abuse by a boss over the worker's alcoholism, against a worker with multiple sclerosis who faced a tirade from a human resources representative about her intention to file an EEOC charge, and against a worker suffering from the long-term aftereffects of a subcranial hemorrhage who withstood mocking comments about his speech problems.[46] Courts have also rejected cases involving conduct more outrageous than verbal abuse. In *Shaner v. Synthes (USA)*, a federal court of appeals affirmed a grant of summary judgment on an intentional-infliction case brought by an employee who alleged that on four or five occasions someone turned up the heat in his work area to aggravate his multiple sclerosis.[47]

Some cases that fail seem virtually indistinguishable from those that succeed. In *Van Stan v. Fancy Colours & Co.*, a case concerning a humiliating termination, the Seventh Circuit Court of Appeals overturned a jury decision in favor of a worker with bipolar disorder.[48] The jury had awarded the worker $150,000 for intentional infliction of emotional distress on the basis of evidence that the company's supervisors knew of the plaintiff's disabling condition, fired him because his disorder required him to work fewer hours, telephoned him at home while he was on vacation to tell him he was fired, and, after being asked for an explanation, falsely told him he was being fired for low productivity. The case is hard to distinguish from *Archer* and seems especially similar to *Moysis*, both discussed above, in which a humiliating method of termination was deemed sufficient to support a claim for intentional infliction of emotional distress. Reversing the pattern suggested by a few of the successful cases analyzed above, some courts have upheld claims under the ADA for harassing conduct while holding that the same conduct would not support a claim for intentional infliction of emotional distress.[49]

Other cases that fail involve schools, public services, and public accommodations. One example is *Costello v. Mitchell Public School District 79*, in which a seventh grader alleged that after she asked her band teacher for after-class help on a regular basis at the beginning of the semester, the teacher tired of her requests and, every day for a month, told her in front of her classmates that she was "retarded, stupid, and needed to go to a school where retarded people were taught."[50] He told her, in response to a request for help, "If you're so retarded, you don't need to be in this classroom."[51] On one occasion, while grading her band notebook in front of the class, the teacher called her stupid and threw the notebook at her, hitting her in the face. The student withdrew from band but had to take a music appreciation class instead, and that class was taught by the same teacher. During the nine weeks she attended that class, the teacher frequently called her stupid and retarded in front of her class-mates, even after he learned that she had undertaken mental health coun-seling. Eventually, the child developed major depression and suicidal thoughts and withdrew from school on her therapist's advice. Despite this pattern of abusive conduct, the court affirmed a grant of summary judg-ment on the intentional infliction of emotional distress claim against the teacher.

Contrast this decision with *Baird v. Rose,* the case of the child vilified by the teacher in front of the class after being excluded from the perfor-mance on account of the teacher's attitude about students with depres-sion. Relying on *Baird* and authority interpreting the Nebraska common law that applied to the case, the dissenting opinion in *Costello* would have upheld the intentional-infliction claim. Indeed, little seems to sepa-rate the two cases but the attitude of the majority in *Costello* that genuine distress willfully inflicted on someone perceived to have a mental disabil-ity by a person with power and authority charged with that person's pro-tection is not a matter to be taken seriously. The *Costello* court identified with the aggressor and endorsed the view that between the oppressor and the oppressed it is the oppressed who does not belong.

One unsuccessful case involving public transportation further demon-strates that different courts are relying more on their ingrained, often prejudiced, attitudes than on differences of fact in imposing different standards for what constitutes outrageous conduct. In *Stauber v. New York City Transit Authority,* the bus lift lowering the plaintiff's motorized wheelchair malfunctioned.[52] Rather than helping move the chair or per-mitting others to do so, the bus driver took the bus out of service and called for service personnel to come and help. The plaintiff struggled off the bus using two canes but slumped down and had to lie on the sidewalk during the half-hour wait for help to arrive. Eventually, two bystanders boarded the bus without the driver's permission and carried the wheel-chair off the bus for her. Throughout the incident, the bus driver was rude to the plaintiff, frequently using profanity. The court affirmed a grant of summary judgment against the plaintiff on the claim of intentional inflic-tion of emotional distress, saying that the conduct was not sufficiently outrageous and that the fact the driver was following company policy in not providing assistance contradicted any conclusion that he intended to inflict distress.

The comparison to *Williams v. Tri-County Metropolitan Transporta-tion District* is inescapable. In both cases, the bus driver publicly addressed rude and profane comments to the bus patron with a disability while balking at providing assistance. The conduct in *Stauber* hardly seems less outrageous than in *Williams,* but only the *Williams* court was willing to recognize that persons with disabilities are a historically disfavored and isolated group that the law needs to grant redress in order to keep those in positions of power from further abusing their authority and punishing them for occupying public space.

A public accommodations case that displays negative attitudes similar to that of *Stauber* is *Sanglap v. LaSalle Bank, FSB.*[53] In that case, the Seventh Circuit Court of Appeals ruled that there was insufficient evidence for a reasonable jury to conclude that a bank knew to a high degree of probability that its closing of the account of a customer after he had several epileptic fits on its premises would cause him severe emotional distress. In a case with similar overtones, a federal court applying Alabama law granted summary judgment on the intentional-infliction claim brought by a person who was blind and had an artificial limb who was forced to leave his motel room when the proprietor discovered the presence of his guide dog. Even though the proprietor had ranted and been abusive to the plaintiff, the court stated that Alabama courts had applied intentional-infliction liability in only a few categories, including sexual but not disability harassment, and rejected the claim.[54]

The Scope of Intentional-Infliction Remedies

Most courts hold that there is no personal liability for the harasser under the ADA and section 504 absent proof of coercion or retaliation.[55] Under the common-law action for intentional infliction of emotional distress, however, the person inflicting the emotional distress will be liable even if the employer or other entity is not. This represents an important reason to pursue the intentional-infliction remedy. There are numerous instances in which intentional-infliction liability was imposed on individuals, but the employer either was not in the case or escaped without a finding of liability. For example, in *Campbell v. Wal-Mart Stores,* the court sustained a cause of action against a co-worker of a woman who was deaf and legally blind and had limited reasoning and communication skills.[56] Phyllis Campbell and the co-worker unpacked, sorted, and hung clothes. Wal-Mart terminated Campbell after eleven years of service because the co-worker reported that the plaintiff had hit her in the back and pushed two shopping carts at her and because of one other alleged, previously unreported assault on another co-worker. Campbell denied harming the co-worker and said that the co-worker had repeatedly poked, prodded, pinched, slapped, made fun of, and otherwise harassed her by moving items from her table and ordering her to do work that was the co-worker's responsibility (Campbell said that other co-workers also teased her and touched her in demeaning ways). She said she was merely attempting to protect herself by pushing the co-worker away when the co-worker was hitting her. The prior incident, according to Campbell, involved her attempt to push the other worker off her after she had grabbed her. The ADA claim against Wal-Mart focused on its failure to provide accommodations for her to communicate as well as its maintenance of a hostile work environment and its discriminatory termination of her employment.

Campbell brought a claim of intentional infliction of emotional distress solely against the co-worker.[57] The court denied summary judgment on the intentional-infliction claim against the co-worker, saying that the conduct could be viewed as sufficiently outrageous to trigger liability, given Campbell's physical disabilities. An ADA claim against Wal-Mart presented obstacles of showing the company's knowledge and responsibility, but these concerns were not relevant to the intentional-infliction claim against the co-worker. In fact, if the co-worker managed to conceal her misconduct from Wal-Mart, that would appear simply to have strengthened the case against her individually by making the behavior that much more outrageous. Thus individual liability under the law of intentional infliction may step into the breach and provide an avenue of relief even if a plaintiff fails to succeed on claims against a defendant covered by the ADA. At the same time, of course, the *Campbell* case shows the limits of the benefit conferred by having a cause of action against individuals. Few clothes sorters at Wal-Mart would be able to pay a substantial judgment.

Perhaps an example of a more economically viable individual-only claim is *Rodgers v. Wells Fargo Bank of Nebraska,* involving a bank vice-president/senior trust administrator whose disabling conditions included vision problems, circulation and respiration difficulties, depression, and anxiety.[58] Rodgers alleged that her manager and a co-worker ridiculed her, harassed her about her corrective eyewear and reading devices, made derogatory comments to others, refused to allow her to go to the bathroom during a meeting, and removed special glasses from her office so that she could not find them. The manager, she said, forced her to write a resignation letter, bruising her hand in the process. The court denied a motion to dismiss the intentional-infliction claim based on these allegations. In *Rodgers,* the co-workers who were sued were at a level of employment such that they may well have been able to provide compensation. Indeed, in *Rodgers* the individual case may have been the most likely avenue of relief, for one can easily imagine a court ruling that the conduct, however outrageous it may have been, failed to meet the severe-or-pervasive requirement for an ADA hostile-environment claim.

Intentional-infliction actions afford money damages. Perhaps monetary awards can never make a person whole for humiliation or insult, but in our society damages are the ordinary means for compensating a person for all past wrongs, including those that entail emotional injury. Moreover, damages punish the wrongdoer and deter future abuses. They correct the injustice that has been done by redressing the balance of harm. They also vindicate and reinforce the sense of the community that an injustice has been done by the defendant's wrongful conduct.[59] As noted above, the damages are not subject to the ADA damages limits for employment cases.

Proposed Interpretations

Justice Cardozo observed that "the [judicial] process in its highest reaches is not discovery but creation."[60] Lawyers continually propose creative new interpretations of common-law claims and defenses, and judges adopt them (or refuse to do so) on the basis of considerations of policy. Thus the tort of intentional infliction itself emerged in a series of decisions in the 1940s and 1950s when judges realized that the judicial system needed to provide a response to intentional harmful conduct that did not fit into the traditional categories of assault, battery, or defamation.

With regard to the basics of intentional-infliction law, the reform that needs to be undertaken is less that of the standards the courts apply than that of the attitudes they bring to the applying. Plainly, what inspires some courts to say "Outrageous!" is not what inspires a similar reaction from other courts. What is perhaps more disturbing, however, is the willingness of some courts to second-guess juries who are using their own wisdom and sense of community standards of behavior to find disability harassment to meet the outrageousness standard. Thus particularly reprehensible are the decision of the intermediate appellate court in the *Robel* case (fortunately overturned by the Washington Supreme Court) and the decisions of the Seventh Circuit Court of Appeals in *Van Stan* and *Sanglap*. Although courts of appeals are charged with the task of over-turning decisions that no reasonable jury could reach, the decisions in these cases were fair applications of what ordinary people feel about the behavior of their peers. The judiciary is lagging behind the population in the development of its moral sense. What is needed is less law reform than judicial reformation.

Beyond the adjustment of judicial attitudes, some more specific legal issues need to be resolved in ways that are more hospitable to claims of intentional infliction of emotional distress. One issue is the liability of em-ployers for the conduct of employees, either the co-workers of a person with a disability in a workplace case or a teacher or other employee in an education or public accommodations case. The second principal issue, one of special importance in employment cases, is potential preemption of common-law claims by workers' compensation or disability discrimi-nation laws. A final issue is the immunity defense.

The better-reasoned cases impose liability on employers for the acts of employees (against co-workers or customers or others), using ordinary principles of *respondeat superior*. *Respondeat superior* is the doctrine that provides for liability of employers for the tortious acts of their em-ployees committed within the scope of employment. It is the ordinary principle that allows a pedestrian to recover against the bus company when the bus driver ignores a traffic signal and strikes the pedestrian. The pedestrian need not show that the company committed negligence itself, say in the selection or training of the driver. It is sufficient to show that the driver was negligent and was acting in the scope of employment. The doctrine applies to intentional torts as well. If a bouncer in a bar commits assault or battery while acting within the scope of employment, the em-ployer is liable.

Many courts simply attribute the conduct of employees to the com-pany for all actions that occurred on the job and without further discus-sion hold the employer liable for the tort on the basis of the employees' intentional inflicting of distress.[61] Other courts engage in more extensive discussion. In *Robel*, the case involving the deli worker who suffered an injury on the job, went on light duty, and was harassed by fellow work-ers and a supervisor, the court acknowledged the general rule that inten-tional torts outside the scope of employment do not carry liability for the employer.[62] The test for conduct outside the scope of employment is that the conduct is different in kind from that authorized, far beyond the authorized time or space limits, or too little actuated by the purpose of serving the employer. The court declared, "The proper inquiry is whether the employee was fulfilling his or her job functions at the time he or she was engaged in the injurious conduct."[63] Although an employer is not responsible for sex harassment conduct when the activity is directed toward the personal sexual gratification of the employee, that proposition does not affect the employer's liability in an intentional-infliction case premised on disability harassment. The court pointed out that the deli employees "tormented Robel on company property during working hours, as they interacted with co-workers and customers and performed the duties they were hired to perform."[64] They did not leave "their job stations or neglect[] their assigned duties to launch the verbal attacks on Robel."[65] Another court applying the same approach denied a motion to dismiss an intentional-infliction claim against an employer when a supervisor had pestered and harassed an employee with a mental disability. The court said the standard was whether the conduct was in the scope of employment and ruled that the issue was one for a jury to decide on the basis of facts presented to it.[66]

A case taking a different tack is *Wheeler v. Marathon Printing, Inc.,* in which the court upheld a judgment against a co-worker for intentional infliction of emotional distress but overturned an award against the employer.[67] The plaintiff was a printing press operator with mental illness who was the subject of a campaign of harassment by a co-worker, Wilkinson, that included constant verbal attacks, property damage, obscene gestures, and other conduct. The owner of the company made some efforts to stop the harassment, but they were ineffective. In that case, the jury found that the co-worker's conduct was within the scope of employment but awarded no damages against the employer for intentional infliction of emotional distress. In light of this result, the court considered only whether there was sufficient support for liability on the part of the employer based on its own conduct—that is, the failure to take sufficiently aggressive action against the harasser. Citing the case law regarding sex harassment, the court held the inaction could not ground liability. The *Wheeler* court apparently viewed the failure on the part of the jury to award damages on the basis of *respondeat superior* as undermining the jury determination that the employee acted within the scope of employment. Therefore, the case does little to undermine the authority of *Robel* and other cases that apply a straight scope-of-employment test and impose liability when the salient fact is that the harassment occurred in the workplace on company time.

Not all secondary authorities have fallen in line with the courts' general approach that *respondeat superior* requires no extraordinary facts beyond harassment on the premises during work hours. In addressing the problem of an employer's tort liability for an employee's hostile-environment sexual harassment, one commentator looks to the test of *Burlington Industries, Inc. v. Ellerth,*[68] which determines when an employer is liable for hostile-environment sexual harassment under title VII of the Civil Rights Act of 1964.[69] Under the *Burlington* test, the employer is liable for the harms caused by its supervisors' creation of a hostile environment unless the employer shows that it took reasonable measures to prevent and correct the conduct and that the employee-victim unreasonably failed to use the corrective measures the employer made available.[70] To the extent that this liability is imposed on the basis of such a test, it might be characterized more as the active negligence of the employer in placing the employee in a position where that person could cause harm. The analogy is thus to other instances of negligent entrustment or supervision. *Respondeat superior* on the basis of the employee's actions is a different source of liability based on different facts.[71]

An entity that employs someone who engages in disability harassment should be liable in tort at the very least in the same situations in which an employer would be liable for hostile-environment sexual harassment committed by employees if a case were brought under title VII.[72] Thus if the defendant places a person in a position of authority over the individual with a disability, and that person creates an environment that is pervasively hostile or abusive, the entity itself should be liable, and that liability should be defeated only by the entity showing that it exercised reasonable care to prevent and promptly correct the harassing behavior and that the plaintiff failed to use opportunities provided for prevention or correction of the conduct. This reasonable-care standard and related shift in the burden of proof would occasion liability in a greater range of circumstances than a test derived from title IX sexual harassment cases, which requires deliberate indifference to known acts of harassment. It is, nevertheless, more protective of defendants' interests than a *respondeat superior* standard.

An approach that relies on *respondeat superior* is a better view of the law, however. *Respondeat superior* gives a stronger incentive to employers to screen out those who are likely to commit harassing acts and to use training and discipline processes even beyond the application of a reasonable-care standard. Moreover, *respondeat superior* spreads the cost of harassment beyond the employee who is harassed, and even beyond the harasser who faces individual liability, to an entity that can more easily afford to pay for the liability and is likely to respond to the threat of liability by taking steps to eliminate harassment by the people it employs.[73]

As with the statutory claims that relate to disability harassment in education, common-law cases frequently fail on the basis of defenses rather than on the merits of the claims themselves. A crucial example is preemption. A number of courts have held that state common-law claims for intentional infliction of emotional distress are preempted by state statutory causes of action; these decisions depend on the peculiarities of individual state statutes. Thus although the basis for intentional infliction of emotional distress liability reflects a national consensus on the content of the law, preemption defenses tend to be state specific. One example of preemption of the intentional-infliction action by the Illinois disability discrimination statute is *Krocka v. City of Chicago*.[74] There, the Seventh Circuit Court of Appeals ruled that an intentional-infliction claim based on the comments of co-employees of a police officer that referred to the officer's mental condition were "inextricably linked to Krocka's disability discrimination claim because they were only offensive to the extent that they referred to Krocka's disability."[75] Ironically, the court held that Krocka was not actually disabled or regarded as disabled, affirming the rejection of his ADA claim. Nevertheless, it believed that any connection that the conduct complained of had to disability would trigger application of the state disability discrimination law, which had been construed by the state courts to prohibit courts from exercising jurisdiction over tort claims inextricably linked to civil rights violations. The Seventh Circuit extended the preemption defense to the intentional-infliction-of-emotional-distress claim by a customer, rather than an employee, in the *Sanglap* case, involving the person with epilepsy whose bank account was summarily closed. As noted above, the court had other bases for the result it reached, but it also held that preemption furnished another basis to overturn the jury verdict in favor of the plaintiff.[76]

The actual decision of the state courts on which the *Krocka* and *Sanglap* opinions relied gives scant support to their view of the Illinois law's preemptive scope. In *Maksimovic v. Tsogalis*, the Illinois Supreme Court decision establishing the "inextricably linked" test, the court rejected a defense that the state Human Rights Act preempted common-law claims against the plaintiff's co-worker for assault, battery, and false imprisonment when the co-worker engaged in sexual harassment of her on the job.[77] It overturned a decision of the intermediate appellate court that found all tort actions factually related to incidents of sexual harassment to be barred. The court distinguished the situation of the case against the co-worker for assault, battery, and false imprisonment from one in which the plaintiff brings a negligent hiring or retention action against an employer when a co-worker has sexually harassed her.[78] When the reason that the retention of the offending employee is negligent on the part of the company is that the employee harasses the plaintiff, the claims are inextricably linked and the negligence action is preempted. But, said the supreme court, when ordinary common-law tort claims "exist wholly separate and apart from a cause of action for sexual harassment under the Act," and the plaintiff "has alleged the elements of each of these torts without reference to legal duties created by the Act, she has established a basis for imposing liability on the defendants independent of the Act."[79] In a case like *Krocka,* the intentional-infliction action based on the co-worker's conduct is a tort claim that exists wholly separate and apart from a disability harassment cause of action under state law. Indeed, as was true in the *Krocka* case itself, the plaintiff need not be found disabled for the intentional-infliction action to succeed. The plaintiff's argument was not that the employer was negligent in allowing a violation of the state disability discrimination statute to occur. The argument was that the co-workers committed a tort under state law that exists completely apart from that statute. Law reform consisting of judicial decision making that restricts preemption to cases like those premised on negligent hiring and retention would be welcome.[80]

With regard to workers' compensation, a few courts have found the intentional-infliction claim preempted, but the majority have concluded that there is no barrier. For example, a court applying Illinois law ruled that to escape the operation of the workers' compensation bar, the employee need show merely that the injury complained of was not accidental.[81] Because the intentional infliction of emotional distress entails intentional, rather than accidental, conduct, there is no barrier.

In contrast, the court in *Haysman v. Food Lion, Inc.,* discussed in chapter 3 in connection with the ADA and disability harassment, the court ruled that battery and intentional infliction of emotional distress claims were preempted by the Georgia workers' compensation law.[82] As interpreted by the court in that case, however, the state workers' compensation statute did not treat conduct differently on the basis of whether the conduct was intentional or unintentional. Instead, intentional torts were covered by the statute as long as the mistreatment stemmed from animosity related to the victim's performance at work. A test of that type will necessarily preempt some intentional-infliction cases that arise in the employment context. There nevertheless will be many instances in which it might persuasively be argued that the hostility was related to the worker's disability but that the performance on the job was unexceptionable and thus that the work performance itself was unrelated to the animosity that motivated the conduct. When the hostility is related to the mere presence of the person in the workplace, it is hardly related to job performance, and that is a common situation in instances of disability harassment.

Any preemption defense is based on the assumption that the legislature meant to exclude the existing remedy for a condition by creating a new one. Sometimes, the legislature explicitly says it is preempting common-law remedies, as with the adoption of workers' compensation statutes that provide a means for employees injured on the job to recover for their losses and specifically bar negligence suits against the employer. In the typical case involving disability harassment, however, the statute said to supplant the common-law remedy rarely does so explicitly. Legislatures know how to exclude, as in the workers' compensation situation. Why assume that they mean to exclude common-law remedies for harassment when they simply say nothing? If the common-law remedy may be more effective in a given case than the remedy created by, say, a state employment discrimination law, why assume that the legislature intended to limit the rights of the employee to a less effective means of redress? Moreover, if the remedy, such as the tort action for intentional infliction of emotional distress, does not require a showing of discrimination, there is no reason for a law targeted at employment discrimination to preempt it.

Another barrier to liability, one that applies to governmental entities and arises frequently in cases concerning the public schools or other governmental agencies, is immunity. Courts have applied immunity both to school districts and to individuals in situations involving both teacher and peer harassment. In *Doe v. S & S Consolidated Independent School District*, a federal court in Texas found a school system immune from tort liability over the use of body wrapping and tape to restrain a child.[83] In

Willhauck v. Town of Mansfield, a federal court in Massachusetts found a school authority immune to negligence liability over the failure to protect a child against assault by peers.[84] *Valentino C. v. School District* applied immunity not only to a school district but also to two individual defendants in a claim for intentional infliction of emotional distress.[85] In other cases, applying other statutes and considering other sets of facts, however, courts have refused to apply immunity.[86] Legislatures create immunities, and the courts are not free to disregard immunity statutes or construe them in ways that subvert the intention of the legislatures that passed them. Policy makers, however, might reexamine whether the immunity protection is truly needed to afford protection for proper decision-making processes or whether it is operating instead as a mechanism to keep real, obvious wrongs from being remedied. They should push for repeal of statutes that serve only the latter function.

8

Constitutional Objections
to Antiharassment Policies

Many academics and several courts have considered whether liability for harassing speech violates First Amendment protections. Though academic authorities have split on the issue, the courts have uniformly concluded that workplace harassment liability does not violate the First Amendment.[1] By creating liability for harassing speech in a greater range of circumstances than existing hostile-environment law does, the interpretations of the law proposed in this book might be thought to pose a more difficult problem, the constitutionality of a form of liability more likely to offend free speech rights than the more limited prohibition on harassment established for employment situations by title VII and applied by analogy to claims under the ADA both in workplaces and in other settings to which the ADA is applicable. The question is whether it violates the First Amendment to extend liability to cases in which the harassing conduct is not severe or pervasive under a title VII standard but nevertheless intimidates, coerces, threatens, or interferes with an employee exercising the ADA-protected right to work or to participate in education or public services. A similar question might be raised concerning harassment cases in which liability is imposed under principles of intentional infliction of emotional distress. School cases present some additional issues as well.

The free speech objection to harassment liability for speech at work or other restricted settings such as schools may seem strange at first, and in truth it is strange. An employee has no free speech while at the workplace. The employer can punish the employee for nearly any sort of expressive behavior, from disparaging company policies to praising a competitor's product.[2] Students are routinely penalized for the content of their speech—for example, by receiving lower grades on a test if they say something other than what the teacher wanted for the correct answer. The right at issue appears to be more that of the employer or manager of others' speech not to be told what to prohibit in order to avoid liability. Or perhaps it is some residual right of persons whose speech is subject to plenary control by the employer or other figure of authority to engage in the limited speech that would not incur the wrath of the relevant powers if those powers were free to act solely on their own preferences. In any instance, courts and commentators have assumed that a free speech right exists, and this treatment will do the same.

Under the precedents established by the Supreme Court, some categories of speech fall outside the protection of the First Amendment entirely or receive only very limited protection.[3] Political and artistic expression receive the highest level of protection. By contrast, among the categories of speech that government can freely prohibit are obscenity (defined by an exacting standard), fighting words, true threats, and incitement of imminent violence. Speech receiving lesser protection includes general commercial communication, such as advertising. With regard to disability harassment, government has adequate power to prohibit what this book proposes be subject to sanction. Even if the activity of the harasser is solely verbal, the speech has little or no First Amendment protection because it is intimidation specific to the workplace and similar settings, because there is a captive-audience aspect to disability harassment, because of the individually directed nature of harassing speech, because the speech frequently includes threats, and because the speech is linked to action. The various categories applicable to verbal harassment that take it outside of the scope of First Amendment protection overlap with each other, but for explanatory purposes they will be treated separately.

This chapter turns first to harassment in a work setting that would be actionable under the reading of section 12203(b) expounded in chapter 4 but not necessarily actionable under existing constructions of hostile-environment liability under the ADA. In many instances, the issues can be generalized to other contexts, such as public agency settings, privately operated places of public accommodation, and schools, where section 12203(b) liability would also be appropriate as a remedy for harassment. The chapter then takes up some special issues relevant to the constitutionality of imposing liability for harassment at school, both at the university and at the elementary and secondary levels.

The Workplace and Analogous Settings

The Supreme Court ruled in *NLRB v. Gissel Packing Co.* that the labor law provision analogous to ADA section 12203(b) is consistent with the First Amendment.[4] That statutory provision protects union organizing by forbidding employer conduct, including pure speech—that is, speech not directly linked to action—that works interference, restraint, or coercion of employees in their right to labor organization. The Court in *Gissel* did not apply any of the various tests that the Court sometimes applies to content-based regulation of speech. Instead, it looked at the realities of the labor-organizing situation:

> Any assessment of the precise scope of employer expression, of course, must be made in the context of its labor relations setting. Thus, an employer's rights cannot outweigh the equal rights of the employees to associate freely . . . [a]nd any balancing of those rights must take into account the economic dependence of the employees on their employers, and the necessary tendency of the former, because of that relationship, to pick up intended implications of the latter that might be more readily dismissed by a more disinterested ear.[5]

The Court distinguished the employment setting from that of a political election, in which debate takes place in the public forum, and upheld the provision.

The comparison to *Gissel* supports the constitutionality of the ADA's protections from coercion, interference, threats, and intimidation, as applied to situations that would not trigger liability under a title VII standard for hostile environment. Continual name-calling, shunning, threats, and infliction of humiliation coerce employees with disabilities to give up their right to be on the job just as surely as predictions of economic catastrophe or promises of economic benefits induce employees not to organize. In both cases, the defendant wields extraordinary economic power in comparison to the worker who is the target of the intimidation. The whole point of disability harassment is an exercise in power, both establishing dominance and coercing the object of hostility to leave. The speech in *Gissel* was an implied threat that the plant would be closed if the workforce organized and struck. The conduct in cases in which ADA section 12203(b) should confer liability is the execution of the threat, the punishment for continuing to stay on the job. In both situations, the economic dependence of the targeted worker renders him or her unable simply to withdraw from the scene.

It is the very right not to withdraw from the scene that the law protects. Even one of the most prominent critics of hostile-environment sex harassment liability stresses that workplace speech that threatens or coerces should not be protected by the First Amendment: "The statement 'when plants are unionized, many people lose their jobs'—or 'women sometimes benefit professionally when they are romantically involved with their supervisors'—means one thing when written in the newspaper. It means quite another when said by a supervisor to a subordinate. In one context it's protected speech, in another a punishable threat."[6]

Context is everything. In the context of the workplace, speech that threatens, intimidates, or coerces deserves no constitutional protection. The point may, of course, be generalized to some settings other than work. In schools, for example, teachers or principals wield extraordinary power over students, power that compares with that of employers over employees. Similarly, a citizen asking for assistance from a government agency or even a passenger riding on a bus is in a subordinate position to the person with the capacity to give or deny a service that the person needs. Threats, coercive words, or intimidation from those sources in those settings are sufficiently similar to workplace communications of the same type to fall outside free speech protections.

Captive Audiences

The inability to withdraw from the workplace suggests a second strand to the analysis supporting the constitutionality of liability for harassment even when based on standards easier to meet than those drawn from an analogy to title VII. Persons with disabilities at work are a captive audience.[7] The Supreme Court has recognized that persons forced to listen to speech may be protected by government regulation of expression to a greater degree than others may be. Thus the Court has upheld restrictions on individually directed residential picketing, on offensive but not obscene radio broadcasts, on political advertising in mass transit vehicles, on sexual materials sent to private mailboxes, and on intrusive picketing outside abortion clinic entrances.[8] The inability of the targets of the speech to escape distinguishes these cases from those in which the audience could simply pay no attention or move on. Although the Court has in some of these cases declared that the restrictions were content neutral or at least viewpoint neutral and subject to lesser constitutional protection on that ground, commentators have pointed out that the laws that were upheld effectively favored some content or viewpoints over others— for example, treating nonprofane radio broadcasts or nonsexual mailings or nonhostile abortion clinic picketing differently from communications with other messages.[9] It is the captive-audience nature of the situation, not the content-neutral nature of the prohibition, that justifies the lesser protection for the speech.

The inability to escape is, of course, the crucial point with regard to the expansion of liability for harassment that this book proposes. If the target of the harassment simply withdraws and goes away, that person will be giving up the very right to integration in society that is the overriding goal of the ADA and the disability rights movement in general. The right to be there and participate on an equal basis in social activities is what the movement is striving for, as well as what the law protects. Constructions of free speech rights need to recognize that if the proper response of the person at whom harassment is aimed is to leave, that person is rendered a second-class citizen, a second-class human being. The inability to go away without losing part of one's humanity applies not just in work settings but also in other settings where the person has a right to be treated as an equal, such as public agency offices, stores, and school.

Individually Directed Speech

In addition, the speech that would be subject to liability under a proper construction of the disability harassment law must be distinguished from constitutionally protected speech in that the communication is individually directed. The First Amendment critics of liability for sexually hostile environments express the most concern for generally directed expressions of opinion, such as a statement—say, one made in a workplace lunchroom—that women belong in the home.[10] These statements have at least some political content, even if the political content is offensive to part or all of the audience. A stronger constitutional argument exists in favor of protecting speech that is intended to persuade or form a part of public debate than speech that is intended to inflict injury on a specific individual. The former may be a part of public discourse and deliberation, even if many properly find it offensive or inane. The latter lacks the redeeming characteristic of contributing to the development of public ideas and has the harmful trait of inflicting hurt and silencing the minority.[11]

Judicial opinions establish the validity of a distinction between general expression of opinion and individually directed taunting or ridicule. Thus, for example, courts have upheld restrictions on telephone harassment even though the same language would not merit criminal sanctions if addressed to the world at large.[12] That harassing speech targeted at an individual in a workplace or other public setting is not completely private communication—others can hear it—makes it more, not less, subject to regulation. The taunting of another in a public place forces that person to expose reactions and feelings that would otherwise stay concealed, invading an important interest in the target's personal privacy.[13]

The point that individually directed harmful speech lacks First Amendment protection applies with added force to the situations in which liability for intentional infliction of emotional distress is appropriate. First Amendment protection is not totally absent with regard to intentional-infliction liability. In *Hustler Magazine v. Falwell,* a case involving an insulting political parody, the Supreme Court ruled that a public figure may not recover for emotional distress on the basis of a publication unless the publication contains a false statement of fact made with actual knowledge that the statement is false or with reckless disregard of its truth.[14] But the intentional-infliction liability discussed in this book is of nonpublic figures, and unlike that in *Falwell,* does not involve a public statement that expresses opinion on matters of public importance (albeit in what might be an offensive way). Even staunch advocates of First Amendment freedoms would permit intentional-infliction-of-emotional-distress liability when private individuals are individually and intentionally targeted and more generalized participation in political debate is absent.[15]

True Threats

Threatening speech, an important component of that which is forbidden by section 12203(b), is given no protection under the Constitution and may be legally sanctioned. Threats of violence are clearly excluded from protection under the Supreme Court's elaboration of the topic in *Virginia v. Black,* the case in which the Court held that bans on cross burning may be constitutional.[16] Threats of physical violence are the most common ones in disability harassment cases: they are a highly effective way for classmates, co-workers, or others to make the person who causes them discomfort to go away.

Many authorities, even some who are generally hostile to the idea of liability for verbally harassing behavior, note that threats of things other than violence, such as denial of workplace rewards, should be excluded from First Amendment protection as well, as when a supervisor engages in quid pro quo sexual harassment.[17] A threat of workplace retaliation if an employee with a disability persists in asking for an accommodation should fall in the same unprotected category and be similarly subject to legal prohibition.

Speech Linked to Action

Speech that constitutes part of a course of unlawful action is subject to governmental restriction. As one authority explains: "This factor . . . explains why employers can be prohibited from creating or tolerating hostile working environments for racial minorities or women under federal anti-discrimination statutes. Since the government can prohibit the practice of race or sex discrimination in employment, it can also restrict expression that constitutes the implementation of discriminatory policies."[18] The prohibition on harassment may be viewed as simply a "collateral" ban on speech closely connected with the nonspeech conduct of discrimination.[19] Of course, this book has argued for a scope to harassment liability that is broader than the definition of "discrimination" that some courts have employed when they have rejected claims for want of proof of severe or pervasive discriminatory environments. The point remains true, however, that the underlying conduct of limiting the economic and social opportunities of people with disabilities is prohibited, and the ban on the verbal harassment is needed to make effective the statutory right to employment or services on equal terms. Harassment keeps individuals from exercising their rights to a nondiscriminatory workplace or public sphere. Perpetration or toleration of speech that furthers violation of the ADA is subject to proscription just as is perpetration or toleration of speech that violates the antitrust or copyright or unfair trade practices laws. In any of these instances, the speech constitutes or furthers the conduct and may be prohibited on that basis.

Content Discrimination within a
Proscribable Category of Speech

In its 1992 decision *R.A.V. v. City of St. Paul*, the Supreme Court said that even though a category of speech is unprotected by the First Amendment, a restriction of some of the speech within the category may be unconstitutional if it is based on the content or the viewpoint of the speech that is penalized.[20] On one level, this point is obvious. The government cannot outlaw obscene displays only when the displays also criticize the Republican Party. Nevertheless, it seems perverse to protect free speech by adopting a constitutional approach that would require the government to punish all speech within an unprotected category because of the social interest in suppressing some of it. The expansion of intentional-infliction-of-emotional-distress liability proposed in this book would not give rise to problems of the type identified in *R.A.V.* The entire category of speech that intentionally inflicts emotional distress is subject to liability; this book simply argues that more of the activity than some courts now recognize ought to fit when the case is one about disability harassment. But when this book argues that the ADA ought to penalize disability harassment, even when expressive activity that inflicts similar harm based on something other than disability is not, a content-based restriction of a proscribable category might be thought to exist.

The Court has limited the reach of the *R.A.V.* analysis by holding that restriction of speech within a proscribable category is permissible on the basis of the targeted speech's content if the basis for selecting the speech to restrict is the very reason the whole category may be forbidden. Thus threats are a category that may be prohibited, but the government could outlaw only threats against the president because those might be considered more harmful than other threats. Or only the obscene material that is the most obscene might be outlawed because its special prurience relates to the reason obscenity may be forbidden. In *Virginia v. Black*, the case that upheld some applications of a ban on cross burning, the Supreme Court applied this reasoning in a broad, pragmatic fashion, stating that although not all threats are outlawed, cross burning "is a particularly virulent form of intimidation," as demonstrated by its history.[21] The Court did not compare cross burning to other forms of threatening behavior that are not prohibited. It was enough that the communication was one of "the forms of intimidation that are most likely to inspire fear of bodily harm."[22]

As the history recounted in chapter 2 demonstrates, bodily harm imposed on persons with disabilities is one constant of American history. In vast numbers of disability harassment cases, verbal harassment is a prelude or accompaniment to physical violence.[23] Imposing sanctions on a broader range of harassment than imposed by the law as it is currently interpreted merely expands the selection of the worst conduct within a range of actions that may be prohibited. Just as *Black* did not engage in any close comparison of cross burning with other forms of threats that might not be so disfavored, differences in the treatment of disability harassment and race and sex harassment do not matter. Broader liability for race and sex harassment may be a good idea as well. It is merely the questionable approaches of various courts that have restricted the reach of title VII to severe or pervasive (or often severe and pervasive) conduct. Many authorities support an expansion of the coverage of race and sex harassment laws and defend the constitutionality of this step under *R.A.V.*'s approach.[24]

Under *R.A.V.*, another permissible basis for restricting part of a proscribable category of speech is when the selection is made on the basis of secondary effects of the speech.[25] The link of disability harassment speech to the action of discrimination and unjustified social isolation brings this exception into play. Moreover, the *R.A.V.* Court defended the constitutionality of incidental limits on speech created by title VII by saying that "words can in some circumstances violate laws directed not against speech but against conduct" and applying that observation to conclude that while "sexually derogatory 'fighting words,' among other words, may produce a violation of Title VII's general prohibition against sexual discrimination in employment practices" that does not violate the First Amendment.[26] Such a law is considered content neutral in the Court's view. An expansion of liability for harassment beyond that found in title VII is what is being proposed here, but this expansion to cover more speech of the same type would not appear to be any less content neutral than title VII's current ban on harassing speech.

Special Issues Relevant to School Cases

The situation of schools presents some special issues not yet developed. On the one hand, schools, particularly institutions of higher education, have a mission of free academic inquiry, something they may not hold in common with other places of employment or public activity. At the same time, schools, particularly at the elementary and secondary level, have prerogatives and duties to maintain order and to educate children how to behave.

Concerns over academic freedom might suggest giving free speech protection when the Boston University officials in the *Guckenberger* case made speeches attacking students with learning disabilities in general terms.[27] The speech in that case was linked to conduct, however, conduct that included changing policies, denying accommodations, and engaging in other activity directly targeting students with learning disabilities. What is more, the person the university chose to give individual responsibility for doing things such as ruling on accommodation requests was the person who made the derogatory speech. When action occurs, it is no violation of free speech rights to look to the bad actor's contemporaneous speech to determine an evil motive, and to assign liability accordingly.[28] This book does not suggest imposing liability for pure expressions of opinion in public forums. Individually targeted messages given to captive audiences, particularly messages that include threats or are linked to harmful conduct, are something else altogether and ought to be subject to liability in educational environments as in other settings. Although some cases have found that wide-reaching codes of civility adopted by public educational institutions are overbroad in violation of the Constitution's free speech protections, none of these decisions considered the imposition of liability on the narrowly defined standards proposed here.[29]

Students in public elementary and high schools have First Amendment rights, but school authorities may prohibit any speech that is inconsistent with the school's basic educational mission. Thus a lewd speech by a student at a school assembly may be punished, as may speech that is racially offensive or inflammatory.[30] Certainly, taking disciplinary action against a student for harassing another on the basis of disability meets that test. As noted in chapter 5, harassment at school interferes with the education of students with disabilities and constitutes a virulent form of intimidation. Sadly, public school teachers and administrators engage in speech that harasses students just as do classmates of students with disabilities. Public employees have rights to free speech. To be protected, however, the expression must be about matters of public concern. Even if it is, a public employee may be disciplined or otherwise sanctioned if the government can show, on balance, that the efficient operation of the office justified the action. Thus a teacher writing a letter to a newspaper on a school budget issue enjoys First Amendment protection, while a government attorney circulating employment grievances among attorneys in the office does not.[31] Applying these principles to harassment cases involving matters other than disability, courts have upheld a sanction against a public employee for use of derogatory terms toward women and allowed recovery when a sexually hostile environment was created by offensive speech and display of sexual material by workers.[32] Restrictions on public school employee speech that amounts to disability harassment are not limits on expression of opinion in open forums on issues of public concern. Moreover, harassing speech plainly disrupts the educational enterprise. Thus sanctions for harassing public school teachers create no constitutional difficulties and should be upheld.

9

An Agenda for Legal
and Social Change

This chapter summarizes the suggestions made elsewhere in the book about how legal interpretations should be altered, then puts forward a number of other policy reforms that could help diminish or eradicate disability harassment by helping promote full and equal integration of people with disabilities into society. These initiatives concern programs such as vocational rehabilitation, employment assistance, education, and social insurance. As the disability studies movement has recognized, however, achieving disability equality means altering not just legal structures but also social attitudes. The reform agenda has to include cultural and economic change.

Law Reform Measures to Deter and Remedy Harassment

The law reforms proposed in this book include a broadened interpretation of the ADA's section barring coercion, threats, intimidation, and interference with statutory rights, 42 U.S.C. § 12203(b). This step would require merely the extension of existing interpretations of the statute in line with interpretation of identical language in other statutes and with regulatory provisions and other recognized sources of guidance about the meaning of legal terms. This reinterpretation would expand the range of situations in which persons subject to harassment would be able to recover against employers, harassing co-workers, and, in contexts other than employment, those additional institutions and individuals who abuse their power to discourage people with disabilities from exercising the right to participate equally in society.

In the field of public elementary and secondary education, this book proposes a wider recognition that harassing conduct by teachers and peers violates not only the ADA and section 504 of the Rehabilitation Act but also the federal special education law. Moreover, these violations should give rise to damages relief against institutions and individuals. The extension of existing law is modest, for many courts already recognize the claims for damages, and those that do not often seem willfully oblivious to both the facts in the cases before them and the legal interpretations adopted by other courts. An equally modest reform is wider adoption of the better-reasoned views of courts regarding the defenses of exhaustion of administrative remedies and application of immunity in cases for damages over harassment at school. Section 12203(b) claims for damages should be part of the array of ADA remedies for school harassment, just as they should for harassment in employment and other fields covered by the ADA.

In the contexts of school, employment, public services, private economic activity, and the public sphere in general, even where the ADA does not operate, persons who are subjected to harassment should be able to bring claims for damages against their harassers based on common-law principles of intentional infliction of emotional distress. Again, the reform proposed on this topic is incremental, calling for courts to recognize the very real harm that harassment inflicts on its targets and the abuse of power that the misconduct represents, as well as to note the chasm that harassment places between present realities and true integration on a plane of equality. This book proposes no reforms of constitutional law. It simply observes that existing doctrines do not operate to keep courts from providing effective relief to persons adversely affected by harassment from others, even when that harassment takes the form of pure speech.

Law Reform Measures to Promote Integration

The connection between harassment and segregation is close. It is a relationship outlined early in this book and one that drives the discussion of the legal reforms that are advanced here. The connection operates in two directions. Action to reduce harassment will promote integration. But action to promote integration among equals by itself will operate to diminish harassment as well. For that reason, if the goal is to mount an effective legal campaign against harassment, legal reforms should include those that reduce segregation of persons with disabilities and that bring people into the mainstream, even if the proposals do not directly address harassment itself. There is the risk of provoking more harassment in the short term. But if harassment is there to wear down those who would integrate, integration should eventually wear down those who would harass. Integration with legal protection is the way.

Legal initiatives to promote integration are sorely lacking. The legal prohibitions against segregation and exclusion found in the ADA and other laws might be thought to complete the process of integrating people with disabilities, but the ADA provisions have seen little development, a sharp contrast to the extensive development of the definition section and the qualified-individual/reasonable-accommodation provisions. One of the rare ADA employment cases involving an integration claim, *Duda v. Board of Education,* upheld a title I cause of action when a school district learned that a janitor had mental illness and responded by transferring him to a location where he had to work by himself and by instructing him not to speak to anyone.[1] As for public services in general, the Supreme Court ruled in *Olmstead v. L.C.* that providing residential services for persons with mental disabilities only in institutionalized settings ordinarily violates the ADA.[2] Only a few cases have applied *Olmstead*'s principles in other contexts, however.[3] The education cases decided under IDEA go in both directions on the issue of integration of children with disabilities into the mainstream, with significant differences in attitude among the federal judicial circuits.[4]

Apart from the ADA provision enforced in *Olmstead* and the special education law provision relating to the least restrictive environment, there is little in the law or in public programs that affirmatively integrates people with disabilities into mainstream society. Michael Stein observes: "[I]mprovement in blacks' relative earnings has been realized because of the federal government's massive enforcement of antidiscrimination policies, including voting rights and school desegregation, that were concentrated on the South. Currently, there exists no equivalent monumental federal government enforcement policy of employing or integrating the disabled."[5]

What is needed is a legislative agenda that will go beyond ending harassment and forbidding segregation to actively promote interaction between individuals with disabilities and without disabilities on an equal level. This agenda could have several components:

1. Vocational Services Reforms. Currently, vocational services provided to people with disabilities focus on sheltered work and, for individuals who have acquired more skills, supported employment in mainstreamed settings. In recent years, the program's emphasis on supported employment has grown.[6] This growth should continue, for it permits more people with more severe disabilities to succeed in the competitive workplace. The law should also encourage the development of small businesses run by people with disabilities. A program to foster entrepreneurship among individuals with disabilities has seen success in Iowa and should be replicated elsewhere by state legislation.[7] Supported employment brings people into the workplace, but the hazard is that the new workers will not be perceived as equal and may be subject to harassment and other discouragement unless the ADA's harassment protections are vigorously enforced. Entrepreneurship programs seek to avoid the inferiority problem by effectively making the vocational services client the boss, serving customers just as any other merchant does, while receiving support as needed from the vocational services agency or other public sources.[8]

2. Affirmative Action and Job Set-Asides for Qualified Workers with Disabilities. Existing laws require federal agencies and federal contractors to engage in affirmative action to employ individuals with disabilities. These laws should be enforced. It would also be beneficial for the United States to adopt a program similar to those found elsewhere in the developed world requiring employers to set aside a fraction of their jobs for people who have severely disabling conditions.[9] Various aspects of these reforms have been challenged.[10] Of greatest concern here, however, is whether actively promoting hiring of individuals with disabilities, to the point of setting aside a percentage of jobs, furthers or fails to further integration and thus may lead to the blurring of the sharp distinction between "normal" and "disabled." There is certainly a risk that workers who are hired to fulfill a quota or other government mandate might be featherbedded or assigned a marginal status. Nevertheless, the genius of the free enterprise system is that the employer has the incentive to make the maximum profit from whatever employees are there and to permit workers to gravitate to wherever they will contribute the most marginal utility to the company. Enforcement of reasonable-accommodation mandates should help that movement. It is also likely that as the income of workers with disabilities increases their status will rise and that this will help diminish status differentials.[11] Interestingly, the more commonly identified problem with the European job set-aside programs is not segregation of workers but outright evasion of the law, a problem that could be solved with sufficient governmental willpower or the provision of a private right to judicial enforcement by persons entitled to the positions.[12]

3. *Enhancement of Special Education Related Services.* The obligation to mainstream children with disabilities at school has been viewed for far too long as the negative command "Thou shalt not segregate." In fact, the language of the statute imposes a positive obligation: school systems must provide services to permit children to be integrated successfully. The language reads:

> [States must guarantee that, t]o the maximum extent appropriate, children with disabilities . . . are educated with children who are not disabled, and that special classes, separate schooling, or other removal of children with disabilities from the regular education environment occurs only when the nature or severity of the disability is such that education in regular classes with the use of supplementary aids and services cannot be achieved satisfactorily.[13]

The obligation is a positive one, to provide related services, such as those of aides and technology, in order to achieve satisfactory education in regular classes. Often, however, the services are deficient, integrated schooling fails, and the courts declare the child, rather than the school system, to be the problem.[14] States need to legislate the provision of related services and appropriate the money for them in order to comply with the related-services mandate; the federal government needs to hold the states accountable to fulfill their obligations. Activity to prevent harassment is properly thought of as one of several services needed to facilitate integration.

4. *Social Insurance Improvements.* The Social Security disability insurance program should be expanded to provide partial disability benefits for people who have significant limitations on functional capacities but who do not meet the program's existing standard of total incapacity expected to last more than a year or result in death.[15] A program of this type would help pull people with disabilities out of poverty while at the same time encouraging them to seek work in order to have income to supplement the pension amounts. Unlike existing Social Security, the person would not have to drop out of the labor force to receive benefits but would work as much as manageable given whatever limits might be imposed by the disability and the continuing failure of the workplace to

fully accommodate workers with disabling conditions. Having a disability imposes costs on an individual. Not only are medical bills of people with disabilities higher than those for other persons, but disabilities typically reduce the hours a person can work and frequently diminish capacities to move, lift, communicate, and think, the activities that employers pay workers to do. A system of partial disability benefits shifts some of those costs to the public; it is a component of social security systems throughout Europe. An American program would raise the condition of people with disabilities while encouraging integration in employment.

The campaign in favor of the ADA was instrumental in bringing the disparate special interest disability groups into a formidable political movement.[16] Legislative reform efforts need to recapture that momentum. The current array of political power at the federal level may not look favorable as of 2006, but disability issues may be among those most effective in motivating a political change. Moreover, important reforms can be won today at state and local levels of government.

Social Reform

Does society alter the law, or does the law alter society? Some of both, of course. Voluntary social action to promote integration of individuals with disabilities into ordinary settings would go far to accomplish the ADA's legal goal of ending forced separation. One place to start would be voluntary action by employers, schools, and other entities to prevent harassment. They need to adopt policies against harassment, train supervisors and co-workers, encourage the making of harassment complaints, investigate the complaints, and impose effective sanctions when harassment occurs.[17]

The greater task, and one that may remain voluntary for the foreseeable future, is the effort to integrate people with disabilities by altering social conditions, in an effort to deemphasize the social distinction between the normal and the abnormal and to focus more on social relationships than on categories of people.[18] This is an enormous task, particularly when no one can afford to dispense with category-based laws such as the ADA.[19] Nevertheless, there is much to be said for anything that helps redefine disability as part of everyday experience rather than as abnormal, or strange, or "the other." Rosemarie Garland Thomson lauds advertising that works to redefine disability as an ordinary part of life and society:

In the aggregate, contemporary advertising casts disabled people as simply one of many variations that compose the market to which they appeal. Such routinization of disability imagery not only brings disability as a common human experience out of the closet but enables people with disabilities—especially those who acquire impairments as adults—to imagine themselves as part of the ordinary world, rather than as a special class of untouchables and unviewables. . . . This form of realism constitutes a rhetoric of equality radical in its refusal to foreground disability as a difference.[20]

The absence of economic power on the part of people with disabilities operates as a limit on what can be accomplished. Because of the poverty of people with disabilities, and the difficulty of using employment to get out of poverty, people with disabilities remain at the margins of the economy. Simon Ungar comments:

Disabled people, as a relatively small and generally economically challenged group, have therefore not generally benefited from [accommodations]. Where businesses have made alterations, these have often been made for publicity purposes rather than specifically for the benefit of disabled customers; in other words, the businesses want to be seen to be making adaptations for disabled people so as to be viewed as caring and charitable by the economically strong (generally able-bodied) members of society.[21]

In other words, economic power is the prerequisite for success. Thus economic advances furthered by employment and social insurance reform may be the crucial first step in the effort for change in social attitudes that will lead to integration on a plane of equality. Samuel Bagenstos is quite correct in saying that the future of disability law lies as much in social welfare as in antidiscrimination efforts.[22]

Law is an imperfect tool, but it has an important role in stopping harassment and promoting integration of people with disabilities into the mainstream. The recasting of approaches to existing law that I suggest are a first step. Legislative reform with regard to vocational services, affirmative action and job set-asides, and welfare policy improvements makes a more ambitious agenda. Reforming the whole of society's attitudes is an enormous, though quite realistic task.

Notes

CHAPTER 1

1. Numbers are difficult to come by on this topic. One study of statistics from the Equal Employment Opportunity Commission indicates that it received eighty thousand Americans with Disabilities Act complaints regarding employment discrimination over a five-year period, of which 12 percent, about 9,600, alleged disability harassment. *Employment Rate of People with Disabilities Increases since Enactment of ADA*, GREAT LAKES DISABILITY BUS. & TECHNICAL ASSISTANCE CTR. REGION V NEWS, Summer, 1996, at 4.

2. The facts here are recounted in *Casper v. Gunite Corp.*, No. 3:98-CV-173RM, 1999 U.S. Dist. LEXIS 13554 (N.D. Ind. June 11, 1999), *aff'd*, 221 F.3d 1338 (7th Cir. 2000) (table). The court was bound to view the facts in the light most favorable to Casper, and here his statements are assumed to be true.

3. This account is found in *Flowers v. Southern Regional Physician Services*, 247 F.3d 229 (5th Cir. 2001). A jury in that case found in favor of Flowers.

4. *Charlie F. v. Board of Educ.*, 98 F.3d 989, 990 (7th Cir. 1996). This account is taken from the plaintiffs' allegations reported in the opinion. The facts were assumed to be true, as they are here.

5. Michelle Fine & Adrienne Asch, *Disability beyond Stigma: Social Interaction, Discrimination, and Activism*, 44 J. SOC. ISSUES 3, 9 (1988).

6. ERVING GOFFMAN, STIGMA: NOTES ON THE MANAGEMENT OF SPOILED IDENTITY (1963).

7. See Aaron J. Prero, *Quantitative Outcomes of the Transitional Employment Training Demonstration*, in DISABILITY, WORK, AND CASH BENEFITS 273, 274, 277 (Jerry L. Mashaw et al. eds. 1996) (discussing prevalence of mental retardation disability in recipients of Supplemental Security Income and low earnings, consistent with sheltered or supported employment).

8. Fine & Asch, *supra* note 5, at 13.

9. See SUSAN SONTAG, AIDS AND ITS METAPHORS (1989).

10. The national average, as of 1999–2000, is 20 percent for all children with disabilities. For children with mental retardation it is 51 percent; for those classified as having emotional disturbance, it is 33 percent. Illinois' numbers, re-

spectively, are 28 percent, 73 percent, and 38 percent. OFFICE OF SPECIAL EDUC. PROGRAMS, U.S. DEP'T OF EDUC., OSEP MONITORING REPORT—ILLINOIS 37 (2002).

11. This information is from *Harshbarger v. Sierra Pacific Power Co.,* 128 F. Supp. 2d 1302 (D. Nev. 2000), *aff'd in part and rev'd in part,* 28 Fed. Appx. 707 (9th Cir. 2002). Again, the account of the employee is assumed to be true.

12. The facts reported here are from *Haysman v. Food Lion, Inc.,* 893 F. Supp. 1092 (S.D. Ga. 1995), and are based on the assumption that Neil Haysman's account is true, an assumption the court had to make in the procedural posture of the case at the point of decision.

13. The facts here are from *Kubistal v. Hirsch,* No. 98 C 3838, 1999 WL 90625, at *1 (N.D. Ill. Feb. 9, 1999). This account assumes that the plaintiffs' allegations are true—an assumption the court was required to make.

14. SIMI LINTON, CLAIMING DISABILITY 100 (1998).

15. Vicki Schultz, *Reconceptualizing Sexual Harassment,* 107 YALE L.J. 1683, 1720–28 (1998).

16. GORDON W. ALLPORT, THE NATURE OF PREJUDICE 264, 268, 276–78 (1954).

17. *Witte v. Clark County Sch. Dist.,* 197 F.3d 1271, 1272–73 (9th Cir. 1999). Again, this account is based on the plaintiffs' allegations.

18. The account here is drawn from *Fox v. General Motors Corp.,* 247 F.3d 169 (4th Cir. 2001). A jury in that case accepted Fox's account and ruled in his favor.

19. PHILIPPE BOURGOIS, IN SEARCH OF RESPECT: SELLING CRACK IN EL BARRIO 188–89 (2d ed. 2003).

20. Samuel R. Bagenstos, *Subordination, Stigma, and "Disability,"* 86 VA. L. REV. 397, 418 (2000).

21. Martha Minow, *Surviving Victim Talk,* 40 UCLA L. REV. 1411, 1420 (1993).

22. Ruth Colker, *Anti-subordination above All: Sex, Race, and Equal Protection,* 61 N.Y.U. L. REV. 1003, 1007 (1986).

23. Bagenstos, *supra* note 20, at 445 ("The statutory 'disability' category should embrace those actual, past, and perceived impairments that subject people to systemic disadvantages in society. And the concept of stigma should play an important evidentiary role.").

24. *Fox,* 247 F.3d at 174.

25. LENNARD J. DAVIS, BENDING OVER BACKWARDS: DISABILITY, DISMODERNISM AND OTHER DIFFICULT POSITIONS 146–47 (2002).

26. *Id.* at 147 (citing unpublished research of Dick Sobsey).

27. *Flowers,* 247 F.3d at 239. The trial judge reduced the verdict to conform with the limits imposed by 42 U.S.C. § 1981a(b)(3)(B). Nominal damages are those in name only, given to vindicate a right symbolically. The amount is typi-

cally six cents or one dollar. See DAN B. DOBBS, LAW OF REMEDIES § 3.3(2), at 221–22 (2d ed. 1993).

28. *Casper,* 1999 U.S. Dist. LEXIS 13554, at *11.

29. *Charlie F.,* 98 F.3d at 993.

30. *Harshbarger,* 128 F. Supp. 2d at 1310.

31. 26 Fed. Appx. at 709–10.

32. *Kubistal,* 1999 U.S. Dist. LEXIS 1613, at *21.

33. *Witte,* 197 F.3d at 1272.

34. *Eason v. Clark County Sch. Dist.,* 303 F.3d 1137, 1144 (9th Cir. 2002).

35. *Fox,* 247 F.3d at 181.

36. DAVID M. ENGEL & FRANK W. MUNGER, RIGHTS OF INCLUSION: LAW AND IDENTITY IN THE LIFE STORIES OF AMERICANS WITH DISABILITIES 239, 242–53 (2003).

CHAPTER 2

1. Among the earliest sources developing this idea is Michelle Fine & Adrienne Asch, *Disability beyond Stigma: Social Interaction, Discrimination, and Activism,* 44 J. SOC. ISSUES 3, 6–14 (1988).

2. See Harlan Hahn, *Advertising the Acceptably Employable Image: Disability and Capitalism,* in THE DISABILITY STUDIES READER, 172, 174 (Lennard J. Davis ed. 1997) (describing "minority-group model of disability"); see also JAMES I. CHARLTON, NOTHING ABOUT US WITHOUT US: DISABILITY OPPRESSION AND EMPOWERMENT 127 (1998) (defending minority group–civil rights model of disability); SIMI LINTON, CLAIMING DISABILITY 9 (1998) (describing oppression against people with disabilities); Jacobus tenBroek & Floyd W. Matson, *The Disabled and the Law of Welfare,* 54 CAL. L. REV. 809, 814–16 (1966) (applying civil rights approach to disability); Jonathan C. Drimmer, Comment, *Cripples, Overcomers, and Civil Rights: Tracing the Evolution of Federal Legislation and Social Policy for People with Disabilities,* 40 UCLA L. REV. 1341, 1357–58 (1993) (describing civil rights model of disability). See generally Paula E. Berg, *Ill/legal: Interrogating the Meaning and Function of the Category of Disability in Antidiscrimination Law,* 18 YALE L. & POL'Y REV. 1, 9 (1999) ("This social-political model rejects the premise of the moral and biomedical perspectives that disability is inherent within the individual. . . . [I]t understands disability as contextual and relational, . . . as a broader social construct reflecting society's dominant ideology and cultural assumptions. While it acknowledges the existence of biologically based differences, the social-political model locates the meaning of these differences—and the individual's experience of them as burdensome—in society's stigmatizing attitudes and biased structures rather than in the individual.") (footnotes omitted).

3. For a concise description of the "biomedical model," see Berg, *supra* note 2, at 6–7 (collecting sources).

4. See tenBroek & Matson, *supra* note 2, at 816. Some contend that the medical model continues to prevail in the population as a whole, despite the passage of antidiscrimination legislation. See, e.g., MARY JOHNSON, MAKE THEM GO AWAY: CLINT EASTWOOD, CHRISTOPHER REEVE AND THE CASE AGAINST DISABILITY RIGHTS 27 (2003).

5. Marta Russell & Ravi Malhotra, *The Political Economy of Disablement: Advances and Contradictions,* Socialist Register 2002: A World of Contradictions, available at http://www.yorku.ca/socreg/RusMal.htm (visited Aug. 17, 2005) ("Reconceptualizing disability as an outcome of the political economy, however, also requires acknowledging the limitations of the 'minority' model of disability, which views it as the product of a disabling social and architectural environment. . . . In contrast, we take the view that disability is a socially created category derived from labour relations, a product of the exploitative economic structure of capitalist society: one which creates (and then oppresses) the so-called 'dis-abled' body as one of the conditions that allow the capitalist class to accumulate wealth."); see also CHARLTON, *supra* note 2, at 23, 48–50; Marta Russell, *Backlash, the Political Economy, and Structural Exclusion,* 21 BERKELEY J. EMPLOYMENT & LAB. L. 335 (2000) (criticizing liberal policy assumptions behind the ADA).

6. For example, I argue that government should reallocate resources so that a person who, because of chronic fatigue, can work only limited hours can still make a living income. Similarly, if an individual has limits on cognitive capacities that prevent that person from making a marginal contribution to the economic enterprise that supports a decent wage, government should provide a subsidy. Mark C. Weber, *Disability and the Law of Welfare: A Post-Integrationist Examination,* 2000 U. ILL. L. REV. 889. In a somewhat similar vein, Samuel Bagenstos argues that the government should provide medical coverage to permit people with disabilities to go to work without risking the loss of publicly funded medical assistance. Samuel R. Bagenstos, *The Future of Disability Law,* 114 YALE L.J. 1 (2004). Other sources also point out limits of the civil rights approach to disability issues. E.g., Bonnie Poitras Tucker, *The ADA's Revolving Door: Inherent Flaws in the Civil Rights Paradigm,* 62 OHIO ST. L.J. 335 (2001) (noting limits on civil rights approach as embodied in ADA).

7. Some note that cultural institutions surrounding disability, and with them, cultural identity, may be threatened by integration. This point is made most often with respect to deafness and the culture that surrounds the use of sign. See, e.g., Harlan Lane, *Constructions of Deafness,* in THE DISABILITIES STUDIES READER, *supra* note 2, at 161. Others have criticized this position. See, e.g., Bonnie P. Tucker, *Deafness—Disability or Subculture: The Emerging Conflict,* 3 CORNELL J.L. & PUB. POL'Y 265 (1994). Susan Wendell has questioned the goal

of integration with respect to other disabling conditions. Susan Wendell, *Toward a Feminist Theory of Disability*, in THE DISABILITY STUDIES READER, *supra* note 2, at 261.

8. This figure and the rest of the statistics in this paragraph are from H. STEPHEN KAYE, 2 DISABILITY WATCH: THE STATUS OF PEOPLE WITH DISABILITIES IN THE UNITED STATES (2001), available at http://www.dralegal.org/downloads/pubs/disability_watch_v2.txt (visited Sep. 9, 2005). Kaye is with the Disability Statistics Center, University of California, San Francisco.

9. Cook collected studies supporting his contention that "[v]irtually all people with disabilities can and should live and receive services they need in community settings," and the array of authority is indeed overwhelming. See Timothy M. Cook, *The Americans with Disabilities Act: The Move to Integration*, 64 TEMP. L. REV. 393, 442–45 (1991) (collecting sources). Institutions remain open primarily because of politics. State hospitals provide badly needed jobs and other patronage to the small towns in which they are located. Needless to say, political considerations should not establish a defense to deinstitutionalization.

10. See L. Scott Muller et al., *Labor-Force Participation and Earnings of SSI Disability Recipients: A Pooled Cross-Sectional Approach to the Behavior of Individuals*, SOC. SECURITY BULL., Mar. 1, 1996, at 22, 34–36 (discussing prevalence of sheltered and supported employment among recipients of government Supplemental Security Income benefits).

11. This figure is based on 1995 data. See Weber, *supra* note 6, at 899 n.63 (citing Mitchell P. LaPlante et al, *Disability and Employment*, DISABILITY STATISTICS ABSTRACT (Jan. 1996). More recent census data report poverty rates by household, a measure that does not exactly compare to the 1995 information. Nevertheless, poverty rates are extraordinary compared to the general population. "Among families with one or more members with a disability, the poverty rate was 12.8 percent—higher than the 9.2 percent for all families and the 7.7 percent for families without members with a disability." U.S. CENSUS BUREAU, DISABILITY AND AMERICAN FAMILIES 2000, at 10 (July, 2005), available at http://www.census.gov/prod/2005pubs/censr-23.pdf. Of families that have both adults and children with disabilities in them, the poverty rate is 28.9 percent. *Id.* at 12, fig. 4.

12. U.S. DEP'T OF EDUC., TWENTY-THIRD ANNUAL REPORT TO CONGRESS ON THE IMPLEMENTATION OF THE INDIVIDUALS WITH DISABILITIES EDUCATION ACT III-4 to 5 (2002).

13. *Id.* at III-5.

14. U.S. DEP'T OF EDUC., THE TRANSITION EXPERIENCES OF YOUNG PEOPLE WITH DISABILITIES: A SUMMARY OF FINDINGS FROM THE NATIONAL LONGITUDINAL STUDY OF SPECIAL EDUCATION STUDENTS 2–9 (1993).

15. See tenBroek & Matson, *supra* note 2, at 811–16 (describing use of almshouses for custody of persons with disabilities, followed by use of institu-

tions); see also Colin Barnes & Mike Oliver, *Disability: A Sociological Phenomenon Ignored by Sociologists* (June, 1993), *at* www.leeds.ac.uk/disability-studies/archiveuk/Barnes/soc%20phenomenon.pdf ("[D]isabled people . . . were segregated from mainstream economic and social life and incarcerated into a variety of institutions including special schools, asylums, workhouses, and long stay hospitals created specifically for this purpose.").

16. See *Wyatt v. Aderholt,* 503 F.2d 1305, 1310 (5th Cir. 1974) (describing filth, brutality, and malnutrition at state institution for people with mental retardation); *N.Y. State Ass'n for Retarded Children v. Rockefeller,* 357 F. Supp. 752 (E.D.N.Y. 1973) (describing reports of 1,300 injuries, assaults, or fights in eight months at state institution for children with mental retardation).

17. See *Youngberg v. Romeo,* 457 U.S. 307, 316 (1982). Many courts refused to find rights to safety and habilitation when an individual is voluntarily confined rather than civilly committed. See, e.g., *Fialkowski v. Greenwich Home for Children,* 921 F.2d 459 (3d Cir. 1990).

18. *Pennhurst State School & Hospital v. Halderman,* 451 U.S. 1 (1981).

19. See Chicago Code § 36–34 (1966) (repealed 1973) (cited in Martha McCluskey, Note, *Rethinking Equality and Difference: Disability Discrimination in Public Transportation,* 97 YALE L.J. 863, 963 n.8); see also Note, *Facial Discrimination: Extending Handicap Law to Employment Discrimination on the Basis of Physical Appearance,* 100 HARV. L. REV. 2035, 2035 n.2 (1987) (collecting sources).

20. See, e.g., *Department of Pub. Welfare v. Haas,* 154 N.E.2d 265 (Ill. 1958); *Watson v. City of Cambridge,* 32 N.E. 864 (Mass. 1893); *State ex rel. Beattie v. Board of Educ.,* 172 N.W. 153 (Wis. 1919). Statutes permitting administrative exclusion of children with disabilities from public school are collected and described in Richard C. Handel, *The Role of the Advocate in Securing the Handicapped Child's Right to an Effective Minimal Education,* 36 OHIO ST. L.J. 349, 351 (1974).

21. See Act of May 18, 1965, ch. 584, 1965 N.C. SESS. LAWS 641 (amending N.C. Gen. Stat. § 115-165 (1963)).

22. See H.R. REP. No. 94–332, at 11–12 (1975).

23. See *Buck v. Bell,* 274 U.S. 200, 207 (1927) (Holmes, J.) (upholding sterilization of woman deemed "feeble-minded," asserting that "[t]hree generations of imbeciles are enough."). *Buck* itself was a sham case in which the attorney for Carrie Buck was in league with the eugenicists. See Paul A. Lombardo, *Three Generations, No Imbeciles: New Light on* Buck v. Bell, 60 N.Y.U. L. REV. 30, 56 (1985). Attitudes underlying the case have not gone away. See Roberta Cepko, *Involuntary Sterilization of Mentally Disabled Women,* 8 BERKELEY WOMEN'S L.J. 122 (1993) (describing legal procedures for compulsory sterilization that fail to protect rights of women with mental disabilities); Robert L. Hayman, *Presumptions of Justice: Law, Politics, and the Mentally Retarded*

Parent, 103 HARV. L. REV. 1201 (1990) (challenging prevalent presumption that persons with mental retardation are unfit as parents).

24. See Cook, *supra* note 9, at 400–01 (1991) ("In virtually every state, in inexorable fashion, people with disabilities—especially children and youth—were declared by state lawmaking bodies to be 'unfitted for companionship with other children,' a 'blight on mankind' whose very presence in the community was 'detrimental to normal' children, and whose 'mingling . . . with society' was 'a most baleful evil.') (footnotes omitted; quoting statutes and governmental reports).

25. Hugh Gregory Gallagher, *"Slapping Up Spastics": The Persistence of Social Attitudes toward People with Disabilities,* 10 ISSUES L. & MED. 401, 402 (1995) ("In the late 1930s and throughout World War II, physicians of Germany's medical establishment . . . systematically killed their severely disabled and chronically ill mental patients. . . . The officially sanctioned killing program was authorized by Hitler in 1939 at the request of leading figures of the German medical establishment. . . . The program's proponents advanced various arguments for its justification: compassion, eugenics, economics, racial purity."); Stanley S. Herr, *The International Significance of Disability Rights,* 93 AM. SOC'Y INT'L L. PROC. 332, 332 (2000) ("By the 1930s, the killing of German and Austrian nationals with disabilities through so-called euthanasia programs . . . suggested precursors to the genocide and fascist barbarisms to come.").

26. This practice continued at least into the 1930s. See Cook, *supra* note 9, at 403 n.74 (collecting extensive primary sources).

27. In his autobiography, Oliver Sacks records the practice of the matron under his physician mother's supervision drowning newborns with anencephaly or spina bifida. OLIVER SACKS, UNCLE TUNGSTEN 242–43 (2001).

28. See Cook, *supra* note 9, at 403 n.74 (collecting sources).

29. 473 U.S. 432, 461–62 (1985) (Marshall, J., concurring in part and dissenting in part).

30. *Id.* at 461–62 (citations and footnotes omitted; quoting, in first sentence, *University of California Regents v. Bakke,* 438 U.S. 265, 303 (1978) (Powell, J., plurality op.), in last sentence, H. Goddard, *The Possibilities of Research as Applied to the Prevention of Feeblemindedness,* PROC. NAT'L CONF. CHARITIES & CORRECTION 307 (1915)). As Justice Marshall pointed out, people with developmental disabilities were viewed as a threat to society, just as African Americans were. *Id.* at 462 n.8 ("Books with titles such as '"The Menace of the Feeble Minded in Connecticut"' (1915), issued by the Connecticut School for Imbeciles, became commonplace. See C. Frazier (Chairman, Executive Committee of Public Charities Assn. of Pennsylvania), The Menace of the Feeble-Minded in Pennsylvania (1913); W. Fernald, The Burden of Feeble-Mindedness (1912) (Mass.); Juvenile Protection Association of Cincinnati, The Feeble-Minded, Or the Hub to Our Wheel of Vice (1915) (Ohio). The resemblance to such works

as R. Shufeldt, The Negro: A Menace to American Civilization (1907), is striking, and not coincidental.").

31. *Id.* at 462–63 (footnotes omitted; quoting, in second sentence, A. MOORE, THE FEEBLE-MINDED IN NEW YORK 3 (1911), in last sentence, Act of Apr. 3, 1920, ch. 210, § 17, 1920 MISS. LAWS 288, 294). See generally Anita Silvers & Michael Ashley Stein, *Disability, Equal Protection, and the Supreme Court: Standing at the Crossroads of Progressive and Retrogressive Logic in Constitutional Classification,* 35 U. MICH. J.L. REFORM 81, 109 (2001–02) ("Marshall's partial dissent [in *Cleburne*] took the history of oppression of disabled people to be a lens that inexorably distorted assessments of their differences.").

32. Richard K. Scotch, *American Disability Policy in the Twentieth Century,* in THE NEW DISABILITY HISTORY 375, 389 (Paul K. Longmore & Lauri Umansky eds. 2001).

33. This development would not necessarily be bad, for specialized or sheltered workshops segregate workers with disabilities and frequently provide little in the way of an entry point to better-paying, better-integrated work. See Harlan Hahn, *Towards a Politics of Disability,* Institute on Independent Living, at http://www.independentliving.org/docs4/hahn2.html (visited Mar. 10, 2003) ("[D]isabled persons often are trained by rehabilitation programs for positions in the secondary labor market which provide few opportunities for increase[d] income or upward mobility."). Nevertheless, if jobs that people with developmental disabilities can do are not available in other settings, the result of the substitution of machines is a net loss in employment.

34. LENNARD J. DAVIS, BENDING OVER BACKWARDS: DISABILITY, DISMODERNISM & OTHER DIFFICULT POSITIONS (2002).

35. *Id.* at 38. Davis links the creation of the normal by students of statistics and its establishment, paradoxically as an ideal for the modern era, to eugenics. "The rather amazing fact is that almost all the early statisticians had one thing in common: they were eugenicists." Lennard J. Davis, *Constructing Normalcy,* in THE DISABILITY STUDIES READER, *supra* note 2, at 9, 14. In fact, the needs of eugenics demanded the development of statistical methods. *Id.* at 14–15.

36. ERVING GOFFMAN, STIGMA: NOTES ON THE MANAGEMENT OF SPOILED IDENTITY 5 (1963).

37. IRVING KENNETH ZOLA, MISSING PIECES: A CHRONICLE OF LIVING WITH A DISABILITY 120 (1982).

38. ROBERT MURPHY, THE BODY SILENT 116 (1987).

39. ROSEMARIE GARLAND THOMSON, EXTRAORDINARY BODIES: FIGURING PHYSICAL DISABILITY IN AMERICAN CULTURE AND LITERATURE 41 (1997). Thomson also discusses the marking of persons with disabilities as deviant from the idea of the average or normal man in the nineteenth century. See *id.* at 63–64.

40. *Id.* at 80.

41. See Simon Ungar, *Disability and the Built Environment*, Distance Education Centre, University of Sheffield, at http://fhis.gcal.ac.uk/PSY/sun/LectureNotes/city/city.html (visited Mar. 10, 2003) ("[I]t should also be clear that these exclusions themselves help to reproduce negative attitudes to disabled people.").

42. GORDON W. ALLPORT, THE NATURE OF PREJUDICE 264 (25th Anniversary ed. 1979).

43. *Id.* at 276–78.

44. Martha M. Field, *Killing "the Handicapped"—Before and after Birth*, 16 HARV. WOMEN'S L.J. 79, 117 (1993).

45. Michael Ashley Stein, *Disability, Employment Policy, and the Supreme Court*, 55 STAN. L. REV. 607, 631–32 (2002) ("Harlan Hahn . . . asserts that able-bodied society feels 'existential anxiety' towards the disabled. [quoting Harlan Hahn, *Toward a Politics of Disability: Definitions, Disciplines, and Policies*, 22 SOC. SCI. J. 87 (1995); Harlan Hahn, *Civil Rights for Disabled Americans*, in IMAGES OF THE DISABLED, DISABLING IMAGES 181, 182 (Alan Gartner & Tom Joe eds. 1987)] The combination of repugnance to disabled bodily difference and fear of also attaining such variation in the future, according to Hahn, result in a sociological desire to segregate people with disabilities from the mainstream." [citing Harlan Hahn, *Antidiscrimination Laws and Social Research on Disability: The Minority Group Perspective*, 14 BEHAV. SCI. & L. 41 (1996)]); see also David M. Engel, *Law, Culture, and Children with Disabilities: Educational Rights and the Construction of Difference*, 1991 DUKE L.J. 166, 183–84 (discussing psychological origins of negative attitudes toward persons with disabilities).

46. Several years before the passage of the ADA, the United States Civil Rights Commission linked forced separation and the negative attitudes that lead to discrimination: "Historically, society has tended to isolate and segregate handicapped people. Despite some improvements, particularly in the last two decades, discrimination against handicapped persons continues to be a serious and pervasive social problem." U.S. COMM'N ON CIVIL RIGHTS, ACCOMMODATING THE SPECTRUM OF INDIVIDUAL ABILITIES 159 (1983).

47. See Paul Sale & Doris M. Carey, *The Sociometric Status of Students with Disabilities in a Full-Inclusion School*, 62 EXCEPTIONAL CHILDREN 6, 16–17 (1995) (reporting attitude study).

48. Samuel R. Bagenstos, *Subordination, Stigma and "Disability,"* 86 VA. L. REV. 397, 438–39 (2000).

49. 193 F.3d 730, 732 (3d Cir. 1999).

50. 320 F.3d 663 (6th Cir. 2003); see also *Thomas v. Cincinnati Bd. of Educ.*, 918 F.2d 618 (6th Cir. 1990); *DeVries v. Fairfax County Sch. Bd.*, 882 F.2d 876 (4th Cir. 1989). Courts have generally failed to enforce the regulation

providing that the placement of a child with disabilities must be "as close as possible to the child's home," 34 C.F.R. § 300.552 (2003). See, e.g., *Murray v. Montrose County Sch. Dist. RE-1J*, 51 F.3d 921, 929–30 (10th Cir. 1995). The courts have a mixed record applying the least-restrictive-environment duty in public school cases. See MARK C. WEBER, SPECIAL EDUCATION LAW AND LITIGATION TREATISE 9:3 (2d ed. 2002) (collecting cases).

51. 245 F.3d 969, 974 (7th Cir. 2001). The court opined that the no-segregation rule was satisfied when the worker was moved to a setting that included workers without disabilities. *Id.* at 973–74.

52. *Duda v. Board of Educ.*, 133 F.3d 1054, 1059–60 (7th Cir. 1998).

53. 527 U.S. 581, 593–94 (1999).

54. *Id.* at 596 (upholding 28 C.F.R. § 35.130(d)).

55. *Id.* at 604 (applying "fundamental-alteration" defense provided by 28 C.F.R. § 35.130(b)(7)).

56. See *id.* (stating that "the ADA is not reasonably read to impel States to phase out institutions, placing patients in need of close care at risk.").

57. *Id.* at 606.

58. See *Brown v. Board of Education (Brown II)*, 349 U.S. 294, 299 (1955) (allowing delay in implementation of racial integration in public schools for administrative difficulties; stating that integration was to be implemented "with all deliberate speed").

59. *Sacramento Unified Sch. Dist. v. Rachel H.*, 14 F.3d 1398 (9th Cir. 1994).

60. *School Dist. v. Z.S.*, 295 F.3d 671, 677 (7th Cir. 2002).

61. Ruth Colker, *The Disability Integration Presumption: Thirty Years Later,* 154 U. PA. L. REV. 789, 833-34, 853 (2006).

62. See Ungar, *supra* note 41 (cataloguing physical and sensory barriers in environment and effects of isolating persons with disabilities).

63. Hahn, *supra* note 33 ("Disabled persons have confronted barriers in architecture, transportation, and public accommodations which have excluded them from common social, economic, and political activities even more effectively than the segregationist policies of racist governments.").

64. See *Guckenberger v. Boston Univ.*, 957 F. Supp. 306, 312 (D. Mass. 1997). Note that President Jon Westling was using the term "plague" to describe the students, not the condition.

65. See *In re Bendectin Litig.*, 857 F.2d 290, 296 (6th Cir. 1988). Not all judges share this attitude. See, e.g., *Helminski v. Ayerst Labs.*, 766 F.2d 208, 217 (6th Cir. 1985) (holding that individuals with physical abnormalities should not be discriminated against with respect to presence in court).

66. See S. REP. NO. 101–116, at 7 (1989).

67. See 135 CONG. REC. S10,720 (1989) (statement of Sen. Durenberger) (cerebral palsy); H.R. REP. NO. 101–485, pt. II, at 30 (1989) (arthritis).

68. See, e.g., Harriet McBryde Johnson, *Unspeakable Conversations*, NEW YORK TIMES MAGAZINE, Feb. 16, 2003 (describing reaction to Singer among members of disability rights community). See generally HELGA KUHSE & PETER SINGER, SHOULD THE BABY LIVE? 1 (1985) (asserting that killing infants with disabilities is moral); PETER SINGER, ANIMAL LIBERATION 18 (2d ed. 1990) (equating killing of animals and killing of infants with brain damage).

69. Regarding James, Pope, and Milton, see Sharon L. Snyder, *Infinities of Forms: Disability Figures in Artistic Traditions*, in DISABILITY STUDIES: ENABLING THE HUMANITIES 173, 173–79 (Sharon L. Snyder et al. eds. 2002). Regarding Johnson, see the compelling essay by Helen Deutsch, *Exemplary Aberration: Samuel Johnson and the English Canon*, in *id.* 197.

70. These descriptions match respectively, the situations presented by cases such as *Washington v. Glucksberg*, 521 U.S. 702 (1997), and the Terri Schiavo affair. For commentary on the right-to-die cases, see Stephen L. Mikochik, *Assisted Suicide and Disabled People*, 46 DEPAUL L. REV. 987, 999–1002 (1997). For commentary generally critical of the courts' ultimate resolution of the Schiavo case, see *Commentary: Terri Schiavo, Not Dead Yet*, at http://www.notdeadyet.org/docs/schiavo05/index.html.

71. See Karen Schwartz et al., *Social Imagery in the Film* Million Dollar Baby: *An Analysis Based on Wolf Wolfensberger's* Social Role Valorization, DISABILITY STUDIES Q., Summer 2005, available at http://www.des-sds.org/_articles_html/2005/summer/m$b_forum.asp.

72. Frank M. Johnson, *The Constitution and the Federal District Judge*, 54 TEX. L. REV. 903, 909 (1976) (emphasis in original).

73. DICK SOBSEY, VIOLENCE AND ABUSE IN THE LIVES OF PEOPLE WITH DISABILITIES vii (1994) (quoting personal account from patient); see also JOSEPH SHAPIRO, NO PITY: PEOPLE WITH DISABILITIES FORGING A NEW CIVIL RIGHTS MOVEMENT 237–39 (1993).

74. See Doris Zames Fleisher & Frieda Zames, *Compassionate Killings*, in DISABILITY STUDIES Q., *supra* note 71.

75. JOHNSON, *supra* note 4, at xvii.

76. Stephen Drake, Million Dollar Baby *and* Not Dead Yet, DISABILITY STUDIES Q., *supra* note 71.

CHAPTER 3

1. *Harris v. Forklift Sys., Inc.*, 510 U.S. 17 (1993); *Meritor Sav. Bank v. Vinson*, 477 U.S. 57 (1986).

2. *Meritor*, 477 U.S. at 67 (quoting *Henson v. Dundee*, 682 F.2d 897, 904 (11th Cir. 1982).

3. *Harris*, 510 U.S. at 22.

4. 42 U.S.C.A. § 12112(a) (West 2005).

5. 893 F. Supp. 1092 (S.D. Ga 1995).

6. See *id.*

7. *Id.* at 1108.

8. *Id.* at 1108–09.

9. *Id.* at 1109.

10. *Id.* at 1106.

11. *Rohan v. Networks Presentation LLC,* 192 F. Supp. 2d 434 (D. Md. 2002) (denying motion to dismiss); *Swatzell v. Southwestern Bell. Tel. Co.,* No. CA 7:00-CV-139-R N.D. Tex. Oct. 31, 2001) (denying motion for summary judgment); *Armstrong v. Reno,* 172 F. Supp. 2d 11 (D.D.C. 2001) (denying motion for summary judgment); *Hiller v. Runyon,* 95 F. Supp. 2d 1016 (S.D. Iowa 2000) (denying motion for summary judgment); *Arena v. AGIP USA, Inc.,* No. 95 CIV. 1529 (WHP), 2000 WL 264312 (S.D.N.Y. Mar. 8, 2000) (denying motion for summary judgment); *Disanto v. McGraw-Hill, Inc.,* No. 97 Civ. 1090 JGK, 1998 WL 474136 (S.D.N.Y. Aug. 11, 1998) (denying motion for summary judgment); *Hendler v. Intelecom, USA,* 963 F. Supp. 200 (E.D.N.Y. 1997) (denying motion for summary judgment); *Hudson v. Loretex Corp.,* No. 95 CV-844 (RSP/RWS), 1997 WL 159282 (N.D.N.Y. April 2, 1997) (denying motion to dismiss); *Easley v. West,* No. Civ. A. 93–6751, 1994 WL 702904 (E.D. Pa. Dec. 13, 1994) (denying motions to dismiss and for summary judgment); *Davis v. York Int'l,* No. Civ. A. HAR 92–3545, 1993 WL 524761 (D. Md. Nov. 22, 1993) (denying motion for summary judgment); see *Brown v. Lester E. Cox Med. Ctr.,* 286 F.3d 1040 (8th Cir. 2002) (affirming verdict for emotional distress for transfer to position below qualifications on basis of disability); see also *Wheeler v. Marathon Printing, Inc.,* 974 P.2d 207 (Or. App. 1998) (upholding harassment claim on basis of state law).

12. 247 F.3d 169 (4th Cir. 2001).

13. *Id.* at 181. The court considered the hostile-work-environment claim to be something other than a claim of intentional discrimination and overturned an award of $4,000 for unpaid overtime on the ground that it was inconsistent with the jury's finding that General Motors had not intentionally discriminated against the plaintiff. *Id.* Of course, an employer's furtherance or toleration of disability harassment is a policy that has a disparate impact on employees with disabilities, but it appears that the jury may have been somewhat confused in failing to identify the conduct as intentional discrimination. Perhaps it felt that the low-level supervisory personnel and workers who did the harassing were too removed from company decision making to have their intentional conduct attributed to the company.

14. *Id.* at 176.

15. 247 F.3d 229 (5th Cir. 2001).

16. *Id.* at 237.

17. *Id.* at 236. On the topic of remedies, the court held that the plaintiff had not presented adequate evidence of specific emotional injury, and so vacated the damages award and remanded for entry of an award of nominal damages. *Id.* at 239. For further discussion of *Flowers,* see Melinda Slusser, Note, *Flowers v. Southern Regional Physician Services: A Step in the Right Direction,* 33 U. TOL. L. REV. 713 (2002).

18. *Fox,* 247 F.3d at 175–76 (citing *Patterson v. McLean Credit Union,* 491 U.S. 164, 180 (1989) and *Meritor Bank v. Vinson,* 477 U.S. 57, 64–66 (1986)). The *Fox* court pointed out that the similarity of statutory purpose between title VII and the ADA has frequently led to the use of title VII precedent in ADA cases. *Id.* at 176.

19. *Flowers,* 247 F.3d at 233.

20. *Id.* at 234.

21. There is no disagreement among the circuits on this point, though so far only two, the Fourth and the Fifth, have recognized the cause of action in the course of upholding a verdict, at least in part. See *Fox v. General Motors Corp.,* 247 F.3d 169, 176 (4th Cir. 2001); *Flowers v. Southern Reg'l Physician Servs., Inc.,* 247 F.3d 229, 232 (5th Cir. 2001); see also *Quiles-Quiles v. Henderson,* 439 F.3d 1 (1st Cir. 2006) (reversing judgment as a matter of law on hostile-environment claim in federal employment under Rehabilitation Act); *Lanman v. Johnson County,* 393 F.3d 1151 (10th Cir. 2004) (stating that claim exists); *Silk v. City of Chicago,* 194 F.3d 788, 803 (7th Cir. 1999) (suggesting existence of claim); *Cannice v. Norwest Bank Iowa N.A.,* 183 F.3d 723, 725 (8th Cir. 1999) (assuming existence of claim), *cert. denied,* 529 U.S. 1019 (2000); *Walton v. Mental Health Ass'n,* 168 F.3d 661, 666 n.2 (3d Cir. 1999) ("Indeed, we have not discovered any case holding that the claim cannot be asserted under the ADA."); *Wallin v. Minnesota Dep't of Corrections,* 153 F.3d 681, 687–88 (8th Cir. 1998) (assuming existence of claim); *Keever v. City of Middletown,* 145 F.3d 809, 813 (6th Cir. 1998) (same); cf. *McConathy v. Dr. Pepper/Seven Up Corp.,* 131 F.3d 558, 563 (5th Cir. 1998) (assuming existence of claim but stating that case is not authority for its existence). Five elements must be shown for the plaintiff to satisfy to be entitled to relief: (1) that the plaintiff is a qualified individual with a disability; (2) that the plaintiff was subjected to unwelcome harassment; (3) that the harassment was on the basis of the disability; (4) that the harassment was severe or pervasive enough to alter the conditions of employment; and (5) that a factual basis exists to impute liability for the harassment to the employer. *Fox v. General Motors Corp.,* 247 F.3d 169, 177 (4th Cir. 2001). Other courts employ similar formulas. See, e.g., *Flowers v. Southern Reg'l Physician Servs., Inc.,* 247 F.3d 229, 235–36 (5th Cir. 2001). The greatest variations are in the wording of the fifth element. See *id.* ("(5) that the employer knew or should have known of the harassment and failed to take prompt effective remedial action."). Following the analogy to sexual harassment cases liti-

gated under title VII, see *Burlington Indus, Inc. v. Ellerth,* 524 U.S. 742, 765 (1998); *Faragher v. City of Boca Raton,* 524 U.S. 775, 807 (1998), the fifth element, however worded, would be deemed satisfied as a matter of law in cases in which supervisors conducted the harassment. For a discussion of imputation of knowledge to the employer in instances of co-worker sex harassment, see *Hall v. Bodine Elec. Co.,* 276 F.3d 345, 356 (7th Cir. 2002).

22. *Spencer v. Wal-Mart Stores, Inc.,* No. Civ. A. 03–104-KAJ, 2005 WL 697988 (D. Del. March 11, 2005).

23. *EEOC v. Circuit City Stores, Inc.,* No. 1:04CV00183, 2005 WL 1474025 (M.D.N.C. June 21, 2005).

24. *Jackanin v. Mount Sinai Hosp.,* No. 98 Civ. 5752(KTD), 2003 WL 402443 (S.D.N.Y. Feb. 20, 2003).

25. *Farrington v. Bath Iron Works Corp.,* No. 01–274-P-H, 2003 WL 278172 (D. Me. Feb. 7, 2003).

26. *Pantazes v. Jackson,* 366 F. Supp. 2d 57 (D.D.C. 2005). Because the employer was a federal agency, the claim was brought, not under section 504 or the ADA, but under 29 U.S.C. §§ 791, 794d.

27. *Faircloth v. Duke Univ.,* 267 F. Supp. 2d 470 (M.D.N.C. 2003).

28. Lisa Eichhorn, *Hostile Environment Actions, Title VII, and the ADA: The Limits of the Copy-and-Paste Function,* 77 WASH. L. REV. 575 (2002).

29. Among recent disability harassment cases that have failed on this ground are *Lanman v. Johnson County,* 393 F.3d 1151 (10th Cir. 2004); *Rohan v. Networks Presentations LLC,* 375 F.3d 266 (4th Cir. 2004); *Wilborn v. Southwestern Bell. Tel. Co.,* No. 303CV0124N, 2005 WL 701045 (N.D. Tex. March 24, 2005); *Papparoth v. E.I. Dupont de Nemours & Co.,* 359 F. Supp. 2d 525 (W.D. Va. 2005); *Holman v. Revere Elec. Supply Co.,* No. 02 C 6351, 2005 WL 638085 (N.D. Ill. March 15, 2005); *Tongalson v. Dreyfus Servs. Corp.,* No. 04 Civ. 2308JSR, 2005 WL 356805 (S.D.N.Y. Feb. 14, 2005); *Chan v. Sprint Corp.,* 351 F. Supp. 2d 1197 (D. Kan. 2005).

30. *Zale v. Sikorsky Aircraft Corp.,* No. 3:97CV00125(JBA), 2000 WL 306943 (D. Conn. Feb. 7, 2000).

31. *Farrington v. Bath Iron Works Corp.,* No. 01–274-P-H, 2003 WL 278172, at *12–*13 (D. Me. Feb. 7, 2003).

32. E.g., *Vande Zande v. Wis. Dep't of Admin.,* 44 F.3d 538, 546 (7th Cir. 1995) (affirming grant of summary judgment against plaintiff on claim based on employer's failure to provide accommodation costing $150 when employer provided other accommodations; stating that "there is no separate offense under the Americans with Disabilities Act called engaging in a pattern of insensitivity. . . .").

33. See *Pantazes v. Jackson,* 366 F. Supp. 2d 57 (D.D.C. 2005).

34. Frank S. Ravitch, *Beyond Reasonable Accommodations: The Availability and Structure of a Cause of Action for Workplace Harassment under the Americans with Disabilities Act,* 15 CARDOZO L. REV. 1475, 1055 (1994).

35. See *Mannie v. Potter*, 394 F.3d 977 (7th Cir. 2005) (inappropriate and insensitive comments not considered sufficient to support cause of action); *Vollmert v. Wis. Dep't of Transp.*, 197 F.3d 293 (7th Cir. 1999) (finding trainer's unfavorable actions not so severe or pervasive as to establish hostile environment); *Cannice v. Norwest Bank Iowa N.A.*, 183 F.3d 723 (8th Cir.1999) (reversing damages award on ground that knowledge of disability did not motivate offensive conduct); *Walton v. Mental Health Ass'n*, 168 F.3d 661 (3d Cir. 1999) (finding conduct not pervasive or severe enough to meet standard for liability); *Wallin v. Minnesota Dep't of Corrections*, 153 F.3d 681 (8th Cir. 1998) (finding incidents isolated and not severe or pervasive); *Keever v. City of Middletown*, 145 F.3d 809 (6th Cir. 1998) (affirming summary judgment based on failure to allege facts to establish severity); *McConathy v. Dr. Pepper/Seven Up Corp.*, 131 F.3d 558 (5th Cir. 1998) (affirming summary judgment on ground that conduct lacked sufficient severity); *Fleetwood v. Hartford Sys., Inc.*, 380 F. Supp. 2d 688 (D. Md. 2005) (finding insufficient support for alteration of terms of employment); *Mohammadian v. Ciba Vision of Puerto Rico*, 378 F. Supp. 2d 25 (D. P.R. 2005) (finding conduct insensitive but not severe); *Cornwell v. Dairy Farmers of America, Inc.*, 369 F. Supp. 2d 87 (D. Mass. 2005) (finding harassment not sufficient to support claim of hostile environment); *Tebo v. Potter*, 345 F. Supp. 2d 61 (D. Mass. 2004) (conduct considered to be trivial, rather than severe harassment); *St. Hilaire v. Minco Prods., Inc.*, 288 F. Supp. 2d 999 (D. Minn. 2003) (finding harassment not severe enough); *Crock v. Sears*, 261 F. Supp. 2d 1101 (S.D. Iowa 2003) (finding conduct not to affect ability to do work); *Overstreet v. Calvert County Health Dep't*, 187 F. Supp. 2d 567 (D. Md. 2002) (granting summary judgment on ground that conduct did not constitute constructive discharge); *Georgy v. O'Neill*, No. 00-CV-0660 (FB), 2002 U.S. Dist. LEXIS 4825 (E.D.N.Y. Mar. 22, 2002) (finding conduct not continuous and pervasive); *Richio v. Miami-Dade County*, 163 F. Supp. 2d 1352 (S.D. Fla. 2001) (finding harassment not severe enough to constitute constructive discharge); *Roeder v. Hendricks Community Hosp.*, No. IP00–0447-C-H/G, 2001 WL 1168151 (S.D. Ind. Sep. 7, 2001) (granting summary judgment on ground conduct lacked severity or pervasiveness); *Griffin v. Jefferson Parish Sch. Bd.*, No. 99–1344 REF, 2001 U.S. Dist. LEXIS 13238 (E.D. La. Aug. 17, 2001) (granting summary judgment on ground harassment not based on disability); *Statzer v. Town of Lebanon*, No. 1:00CV00128, 2001 WL 710103 (W.D. Va. June 4, 2001) (granting summary judgment on ground harassment lacked severity or pervasiveness); *Ballard v. Healthsouth Corp.*, No. Civ. A. 3:00-CV-1011, 2001 WL 585974 (N.D. Tex. May 25, 2001) (granting summary judgment on grounds of severity and pervasiveness); *McCoy v. USF Dugan, Inc.*, No. 99–1504-JTM, 2001 WL 579820 (D. Kan. May 21, 2001) (granting summary judgment on ground conduct not severe enough); *Johnston v. Henderson*, No. 00–6445CIV, 2001 WL 476955 (S.D. Fla. May 1, 2001) (granting summary

judgment on grounds of severity and pervasiveness of conduct); *Jeseritz v. Henderson*, No. CIV-99–1439 RHK JMM, 2001 WL 420164 (D, Minn. Feb. 9, 2001) (granting summary judgment on ground conduct lacked severity or pervasiveness); *Davis-Durnil v. Village of Carpentersville*, 128 F. Supp. 2d 575 (N.D. Ill. 2001) (finding comments and other actions not to constitute severe or pervasive conduct); *Soledad v. United States Dep't of Treasury*, 116 F. Supp. 2d 790 (W.D. Tex. 2000) (granting judgment as a matter of law for defendant overturning jury verdict, ruling conduct not severe or pervasive); *Comber v. Prologue, Inc.*, No. JFM-99–2637, 2000 U.S. Dist. LEXIS 16331 (D. Md. Sep. 28, 2000) (granting summary judgment on ground of no pervasive hostility); *Harshbarger v. Sierra Pac. Power Co.*, 128 F. Supp. 2d 1302 (D. Nev. 2000) (granting summary judgment, finding conduct not severe or pervasive); *Scherer v. GE Capital*, No. 99–2172-GTV, 2000 U.S. Dist. LEXIS 9152 (D. Kan. June 2, 2000) (granting summary judgment for lack of severe or pervasive conduct); *Fitch v. Solipsys Corp.*, 94 F. Supp. 2d 670 (D. Md. 2000) (granting summary judgment for failure to show severe or pervasive conduct); *Veal v. AT & T Corp.*, No. CIV. A. 99–0370 (Mar. 22, 2000) (granting summary judgment, finding conduct insufficiently pervasive and not motivated by disability); *Casper v. Gunite Corp.*, No. 3:98-CV-173RM, 1999 U.S. Dist. LEXIS 13554 (N.D. Ind. June 11, 1999) (granting summary judgment on absence of severity or frequency), *aff'd*, 221 F.3d 1338 (7th Cir. 2000) (table); *Ward v. Massachusetts Health Research Inst.*, 48 F. Supp. 2d 72 (D. Mass 1999) (granting summary judgment on ground of lack of severity and official knowledge); *Schwertfager v. City of Boynton Beach*, 42 F. Supp. 2d 1347 (S.D. Fla. 1999) (granting summary judgment on ground environment not shown to be objectively abusive); *Fosburg v. Lehigh Univ.*, No. Civ. A. 98-CV-864, 1999 WL 124458, *6 (E.D. Pa. Mar. 4, 1999) (finding on allegations of complaint that harassment did not reach level of hostility or pervasiveness needed to state claim); *Pomilio v. Wachtell Lipton Rosen & Katz*, No. 97 Civ. 2230 (MBM), 1999 WL 9843 (S.D.N.Y. Jan. 11, 1999) (granting summary judgment on ground that comments were isolated); *Hoffman v. Brown*, No. 1:96CV225-C, 1997 WL 827526 (W.D.N.C. Oct. 24, 1997) (granting summary judgment due to absence of evidence of impact of utterances on work environment); *Rodriguez v. Loctite Puerto Rico*, 967 F. Supp. 653 (D.P.R. 1997) (granting summary judgment on basis of absence of evidence of pervasive hostility); *Gray v. Ameritech Corp.*, 937 F. Supp. 762 (N.D. Ill. 1996) (granting summary judgment on ground of absence of knowledge of conduct by defendant); see also *Robel v. Roundup Corp.*, 10 P.3d 1104 (Wash. App. 2000) (finding conduct not severe or pervasive; applying state law), *rev'd* 59 P.3d 611 (Wash. 2002). The cases rejecting claims on the grounds of severity or pervasiveness assume that a cause of action exists under the ADA for a hostile work environment.

36. 194 F.3d 788 (7th Cir. 1999).

37. *Id.* at 795. Secondary effects of severe sleep apnea include hypertension and stroke. *Id.* The case was an appeal of the district court's grant of summary judgment, and the court of appeals took the facts alleged by the plaintiff as true, which this narrative does as well. See *id.* at 794 n.1.

38. *Id.* At first, he obtained an accommodation of no night shifts; subsequently he requested and obtained limited-duty status, with a restriction of day shift only. *Id.*

39. *Id.*

40. *Id.* at 807–08.

41. *Harshbarger v. Sierra Pacific Power Co.,* 128 F. Supp. 2d 1302, 1310 (D. Nev. 2000), *aff'd in part and rev'd in part,* 28 Fed. Appx. 707 (9th Cir. 2002). The plaintiff had severe elbow and shoulder injuries from which he had not fully recovered. The court found that this condition did not constitute a disability but considered the harassment claim anyway. *Id.* at 1310. The co-workers' derogatory sex stereotyping may also be noted. The case is discussed at greater length in chapter 1.

42. *Statzer v. Town of Lebanon,* No. 1:00CV00128, 2001 WL 710103 (W.D. Va. June 4, 2001), at *6. The condition rendered the plaintiff's speech about 50 percent intelligible. *Id.* at *1.

43. *Casper v. Gunite Corp.,* No. 3:98-CV-173RM, 1999 U.S. Dist. LEXIS 13554 (N.D. Ind. June 11, 1999), *aff'd,* 221 F.3d 1338 (7th Cir. 2000) (table). The case is also discussed in chapter 1.

44. *McConathy v. Dr. Pepper/Seven Up Corp.,* 131 F.3d 558, 563–64 (5th Cir. 1998). The plaintiff had temporomandibular joint disease. *Id.* at 560.

45. *Shaver v. Independent Stave Co.,* 350 F.3d 716 (8th Cir. 2003).

46. 179 F. Supp. 2d 914, 918–19, 926 (S.D. Ind. 2001).

47. *Id.* at 927.

48. E.g., *Burnett v. Tyco Corp.,* 203 F.3d 980 (6th Cir. 2000) (finding crude remarks and incident of physical contact insufficient to create hostile work environment); *Butler v. Ysleta Indep. Sch. Dist.,* 161 F.3d 263 (5th Cir. 1998) (overturning jury verdict on ground that anonymous letters did not create severe or pervasive hostile environment); *Koelsch v. Beltone Elec. Corp.,* 46 F.3d 705 (7th Cir. 1995) (finding that supervisor's comment that he could not control himself around plaintiff and repeated invitations for drinks and dinner failed to meet standard for harassment). A similar approach has been applied in a case under the Age Discrimination in Employment Act. E.g., *Bennington v. Caterpillar, Inc.,* 275 F.3d 654, 660 (7th Cir. 2001) (assuming existence of claim but ruling that rude or unfair conduct failed to rise to level of actionable discrimination). For a discussion of the difficulty of establishing that conduct is severe or pervasive enough to satisfy the hostile-environment standard for sex discrimination cases, see James C. Chow, Comment, *Sticks and Stones and*

Simple Teasing: The Jurisprudence of Non-cognizable Harassing Conduct in the Context of Title VII Hostile Work Environment Claims, 33 LOY. L.A. L. REV. 133 (1999).

49. See Chow, *supra* note 48, at 133 ("Approximately two-thirds of all Title VII sexual harassment claims in the United States circuit courts are dismissed when the claim involves stray remarks."). Chow proposes a revision of the interpretation of title VII so as to disregard any excuse that the verbal harassment consisted of a stray remark or teasing. *Id.* at 158–59. The vast bulk of what women perceive as sex harassment never even gets reported, often for fear of further exclusion or retaliation. See Beth A. Quinn, *The Paradox of Complaining: Law, Humor, and Harassment in the Everyday Work World*, 25 L. & SOC. INQUIRY 1151, 1154 (2000) (analyzing studies about underreporting), 1177–78 (discussing victims' fears of further exclusion and retaliation); see also Kari Jahnke, *Retaliatory Harassment against Employees by Employees: Should the Employer Be Liable?* 16 LAB. LAW. 465 (2001) (discussing retaliatory harassment that occurs after victims of discrimination file charges). This fact suggests that victims are already screening cases so that those that get to the court are the most serious; in the rest the conduct is simply ignored and the harm absorbed by the victims.

50. *Harris v. Forklift Sys., Inc.*, 510 U.S. 17, 21 (1993).

51. See, e.g., *Schwertfager v. City of Boynton Beach*, 42 F. Supp. 2d 1347, 1366 (S.D. Fla. 1999) (relying on *Harris* language as threshold for actionable discrimination).

52. See Ravitch, *supra* note 34, at 1055–58 (discussing modifications of the hostile-environment standard for disability cases); Christine Neagle, Comment, *An Analysis of the Applicability of Hostile Work Environment Liability to the ADA*, 3 U. PA. J. LAB. & EMP. L. 715, 737–38 (2001) (same). Thus Professor Ravitch proposes asking whether "a reasonable person with the same disability would consider [the abusive conduct] sufficiently severe or pervasive to alter the terms, conditions, or privileges of employment. . . ." Ravitch, *supra* note 34, at 1055. Though this adaptation would be salutary, it would change the results of only a few cases.

53. 957 F. Supp. 306 (D. Mass. 1997). Plaintiffs brought other claims as well, including state law causes of action for breach of contract and intentional infliction of emotional distress.

54. *Id.* at 312.

55. *Guckenberger v. Boston Univ.*, 974 F. Supp. 106 (D. Mass. 1997); see also *Guckenberger v. Boston Univ.*, 957 F. Supp. 306, 321–24 (D. Mass. 1997) (permitting claims to proceed against individual defendants).

56. *Guckenberger v. Boston Univ.*, 957 F. Supp. 306, 315 (D. Mass. 1997).

57. *Id.* at 316.

58. See, e.g., *Rothman v. Emory Univ.*, 123 F.3d 466 (7th Cir. 1997). But see *Pell v. Trs. of Columbia Univ.*, No. 97 Civ. 0193(SS), 1998 WL 19989, at *16–*18 (Jan. 21, 1998) (denying motion to dismiss section 504 hostile-educational-environment claim).

59. 326 F.3d 975 (8th Cir. 2003); see also *M.P. v. Indep. Sch. Dist. No. 721*, 439 F.3d 865 (8th Cir. 2006) (finding damages claim not subject to exhaustion requirement).

60. 326 F.3d at 978.

61. *Id.* at 982.

62. 381 F. Supp. 2d 343 (S.D.N.Y. 2005).

63. *Id.* at 348 (footnotes omitted) (quoting in part from complaint).

64. *Id.* at 360.

65. *Id.*

66. No. 3:03CV2224(PCD), 2005 WL 2072312 (D. Conn. Aug. 26, 2005).

67. *Id.* at *2 (quoting complaint).

68. *Id.* at *9. The court also upheld various other claims under IDEA and the United States Constitution.

69. 192 F.3d 462 (4th Cir. 1999). Other cases have sustained causes of action under the ADA or section 504 for harassment by teachers or peers in elementary and secondary schools. E.g., *Roe v. Nevada*, 332 F. Supp. 2d 1331 (D. Nev. 2004); *Rick C. v. Lodi Sch. Dist.*, 32 Individuals with Disabilities Educ. L. Rep. 232 (W.D. Wis. 2000).

70. 524 U.S. 274 (1998).

71. 526 U.S. 629 (1999).

72. *Id.* at 648.

73. *K.M.*, for example, relies heavily on *Davis. K.M. v. Hyde Park Cent. Sch. Dist.*, 381 F. Supp. 343, 359–60 (S.D.N.Y. 2005).

74. Hence the title of Joseph Shapiro's book about the passage of the ADA, *No Pity*. Joseph P. Shapiro, No Pity: People with Disabilities Forging a New Civil Rights Movement (1993).

75. 229 F. Supp. 2d 437 (D. Md. 2002).

76. *Id.* at 438.

77. 773 F. Supp. 1005 (W.D. Mich. 1991).

78. E.g., *Witte v. Clark County Sch. Dist.*, 197 F.3d 1271 (9th Cir. 1999) (reversing dismissal of claims under section 504 and ADA for psychological and physical abuse of child by teacher and aide); *Baird v. Rose*, 192 F.3d 462 (4th Cir. 1999).

79. By and large, constitutional protections apply only against governmental activity, so constitutional claims based on harassment are unlikely to be brought except against government actors such as school systems or public employers.

CHAPTER 4

1. 42 U.S.C.A. § 12203(b) (West 2005). This language is in addition to the language in title I of the ADA that is comparable to that of title VII of the Civil Rights Act and provides the cause of action for harassment discussed in the cases described in chapter 3. Compare 42 U.S.C.A. § 12112(a) (West 2005) (ADA title I provision prohibiting discrimination in terms. conditions, or privileges of employment) with 42 U.S.C.A. 42 U.S.C.A. § 2000e-2(a)(1) (West 2005) (title VII provision prohibiting discrimination in terms, conditions, or privileges of employment). Compare 42 U.S.C.A. § 12203(a) (West 2005) (ADA prohibition on retaliation) with 42 U.S.C.A. § 2000e-3(a) (West 2005) (title VII prohibition on retaliation). See generally *Patterson v. McLean Credit Union*, 491 U.S. 164, 180 (1989) (stating that "harassment that is sufficiently severe or pervasive to alter the conditions of employment and create an abusive working environment" constitutes discrimination in the terms, conditions, or privileges of employment) (internal quotation omitted).

2. 510 U.S. 17, 21–22 (1993).

3. *Faragher v. City of Boca Raton*, 524 U.S. 775, 788 (1998).

4. *Mackey v. Lanier Collection Agency & Service, Inc.*, 486 U.S. 825, 837 (1988) ("If we were to give ERISA § 514(a) the meaning which petitioners and the United States attribute to it—barring garnishment of all ERISA plan benefits—we would render § 206(d)(1) substantially redundant with § 514(a), as they concede. See Tr. of Oral Arg. 8–9, 14. As our cases have noted in the past, we are hesitant to adopt an interpretation of a congressional enactment which renders superfluous another portion of that same law.").

5. See, e.g., *Selenke v. Medical Imaging*, 248 F.3d 1249 (10th Cir. 2001); *Silk v. City of Chicago*, 194 F.3d 788, 799 (7th Cir. 1999); *Powers v. Tweco Prods., Inc.*, No. Civ. A. 00–1136-MLB, 2002 WL 1225280 (D. Kan. June 5, 2002).

6. Although Silk did not quit, he "became a scorned individual." *Silk*, 194 F.3d at 803. The case is discussed in greater detail in chapter 3.

7. WEBSTER'S NEW SCHOOL AND OFFICE DICTIONARY 400 (Fawcett Crest ed.1960) (defining intimidation as "the use of threats or violence to influence the actions of another").

8. *Harshbarger v. Sierra Pacific Power Co.*, 128 F. Supp. 2d 1302, 1310 (D. Nev. 2000), *aff'd in part and rev'd in part*, 28 Fed. Appx. 707 (9th Cir. 2002).

9. *Statzer v. Town of Lebanon*, No. 1:00CV00128, 2001 WL 710103 (W.D. Va. June 4, 2001), at *6.

10. *McConathy v. Dr. Pepper/Seven Up Corp.*, 131 F.3d 558, 563–64 (5th Cir. 1998).

11. See *Conley v. United Parcel Serv.*, 88 F. Supp. 2d 16, 20 (E.D.N.Y. 2000) (upholding section 12203(b) claim when employer took adverse action against employee who requested accommodation; applying section 12203(a)

to claim for retaliation for filing charge); see also *McClurg v. GTECH Corp.*, 61 F. Supp. 2d 1150, 1162 (D. Kan. 1999) (applying section 12203(b) to claim for retaliation for requesting accommodation). Compare 42 U.S.C.A. § 12203(a) (West 2005) ("No person shall discriminate against any individual because such individual has opposed any act or practice made unlawful by this chapter or because such individual made a charge, testified, assisted, or participated in any manner in an investigation, proceeding, or hearing under this chapter.") with 42 U.S.C.A. § 12203(b) (West 2005) ("It shall be unlawful to coerce, intimidate, threaten, or interfere with any individual in the exercise or enjoyment of, or on account of his or her having exercised or enjoyed, or on account of his or her having aided or encouraged any other individual in the exercise or enjoyment of, any right granted or protected by this chapter.").

12. 42 U.S.C.A. § 12101(a)(2) (West 2005); see Stephen F. Befort & Tracey Holmes Donesky, *Reassignment under the Americans with Disabilities Act: Reasonable Accommodation, Affirmative Action, or Both?* 57 WASH. & LEE L. REV. 1045, 1046 (2000) ("One of Congress's principal motivations for enacting the Americans with Disabilities Act . . . was to help disabled individuals enter into and remain in the American workplace.").

13. See Timothy M. Cook, *The Americans with Disabilities Act: The Move to Integration,* 64 TEMP. L. REV. 393, 416 (1991) (describing ADA's legislative goal of integrating people with disabilities into mainstream of American life); see also Jacobus tenBroek & Floyd W. Matson, *The Disabled and the Law of Welfare,* 54 CAL. L. REV. 809, 811 (1966). This prescient and highly influential article details the history of what the authors term "custodialism," the practice of keeping individuals with disabilities separate from the rest of the population, and viewing the people with disabilities as objects of charity at best and elimination at worst. See *id.* at 816 (describing custodialism); cf. Stanley S. Herr, *The International Significance of Disability Rights,* 93 ASIL PROC. 332, 332–33 (2000) (describing systematic killing of persons with disabilities by Nazi regime).

14. *Mondzelewski v. Pathmark Stores, Inc.,* 163 F.3d 778 (3d Cir. 1998) (allowing retaliation claim based on shift change); see *Crane v. Vision Quest Nat'l,* No. Civ. A. 98–4797, 2000 WL 1230465 (E.D. Pa. Aug. 23, 2000) (denying motion for summary judgment in sex discrimination retaliation case based on transfer to different position). Retaliation claims of other types, such as claims that a government entity retaliated against a citizen or employee for exercising free speech rights, do not require a showing of adverse employment action. A "campaign of minor harassment" suffices. *Mosely v. Bd. of Educ.,* 434 F.3d 527, 534 (7th Cir. 2006) (collecting cases). In a very recent case under title VII, the Supreme Court ruled that a claim for retaliation exists even when the employer's actions do not affect the terms and conditions of employment, as long

as the actions would be materially adverse to a reasonable employee or job applicant. *Burlington N. & Santa Fe Ry. Co. v. White*, 126 S. Ct. 2405 (2006).

15. E.g., *Finnegan v. Department of Pub. Safety & Correctional Servs.*, 184 F. Supp. 2d 457 (D. Md. 2002) (rejecting hostile-environment claim on basis of severe-or-pervasive standard but upholding retaliation claim on same facts).

16. *Rodriguez v. Loctite Puerto Rico*, 967 F. Supp. 653, 662 (D.P.R. 1997). The court quoted the "terms, conditions, or privileges" language of title VII, 42 U.S.C.A. § 200e-2(a)(1), rather than the comparable language of the ADA, which is "terms, conditions, and privileges." 42 U.S.C.A. § 12112(a) (West 2005).

17. *Flowers v. Southern Regional Physician Servs.*, 247 F.3d 229 (5th Cir. 2001); *Fox v. Gen. Motors*, 247 F.3d 169 (4th Cir. 2001). Both cases are discussed extensively in chapter 3.

18. Perhaps the majority of cases, however, are cases where the plaintiff asserts retaliation per se, typically citing subsection (a), but in which the courts lump together subsections (a) and (b), rendering (b) superfluous. See, e.g., *Selenke v. Medical Imaging*, 248 F.3d 1249 (10th Cir. 2001); *Silk v. City of Chicago*, 194 F.3d 788, 799 (7th Cir. 1999); *Powers v. Tweco Prods., Inc.*, No. Civ. A. 00–1136-MLB, 2002 WL 1225280 (D. Kan. June 5, 2002); *Bull v. Coyner*, No. 98 C 7583, 2000 WL 224807 (N.D. Ill. Feb. 23, 2000). Some cases applying a subsection (a) interpretation to both (a) and (b) uphold the plaintiffs' retaliation claims. *Butler v. City of Prairie Village*, 172 F.3d 736, 751 (10th Cir. 1999); *Jackson v. Lake County*, No. 01-C 6528, 2002 WL 808351, at *5–*7 (N.D. Ill. Apr. 30, 2002) Additional cases apply section 12203(b) to actions taken against the plaintiff because a person associated with the plaintiff made an ADA complaint. Compare *Fogleman v. Mercy Hosp., Inc.*, 283 F.3d 561, 564 (3d Cir. 2002) (upholding claim regarding termination of son in retaliation for father's assertion of claim) and *Barker v. International Paper Co.*, 993 F. Supp. 10 (D. Me. 1998) (upholding claim regarding retaliation against worker for advocacy on behalf of wife and co-worker) with *Braverman v. Penobscot Shoe Co.*, 859 F. Supp. 596 (D. Me. 1994) (granting summary judgment against plaintiff in claim based on retaliation for keeping co-worker's cancer secret). For a brief but helpful discussion of *Fogleman*, see *Employment Discrimination: ADA Retaliation Ban Shields Inactive Targets, Broader Than ADEA, State Law Counterparts*, U.S.L.W., Apr. 4, 2002, at d4. At least some of these associational claims would fit under the "opposed any act or practice made unlawful" language of subsection (a), as well as under subsection (b). Some section 12203(b) cases fail on causation grounds, with courts holding that any untoward conduct was not based on the plaintiff's disability. E.g., *Wray v. National RR. Passenger Corp.*, 10 F. Supp. 2d 1036, 1040–41 (E.D. Wis. 1998) (also finding removal of train passenger with disabilities who lacked reservation from seat previously reserved by other person with disabilities to not constitute "discrimination" in vi-

olation of section 12203(b)). Still other cases fail on the ground that the plaintiff was not exercising or enjoying a right protected by the ADA. *Alford v. City of Cannon Beach,* No. CV-00–303-HU, 2000 WL 33200554 (D. Or. Jan. 17, 2000) (finding no violation of section 12203(b) in public accommodations claim on ground plaintiff not exercising right under ADA); *Barnes v. Benham Group, Inc.,* 22 F. Supp. 2d 1013 (D. Minn. 1998) (finding no violation in requested disclosure of insurance-related information).

19. 336 F.3d 1181 (9th Cir. 2003).

20. *Id.* at 1193.

21. *Id.* at 1190.

22. 263 F.3d 208 (2d Cir. 2001).

23. *Id.* at 213–14.

24. *Id.* at 223.

25. *Franklin v. Consolidated Edison Co.,* No. 98 Civ. 2286(WHP), 1999 WL 796170 (S.D.N.Y. 1999).

26. *Conley v. United Parcel Serv.,* 88 F. Supp. 2d 16, 21 (E.D.N.Y. 2000) (denying summary judgment on claim of delivery driver subjected to having supervisor accompany her on trips); see also *Galenbeck v. Newman & Newman, Inc.,* No. 02–6278-HO, 2004 WL 1088289 (D. Or. May 14, 2004) (reserving issue whether plaintiff may invoke section 12203(b) when defendant allegedly increased lifting duties in response to request for accommodation). In *McClurg v. GTECH Corp,* 61 F. Supp. 2d 1150, 1162 (D. Kan. 1999), the court denied defendant's summary judgment motion with regard to a claim under section 12203(b) that the defendant retaliated against the plaintiff for making requests for accommodation, emphasizing that activity protected under subsection (b) includes more than administrative complaints or lawsuits.

27. *Fleetwood v. Hartford Sys., Inc.,* 380 F. Supp. 2d 88, 705 (D. Md. 2005).

28. 866 F. Supp. 190 (E.D. Pa.1994). In a similar vein, a court upheld a claim under section 12203(b) when a person with a psychiatric disability was allegedly threatened with arrest for what she said was an unfounded charge of theft if she attempted to pursue redress after being barred from her place of employment. *Coleman v. Town of Old Saybrook,* No. 3:03CV01275(RNC), 2004 WL 936174 (D. Conn. Apr. 28, 2004).

29. *Mondzelewski v. Pathmark Stores, Inc.,* 163 F3d 778, 789 (3d Cir. 1998).

30. See *Rhoads v. FDIC,* 257 F.3d 373, 391–94 (4th Cir. 2001). Refusing a request for an accommodation may itself be adverse action in violation of section 12203(a) when the refusal constitutes a denial of benefits. *Bayonne v. Pitney Bowes, Inc.,* No. 3:03cv712, 2004 WL 213168 (D. Conn. Jan. 27, 2004).

31. Still other statutes that include similar language are the Voting Rights Act, 42 U.S.C.A. § 1971(b) (West 2005), and the law providing for automotive dealer suits against manufacturers, 15 U.S.C.A. § 1221(e) (West 2005).

32. The Fair Housing Act provides:
It shall be unlawful to coerce, intimidate, threaten, or interfere with any person in the exercise or enjoyment of, or on account of his having exercised or enjoyed, or on account of his having aided or encouraged any other person in the exercise or enjoyment of, any right granted or protected by section 3603, 3604, 3605, or 3606 of this title.
42 U.S.C.A. § 3617 (West 2005). One court gave the following description of what the ban covers:
Section 3617 is not limited to those who used some sort of "potent force or duress," but extends to other actors who are in a position directly to disrupt the exercise or enjoyment of a protected right and exercise their powers with a discriminatory animus. Under this standard, the language "interfere with" encompasses such overt acts as racially motivated firebombings, Stirgus v. Benoit, 720 F. Supp. 119 (N.D. I11.1989), sending threatening notes, Sofarelli v. Pinellas County, 931 F.2d 718 (11th Cir.1991), and less obvious, but equally illegal, practices such as exclusionary zoning, United States v. City of Birmingham, 727 F.2d 560 (6th Cir.), cert. denied, 469 U.S. 821, 105 S. Ct. 95, 83 L.Ed.2d 41 (1984), deflating appraisals because of discriminatory animus, United States v. American Inst. of Real Estate Appraisers, supra, and insurance redlining, Laufman v. Oakley Bldg. & Loan Co., 408 F. Supp. 489 (S.D.Ohio 1976). *Michigan Protection & Advocacy Serv. v. Babin,* 18 F.3d 337, 347 (6th Cir. 1994).

33. 931 F.2d 718 (11th Cir. 1991). The court described the allegations in this fashion:
Sofarelli alleges that members of Hibbing's community committed certain actions—such as leaving a note threatening "to break [Sofarelli] in half" if he did not get out of the neighborhood and running up to one of Sofarelli's trucks, hitting it, shouting obscenities and spitting at Sofarelli—which would clearly constitute coercion and intimidation under § 3617.
Id. at 722.

34. 127 F. Supp. 2d 1059, 1063 (W.D. Mo. 2000) (following *Sofarelli* and *United States v. City of Hayward,* 36 F.3d 832 (9th Cir. 1994); declining to follow *Frazier v. Rominger,* 27 F.3d 828 (2d Cir. 1994))

35. 388 F.3d 327, 330–31 (7th Cir. 2004). The court relied in part on regulations barring interference with the enjoyment of a dwelling. *Id.* at 330. It distinguished the claim from one of discrimination in the sale or rental of housing, finding a claim brought under the section barring that activity to be properly dismissed. *Id.* at 328–29.

36. National Labor Relations Act, § 8(a)(1), 29 U.S.C.A. § 158(a)(1) (West 2005).

37. *ITT Automotive v. NLRB*, 188 F.3d 375, 384 (6th Cir. 1999) (quoting *Peabody Coal v. NLRB*, 725 F.2d 357, 363 (6th Cir.1984)).

38. *NLRB v. Gissel Packing Co.*, 395 U.S. 575, 617 (1969).

39. Railway Labor Act, § 2, subds. 3, 4, 45 U.S.C.A. § 152, subds. 3, 4 (West 2005).

40. *Konop v. Hawaiian Airlines*, 236 F.3d 1035, 1052–53 (9th Cir. 2001).

41. *New York Univ. Med. Ctr. v. NLRB*, 156 F.3d 405, 411 (2d Cir. 1998).

42. *NLRB v. Overnite Transp. Co.*, 938 F.2d 815, 819 (7th Cir. 1991).

43. National Industrial Recovery Act, ch. 90, § 1, 48 Stat. 195 (1933) (expired 1935).

44. See S. Rep. No. 73–114, at 2 (1933) (noting intention to protect free choice of employees; specifying freedom from "interference, restraint, or coercion" but not directly addressing retaliation).

45. See 29 C.F.R. § 1630.12(b) (2005) (emphasis added). Section 12203(b) is found in title V of the statute, but it applies to employment, the subject matter of title I, and incorporates the remedies of title I with respect to employment. See *infra* text accompanying notes 77-89 (discussing remedies).

46. Compare *Sutton v. United Air Lines, Inc.*, 527 U.S. 471, 482 (1999) (rejecting EEOC and Department of Justice regulation defining "substantially limited" term defining persons with mitigated impairments), with *id.* at 491–92 (deferring to EEOC regulation defining "substantially limited" term with regard to working).

47. See *Chevron U.S.A., Inc. v. Echazabal*, 536 U.S. 73, 87 (2002). Regarding the degree of deference to which EEOC interpretations of the ADA should be entitled, see Rebecca Hanner White, *Deference and Disability Discrimination*, 99 Mich. L. Rev. 947 (2000) (contending that courts should afford deference).

48. A regulation interpreting disability discrimination to include title VII-grade harassment arrives supported by a similar EEOC interpretation of similar language in title VII. See 29 C.F.R. § 1604.11 (2005). In the first hostile-environment sex harassment case under title VII, the Court relied on EEOC Guidelines establishing harassment as a form of discrimination. *Meritor Sav. Bank v. Vinson*, 477 U.S. 57, 65 (1986).

49. U.S. Const. art. II, § 4.

50. See Charles L. Black, Jr., Impeachment: A Handbook 36–37 (1974); 1 Laurence H. Tribe, American Constitutional Law § 2–7, at 170 (3d ed. 2000); see also 2A Jabez Gridley Sutherland, Statutes and Statutory Construction § 47.17 (Norman J. Singer 5th ed.1991) ("Where general words follow specific words in a statutory enumeration, the general words are construed to embrace only objects similar in nature to those objects enumerated by the preceding specific words.").

51. WEBSTER'S NEW SCHOOL AND OFFICE DICTIONARY, *supra* note 7, at 339.

52. THE RANDOM HOUSE DICTIONARY OF THE ENGLISH LANGUAGE 645 (unabridged ed. 1971).

53. 145 F.3d 809 (6th Cir. 1998).

54. *Id.* at 813.

55. See, e.g., *Ballard v. Healthsouth Corp.*, No. CIV.A. 3:00-CV-1011, 2001 WL 585974, at *7 (N.D. Tex. May 25, 2001)

56. See, e.g., *Veal v. AT&T Corp.*, No. CIV.A. 99–0370, 2000 WL 303299, at *8 (E.D. La. March. 22, 2000).

57. See, e.g., *Roeder v. Hendricks Community Hosp.*, No. IP00–0447-C-H/G, 2001 WL 1168151, at *9 (S.D. Ind. Sep. 7, 2001).

58. The availability of attorneys' fees does not change the reality that costs must be balanced against recoveries. The fees are simply an element of the prospective gain from the case, which must be discounted by the probability of losing and balanced against the costs that are not recoverable. See RICHARD A. POSNER, ECONOMIC ANALYSIS OF THE LAW 572 (1992) (describing effects of availability of attorneys' fees). Moreover, under the current interpretation of the attorneys' fees statutes, the award may be diminished (even to zero) based on the limited extent of the recovery. *Farrar v. Hobby*, 506 U.S. 103, 115 (1992) (holding that no fees should be awarded under Civil Rights Attorneys' Fees Act when plaintiff recovered only nominal damages); see also *Holmes v. Milcreek Township Sch. Dist.*, 205 F.3d 583 (3d Cir. 2000) (reducing IDEA attorneys' fees by 75 percent for limited success and disproportionate investment of time).

59. See *Sutton v. United Air Lines, Inc.*, 527 U.S. 471, 482 (1999); *Murphy v. United Parcel Serv., Inc.*, 527 U.S. 516, 521 (1999); *Albertsons, Inc. v. Kirkingburg*, 527 U.S. 555, 564 (1999). The Court further restricted the definition of being regarded as having a disability. See *Sutton*, 527 U.S. at 489; *Murphy*, 527 U.S. at 525. Numerous sources challenge the Court's rulings in the *Sutton* trilogy. See, e.g., Samuel R. Bagenstos, *Subordination, Stigma, and "Disability,"* 86 VA. L. REV. 397 (2000); Frank S. Ravitch & Marsha B. Freeman, *The Americans with "Certain" Disabilities Act: Title I of the ADA and the Supreme Court's Result Oriented Jurisprudence*, 77 DENV. U. L. REV. 119 (1999); Bonnie Poitras Tucker, *The Supreme Court's Definition of Disability under the ADA: A Return to the Dark Ages*, 52 ALA. L. REV. 321 (2000); Mark C. Weber, *Disability Discrimination in Higher Education*, 26 J.C. & U. L. 351, 354–55 (1999).

60. *Sorensen v. Univ. of Utah Hosp.*, 194 F.3d 1084 (10th Cir. 1987).

61. *Zale v. Sikorsky Aircraft Corp.*, No. 3:97CV00125(JBA), 2000 WL 306943 (D. Conn. Feb. 7, 2000) (granting summary judgment in harassment claim based on co-workers making loud noises and then laughing when plaintiff hid under furniture).

62. *Schwertfager v. City of Boynton Beach,* 42 F. Supp. 2d 1347 (S.D. Fla. 1999) (granting summary judgment in discrimination and harassment claim).

63. 42 U.S.C.A. § 12203(b) (West 2005).

64. *Muller v. Costello,* 187 F.3d 298, 311 (2d Cir. 1999); *Settle v. S.W. Rodgers, Co., Inc.,* 998 F. Supp. 657 (E.D. Va.), *aff'd* 182 F.3d 909 (4th Cir. 1998); *Barker v. International Paper Co.,* 993 F. Supp. 10 (D. Me.1998); see *Sullivan v. River Valley Sch. Dist.,* 197 F.3d 804 (6th Cir. 1999) (not listing disability of plaintiff as element of ADA retaliation claim).

65. 524 U.S. 742, 765 (1998).

66. 524 U.S. 775, 805 (1998).

67. "'A [t]angible employment action constitutes a significant change in employment status, such as hiring, firing, failure to promote, reassignment with significantly differing responsibilities, or a decision causing a significant change in benefits' as well as the 'denial of a raise or promotion.'" *Id.* at 804 n.16 (quoting *Ellerth,* 524 U.S. at 761).

68. See *Ellerth,* 524 U.S. at 765 (explaining basis for defense); *Faragher,* 524 U.S. at 805 (same).

69. See, e.g., *Silk v. City of Chicago,* 194 F.3d 788, 805 (7th Cir. 1999) (discussed *supra* chapter 4).

70. 42 U.S.C.A. § 12203(b) (West 2005).

71. E.g., *Shotz v. City of Plantation,* 344 F.3d 1161, 1178 (11th Cir. 2003); *Reg'l Econ. Cmty. Action Program, Inc. v. City of Middletown,* 294 F.3d 35, 45 n.1 (2d Cir. 2002); *Coleman v. Town of Old Saybrook,* No. 3:03CV01275(RNC), 2004 WL 936174 (D. Conn. Apr. 28, 2004) (upholding claim for individual liability of public officials under section 12203(b) and denying defense of qualified immunity); see *Higdon v. Jackson,* 393 F.3d 1211 (11th Cir. 2004) (finding that statute provided personal liability, but holding that plaintiff's claim of retaliation failed).

72. E.g., *Baird v. Rose,* 192 F.3d 462, 471 (4th Cir. 1999) (considering claim of retaliation for asserting rights protected by ADA title II); *Hiler v. Brown,* 177 F.3d 542, 545 (6th Cir. 1999) (rejecting individual liability in action under section 12203(a)).

73. 3 F. Supp. 2d 83, 90 (D. Mass. 1998); see also *Harris v. Oregon Health Scis. Univ.,* No. CV-98-1-ST, 1999 WL 778584 (D. Or. Sep. 22, 1999) (retaining individual defendant in retaliation case but reserving issue subject to renewal of dismissal motion); cf. *Ostrach v. Regents of the Univ. of Cal.,* 957 F. Supp. 196 (E.D. Ca1.1997) (declaring counterarguments to be persuasive, but finding individual liability barred by applicable precedent). Some courts applying the ADA's general prohibitions on discrimination have upheld claims against individuals, relying on the statutory provision that defines an employer to include agents of employers. E.g., *Braverman v. Penobscot Shoe Co.,* 859 F. Supp. 596, 602 (D. Me. 1994); *Doe v. Shapiro,* 852 F. Supp. 1246, 1249 (E.D. Pa. 1994).

74. See *Key v. Grayson*, 163 F. Supp. 2d 697 (E.D. Mich. 2001).

75. See 56 Fed. Reg. 35,696, 35,707 (July 26, 1991) (Department of Justice interpretation of 28 C.F.R. § 35.134 to extend section 12203 to cover individuals rather than merely covered entities with regard to title II violations). The EEOC regulations for title I do not have a specific explanation like that of the Department of Justice title II regulations; nevertheless, the title I regulatory language itself serves the same function as the title II explanation, providing explicitly that "it is unlawful" rather than restricting the duty to "private or public entity" as the language of section 35.134 does. See 29 C.F.R. § 1630.12 (2005).

76. The argument advanced here follows that in *Shotz v. City of Plantation*, 344 F.3d 1161, 1178 (11th Cir. 2003).

77. *Shotz v. City of Plantation*, 344 F.3d 1161 (11th Cir. 2003); *Salitros v. Chrysler Corp.*, 306 F.3d 562 (8th Cir. 2002); *Foster v. Time Warner Entertainment Co.*, 250 F.3d 1189 (8th Cir. 2001); *EEOC v. Wal-Mart Stores, Inc.*, 187 F.3d 1241 (10th Cir. 1999); *Muller v. Costello*, 187 F.3d 298 (2d Cir. 1999); *Lovejoy-Wilson v. NOCO Motor Fuels, Inc.*, 242 F. Supp. 2d 236 (W.D.N.Y. 2003); *Niece v. Fitzner*, 922 F. Supp. 1208 (E.D. Mich.1996); see also *Edwards v. Brookhaven Sci. Assocs.*, 390 F. Supp. 2d 225 (E.D.N.Y. 2005) (adopting position after discussion); *Rhoads v. FDIC.*, No. 94–1548, 2002 WL 31755427 (D. Md. Nov. 7, 2002) (same); *Ostrach v. Regents of the Univ. of Cal.*, 957 F. Supp. 196 (E.D. Cal. 1997) (same).

78. 42 U.S.C.A. § 12203(c) (West 2005) ("The remedies and procedures available under sections 12117, 12133, and 12188 of this title shall be available to aggrieved persons for violations of subsections (a) and (b) of this section, with respect to subchapter I, subchapter II, and subchapter III, respectively, of this chapter.").

79. 42 U.S.C.A. § 1981a(a)-(b) (West 2005).

80. 42 U.S.C.A. § 12133 (West 2005); *see Barnes v. Gorman*, 536 U.S. 181 (2002) (barring punitive damages claim against municipality under title II and section 504 in nonemployment case). There is some statutory ambiguity whether an individual suing for employment discrimination by an governmental entity covered by ADA title II is subject to the damages limits. See RUTH COLKER AND ADAM A. MILANI, THE LAW OF DISABILITY DISCRIMINATION 278 (5th ed. 2005).

81. 957 F. Supp. 196 (E.D. Cal. 1997).

82. *Franklin v. Gwinnett County Pub. Schs.*, 503 U.S. 60, 66, (1992) (stating that courts must "presume the availability of all appropriate remedies unless Congress has expressly indicated otherwise."); see *Smith v. Wade*, 461 U.S. 30 (1983) (finding punitive damages appropriate in section 1983 case).

83. *Kramer v. Bank of America Secs.*, 355 F.3d 961 (7th Cir. 2004); *Santana v. Lehigh Valley Hosp. & Health Network*, No. 05–1496, 2005 WL 1941654 (E.D. Pa. Aug. 11, 2005); *Sabbrese v. Lowe's Home Ctrs., Inc.*, 320 F. Supp. 2d

311 (W.D. Pa. 2004); *Johnson v. Ed Bozarth No. 1 Park Meadows Chevrolet, Inc.*, 297 F. Supp. 2d 1286 (D. Colo. 2004); *Sink v. Wal-Mart Stores, Inc.*, 147 F. Supp. 2d 1085, 1101 (D. Kan. 2001); *Boe v. Allied Signal, Inc.*, 131 F. Supp. 2d 1197 (D. Kan. 2001); *Brown v. City of Lee's Summit*, No. 98–0438-CV-W-2, 1999 WL 827768 (W.D. Mo. June 1, 1999).

84. 355 F.3d 961 (7th Cir. 2004).

85. 390 F. Supp. 2d 225 (E.D.N.Y. 2005)

86. *Id.* at 236.

87. *Sink v. Wal-Mart Stores, Inc.*, 147 F. Supp. 2d 1085, 1101 (D. Kan. 2001).

88. *United States v. Am. Trucking Assns., Inc.*, 310 U.S. 534, 543 (1940).

89. See *Jackson v. Birmingham Bd. of Educ.*, 125 S. Ct. 1497 (2005) (upholding damages claim for retaliation under title IX of the Education Amendments, 20 U.S.C. § 1681(a)). Punitive damages may not be available against state and local governmental defendants, however. See *Barnes v. Gorman*, 536 U.S. 181 (2002) (barring punitive damages claim in action against municipality under title II and section 504 in case not having to do with employment).

90. *Guckenberger v. Boston Univ.*, 957 F. Supp. 306 (D. Mass. 1997); see also *Corey H. v. Cape Henlopen Sch. Dist.*, 286 F. Supp. 2d 380 (D. Del. 2003) (analyzing hostile-environment claim under special education law and denying relief under that law and section 504 of Rehabilitation Act and requiring severe or pervasive discrimination); *Spychalsky v. Sullivan*, No. CV0109 58DRHETB, 2003 WL 22071602 (Aug. 29, 2003) (analyzing hostile-environment claim brought by law student under section 504 severe-or-pervasive standard). The statement in the text should not be taken to mean that relief would be appropriate under section 12203(b) in all these cases, simply that the section should have been applied.

CHAPTER 5

1. *Witte v. Clark County Sch. Dist.*, 197 F.3d 1271 (9th Cir. 1999). A caution should be noted that these facts were those alleged in the complaint. The accounts in these and many other cases in the chapter are drawn from allegations that the court had to treat as true for purposes of the decision the court made.

2. 7 F. Supp. 2d 920, 922 (W.D. Mich. 1998).

3. 205 F.3d 912 (6th Cir. 2000).

4. *Kubistal v. Hirsch*, No. 98 C 3838, 1999 WL 90625 (N.D. Ill. Feb. 9, 1999).

5. *Charlie F. v. Board of Educ.*, 98 F.3d 989 (7th Cir. 1996).

6. 192 F.3d 462 (4th Cir. 1999).

7. *Id.* at 466.

8. In cases decided before 1999, claims based on these occurrences were reg-ularly dismissed. See, e.g., *Stevens v. Umsted*, 131 F.3d 697 (7th Cir. 1997) (finding no liability and upholding immunity in case concerning sexual assaults at state school when child was voluntarily enrolled there, despite superinten-dent's knowledge of ongoing attacks); *Larson v. Miller*, 76 F.3d 1446 (8th Cir. 1996) (en banc) (finding insufficient evidence to support section 1983 or section 1985 conspiracy claims in case regarding sexual assault by school bus driver); *Walton v. Alexander*, 44 F.3d 1297 (5th Cir. 1995) (finding immunity and no li-ability when child who was assaulted by another student was voluntarily en-rolled at state school for deaf); *Dorothy J. v. Little Rock Sch. Dist.*, 7 F.3d 729 (8th Cir. 1993) (finding insufficient support for section 1983 case against school district arising from sexual assault of student by other students); *D.R. v. Middle Bucks Area Vocational Technical Sch.*, 972 F.2d 1364 (3d Cir. 1992) (en banc) (finding insufficient support for section 1983 or section 1985 claim against school district arising out of molestation of one student by other students); *Hunter v. Carbondale Area Sch. Dist.*, 829 F. Supp. 714 (M.D. Pa.), *aff'd*, 5 F.3d 1489 (3d Cir. 1993) (granting school district's motion to dismiss section 1983 claim arising from drowning of special education student). It is possible that some of these assaults would now be considered actionable as sexual ha-rassment in light of the Supreme Court's declaration in *Davis v. Monroe County Board of Education*, 526 U.S. 629, 643 (1999), that under sex discrimination laws a damages claim may be made for deliberate indifference to known acts of peer sexual harassment at school. See generally Kelly Dixson Furr, Note, *How Well Are the Nation's Children Protected from Peer Harassment at School? Title IX Liability in the Wake of* Davis v. Monroe County Board of Education, 78 N.C. L. Rev. 1573, 1574 (2000) (noting likely difference in results in some cases after *Davis*). Same-sex harassment is actionable under title VII of the Civil Rights Act of 1964, and it is probable that this rule will be extended to the school actions. See *Oncale v. Sundowner Offshore Servs., Inc.*, 523 U.S. 75 (1998) (recognizing statutory claim for same-sex harassment).

9. 173 F.3d 1226 (10th Cir. 1999).

10. 381 F.3d 194 (3d Cir. 2004) (Alito, J.).

11. 326 F.3d 975, 978 (8th Cir. 2003); see also *M.P. v. Indep. Sch. Dist. No. 721*, 439 F.3d 865 (8th Cir. 2006) (finding damages claim not subject to exhaus-tion requirement).

12. *Scruggs v. Meriden Bd. of Educ.*, No. 3:03CV2224(PCD), 2005 WL 2072312 (Aug. 26, 2005).

13. *Id.* at *2.

14. *K.M. v. Hyde Park Cent. Sch. Dist.*, 381 F. Supp. 2d 343 (S.D.N.Y. 2005).

15. *Id.* at 348.

16. E.g., *Costello v. Mitchell Pub. Sch. Dist.* 79, 266 F.3d 916 (8th Cir. 2001) (finding that child verbally and otherwise abused by teacher was not covered by disability discrimination laws and rejecting claims not relating to disability discrimination); *Biggs v. Bd. of Educ.,* 229 F. Supp. 2d 437 (D. Md. 2002) (finding in the alternative that school district was immune from suit or that district was not deliberately indifferent in action alleging failure to stop constant verbal harassment of child with epilepsy when district threatened suspension of harassers and made other responses).

17. THE COLUMBIA WORLD OF QUOTATIONS (1996), available at http://www.bartleby.com/66/35/42835.html.

18. Even some efforts by schools to increase disability awareness simply reinforce the message that people with disabling conditions are to be gaped at or, at best, pitied. See Dona Avery, *Freaks on Exhibit: A Critical Review Essay of Levinson and St. Onge,* Disability Awareness in the Classroom, 20 DISABILITY STUD. Q. 348, 349 (2000). The author criticizes teaching materials that include flashcard photographs of teenagers with various disabling conditions and messages such as "If Raymond is gradually losing all his abilities, do you think it's a blessing that he's also losing his mental awareness?" She concludes that the messages delivered "by these cards and photos, and by the teachers who use them in class, are perpetuating several stereotypes rather than helping to demystify disability. . . . [The program] may actually crystallize the myth-understandings, as well as increase the frequency of staring that an incoming disabled student will be made to endure." *Id.*

19. Schoolchildren with disabilities are significantly lower in social prestige than other students. See Paul Sale & Doris M. Carey, *The Sociometric Status of Students with Disabilities in a Full-Inclusion School,* 62 EXCEPTIONAL CHILDREN 6, 16–17 (1995) (reporting attitude study). For a revealing personal narrative regarding the treatment by peers and teachers of a deaf student in high school, see BONNIE POITRAS TUCKER, THE FEEL OF SILENCE 31–35 (1995). See generally David M. Engel, *Law, Culture, and Children with Disabilities,* 1991 DUKE L.J. 166, 184 ("Physically disabled persons are viewed with fear and revulsion because they occupy an anomalous social position. . . . Stigma, fear of contagion, stereotyping, and rejection have thus typified the responses of 'normal' society to those labeled physically 'handicapped.'").

20. See Vicki Schultz, *Reconceptualizing Sexual Harassment,* 107 YALE L.J. 1683, 1720–28 (1998); cf. Miranda Oshige, Note, *What's Sex Got to Do with It?* 47 STAN. L. REV. 565, 567 (1995) (proposing reconfiguration of sexual harassment as gender-based different treatment).

21. See Hugh Gregory Gallagher, *"Slapping Up Spastics": The Persistence of Social Attitudes toward People with Disabilities,* 10 ISSUES L. & MED. 401 (1995) (discussing negative social attitudes toward persons with disabilities).

22. Regarding school avoidance, see Susan G. Parker, *School Avoidance Often Signals Child Being Bullied,* PEDIATRIC NEWS, June 1998, at 46 ("Children who refuse to go to school and present with somatic symptoms like chronic headaches and abdominal pain may be victims of bullies."); Leslie Z. Paige, *School Phobia/School Avoidance/School Refusal* ("Many children [who refuse to attend school] have social concerns and may have been teased or bullied at school. . . ."), available at http://www.ldonline.org/ld_indepth/parenting/naspschool_avoidance.html (visited Dec. 21, 2005). Regarding dropout rates of children with disabilities, see U.S. DEP'T OF EDUC., THE TRANSITION EXPERIENCES OF YOUNG PEOPLE WITH DISABILITIES: A SUMMARY OF FINDINGS FROM THE NATIONAL LONGITUDINAL STUDY OF SPECIAL EDUCATION STUDENTS 2–9 (1993). Regarding employment of dropouts with disabilities, see U.S. DEP'T OF EDUC., TWENTY-SECOND ANNUAL REPORT TO CONGRESS ON THE IMPLEMENTATION OF THE INDIVIDUALS WITH DISABILITIES EDUCATION ACT IV-15 (2000). The data reflect similar trends regarding the population as a whole. See 143 CONG. REC. S4311–19 (daily ed. May 12, 1997) (statement of Sen. Kennedy) (reporting that high school dropouts are more than three times as likely to be unemployed as high school graduates and that dropouts constitute disproportionate percentage of welfare family heads and the prison population).

23. There also are potential remedies under the common law. These are discussed in chapter 7.

24. 29 U.S.C.A. § 794 (West 2005).

25. 29 U.S.C.A. § 705(20)(B) (West 2005).

26. 34 C.F.R. § 104.4(b) (2005).

27. See 42 U.S.C.A. § 12132 (West 2005) ("Subject to the provisions of this subchapter, no qualified individual with a disability shall, by reason of such disability, be excluded from participation in or be denied the benefits of the services, programs, or activities of a public entity, or be subjected to discrimination by any such entity."). Compare 28 C.F.R. § 35.130 (2005) (ADA title II), with 34 C.F.R. § 104.4 (2005) (section 504).

28. See generally Mark C. Weber, *Disability Discrimination by State and Local Government: The Relationship between Section 504 of the Rehabilitation Act and Title II of the Americans with Disabilities Act,* 36 WM. & MARY L. REV. 1089, 1109–16 (1995) (discussing differences between section 504 and ADA title II). In one minor difference, the ADA removed the word "solely" from the definition of "discrimination on the basis of disability" to solve the potential coverage problem created if someone were discriminated against on account of disability as well as race or sex. See *id.* at 1110–11 (collecting and discussing sources from legislative history of ADA). The primary difference in coverage is the obvious one: title II of the ADA covers state and local government entities irrespective of their receipt of federal funds, but section 504 covers all entities that receive federal funds irrespective of whether they are government agencies.

29. 192 F.3d 462 (4th Cir. 1999).

30. 197 F.3d 1271, 1272 (9th Cir. 1999). But see *Waechter v. Sch. Dist. No. 14–030*, 773 F. Supp. 1005 (W.D. Mich. 1991). In *Waechter*, a recess supervisor forced a child whom the school knew had a heart defect to run a 350-yard sprint as punishment for talking in class. The child suffered cardiac arrest and died. The court dismissed a claim for violation of section 504, reasoning that the statute does not provide damages relief. *Id.* at 1011. The court appeared to misread applicable section 504 precedent on this point. See *infra* text accompanying notes 40-54 (discussing damages relief under section 504). See generally *infra* note 73 (discussing due process claim in *Waechter*).

31. 247 F.3d 229 (5th Cir. 2001). On the topic of remedies, the court held that the plaintiff had not presented adequate evidence of specific emotional injury, and so vacated the damages award and remanded for entry of an award of nominal damages. *Id.* at 239.

32. 247 F.3d 169 (4th Cir. 2001). The court considered the hostile-work-environment claim to be something other than a claim of intentional discrimination and overturned an award of $4,000 for unpaid overtime on the ground that it was inconsistent with the jury's finding that General Motors had not intentionally discriminated against the plaintiff. *Id.* at 181.

33. Compare 20 U.S.C.A. § 1681(a) (West 2005) (title IX), with 29 U.S.C.A. § 794 (West 2005), with 42 U.S.C.A. § 2000d (West 2005). The similarity of section 504 and title II of the ADA in turn suggests that conduct analogous to that which violates title IX will also violate title II of the ADA in an appropriate case. See generally Adam A. Milani, *Harassing Speech in the Public Schools: The Validity of Schools' Regulation of Fighting Words and the Consequences If They Do Not*, 28 Akron L. Rev. 187, 232 (1995) (discussing claim for hostile environment under section 504).

34. 524 U.S. 274, 277 (1998).

35. 526 U.S. 629, 633 (1999).

36. *Id.* at 648.

37. See *Vance v. Spencer County Pub. Sch. Dist.*, 231 F.3d 253, 259 (6th Cir. 2000) ("[O]ne incident can satisfy a claim. . . ."); *Doe v. School Admin. Dist. No. 19*, 66 F. Supp. 2d 57, 62 (D. Me. 1999) ("Within the context of Title IX, a student's claim of hostile environment can arise from a single incident.").

38. 381 F. Supp. 2d 343 (S.D.N.Y. 2005).

39. *Id.* at 360.

40. The theory is that the general provisions of section 504 apply only to entities that are federal grantees and that the comparable provisions of title II apply only to state and local governmental agencies. Thus courts hold there is ordinarily no liability for persons, just entities. *Alsbrook v. City of Maumelle*, 184 F.3d 999, 1005 n.8 (8th Cir. 1999) (en banc) (ADA), *cert. dismissed sub nom. Alsbrook v. Arkansas*, 529 U.S. 1001 (2000); *Smith v. Maine Sch. Admin.*

Dist. No. 6, No. 00–284-P.C, 2001 WL 68305, at *3 (D. Me. Jan. 29, 2001) (both Rehabilitation Act and ADA); *Thomas v. Nakatani,* 128 F. Supp. 2d 684, 692–93 (D. Haw. 2000) (ADA); *Hallett v. New York State Dep't of Corr. Servs.,* 109 F. Supp. 2d 190, 199 (S.D.N.Y. 2000) (both); *Calloway v. Boro of Glassboro Dep't of Police,* 89 F. Supp. 2d 543, 557 (D.N.J. 2000) (both); *Yeskey v. Pennsylvania,* 76 F. Supp. 2d 572, 574–75 (M.D. Pa. 1999) (ADA); *Montez v. Romer,* 32 F. Supp. 2d 1235, 1241 (D. Colo. 1999) (both). But see *Niece v. Fitzner,* 922 F. Supp. 1208, 1218 (E.D. Mich. 1996) ("There is nothing within Title II which explicitly authorizes or prohibits suits against public actors acting in their official or individual capacities."); *Johnson v. New York Hosp.,* 897 F. Supp. 83, 86 (S.D.N.Y. 1995) (upholding individual liability of hospital president under section 504), *aff'd,* 96 F.3d 33 (2d Cir. 1996); *Chaplin v. Consolidated Edison Co.,* 587 F. Supp. 519, 520 (S.D.N.Y. 1984) (section 504). For an argument that individual liability ought to exist for all intentional ADA title II, Rehabilitation Act section 504, and IDEA violations, and that qualified immunity should not protect defendants subject to the liability, see Gary S. Gildin, *Dis-qualified Immunity for Discrimination against the Disabled,* 1999 U. ILL. L. REV. 897.

41. *Washington v. Davis,* 426 U.S. 229 (1976).

42. 465 U.S. 624 (1984) (permitting action for back pay pursuant to the Rehabilitation Act); see also *Franklin v. Gwinnett County Pub. Schs.,* 503 U.S. 60, 74–75 (1992) (permitting damages action pursuant to title IX of Education Amendments of 1972 for intentional conduct). Regarding the intent requirement, see *Scokin v. Texas,* 723 F.2d 432 (5th Cir. 1984) (requiring showing of intent to support monetary claim); *David H. v. Palmyra Area Sch. Dist.,* 769 F. Supp. 159 (M.D. Pa. 1990) (denying section 504 claim for monetary relief in absence of showing of intent), *aff'd,* 932 F.2d 959 (3d Cir. 1991) (table). This approach has been challenged by various writers. Sande Buhai & Nina Golden, *Adding Insult to Injury: Discriminatory Intent as a Prerequisite to Damages under the ADA,* 52 RUTGERS L. REV. 1121 (2000) (relying on underlying purposes of ADA to conclude that damages should be available for violations without showing of intentional discrimination); Leonard J. Augustine, Jr., Note, *Disabling the Relationship between Intentional Discrimination and Compensatory Damages under Title II of the Americans with Disabilities Act,* 66 GEO. WASH. L. REV. 592, 607–12 (1998) (criticizing intent requirement for damages in title II accommodations actions).

43. 436 U.S. 658, 694 & n.58 (1978).

44. Regarding single decisions of authoritative decision makers, see *Pembaur v. City of Cincinnati,* 475 U.S. 469 (1986) (permitting liability based on county prosecutor's approval of police breaking down doctor's door to serve subpoenas); *City of Canton v. Harris,* 489 U.S. 378, 388 & n.8 (1989). The "deliberate indifference" standard originated in *Estelle v. Gamble,* 429 U.S. 97 (1976), in

which the Supreme Court ruled that failure to provide medical attention to a prisoner is a violation of the Eighth Amendment actionable pursuant to 42 U.S.C. § 1983 if there is "deliberate indifference to serious medical needs of prisoners." *Estelle*, 429 U.S. at 104. The Supreme Court has also applied the standard to generalized complaints that prison conditions violate the Eighth Amendment. *Wilson v. Seiter*, 501 U.S. 294, 303 (1991). The deliberate indifference standard is simply a proxy for the policy or custom that is a form of corporate intent: "Only where a municipality's failure to train its employees in a relevant respect evidences a 'deliberate indifference' to the rights of its inhabitants can such a shortcoming be properly thought of as a city policy or custom. . . .'" *Collins v. City of Harker Heights*, 503 U.S. 115, 123 n.6 (1992) (quoting *Canton v. Harris*, 489 U.S. 378, 389 (1989)).

45. See *T.J.W. v. Dothan City Bd. of Educ.*, 26 Individuals with Disabilities Educ. L. Rep. 999 (M.D. Ala. Aug. 12, 1997) (permitting a damages claim under standard of intentional discrimination or bad-faith conduct). Many cases apply the bad-faith or gross misjudgment standard. E.g., *Thompson v. Board of the Special Sch. Dist. No. 1*, 144 F.3d 574 (8th Cir. 1998) (finding test not met in dispute over services); *K.U. v. Alvin Indep. Sch. Dist.*, 991 F. Supp. 599 (S.D. Tex. 1998) (same), *aff'd*, 166 F.3d 341 (5th Cir. 1998) (table); *Walker v. District of Columbia*, 969 F. Supp. 794 (D.D.C. 1997) (permitting liability).

46. 141 F.3d 524 (4th Cir.), *cert. denied*, 525 U.S. 871 (1998).

47. No. 98-CV-4161, 1999 WL 124381, at *5 (E.D. Pa. Feb. 23, 1999). The court denied the defendants' motion for summary judgment, reasoning that a jury could "reasonably infer that the defendants were acting in bad faith." *Id.*

48. *M.P. v. Indep. Sch. Dist. No. 721*, 326 F.3d 975, 982 (8th Cir. 2003).

49. 526 U.S. 629, 633, 648 (1999).

50. *Gebser v. Lago Vista Indep. Sch. Dist.*, 524 U.S. 274 (1998).

51. *M.P. v. Indep. Sch. Dist. No. 721*, 326 F.3d 975, 982 (8th Cir. 2003).

52. See chapter 7 (discussing intentional-infliction cause of action for disability harassment).

53. See Albert W. Alschuler, *Mediation with a Mugger: The Shortage of Adjudicative Services and the Need for a Two-Tier Trial System in Civil Cases*, 99 HARV. L. REV. 1808, 1808 (1986). In a much-reported incident that occurred in the New York City subway in 1984, Goetz shot several youths when he believed they were about to rob him. *Id.* at 1809–10.

54. See generally EDWARD D. RE & JOSEPH R. RE, REMEDIES 824 (5th ed. 2000) ("[B]y imposing upon tortfeasors the cost of their wrongful acts, [damages] promote the deterrent value of tort law."). In the last generation, the deterrent effects of damages awards have been the special subject of the law and economics movement. See, e.g., Richard A. Posner, *A Theory of Negligence*, 1 J. LEGAL STUD. 29, 32–33 (1972) (discussing self-interest in taking precautions against harm to avoid damages award).

55. 28 C.F.R. § 35.134(b) (2005) ("No private or public entity shall coerce, intimidate, threaten, or interfere with any individual in the exercise or enjoyment of, or on account of his or her having exercised or enjoyed . . . any right granted or protected by the Act or this part."). Regulations applicable to section 504 impose a similar duty. 34 C.F.R. § 104.6 (2005) (incorporating by reference antiretaliation provision of 34 C.F.R. § 100.7(e) ("No recipient or other person shall intimidate, threaten, coerce, or discriminate against any individual for the purpose of interfering with any right or privilege secured by . . . the Act or this part . . . ")). See generally 42 U.S.C.A. § 12203(b) (West 2005) (found in ADA title V) ("It shall be unlawful to coerce, intimidate, threaten, or interfere with any individual in the exercise or enjoyment of, or on account of his or her having exercised . . . any right granted or protected by this chapter.").

56. The retaliation provision is different from the rest of the statute in that it clearly applies to all persons, not just to covered entities or federal grantees. 42 U.S.C.A. § 12203 (West 2005) (stating that no person "shall discriminate against any individual because such individual has opposed any act or practice made unlawful by this chapter" and that it "shall be unlawful to coerce, intimidate, threaten, or interfere with any individual in the exercise or enjoyment of, or on account of his or her having exercised . . . any right granted or protected by this chapter"). The retaliation-coercion provision is found in ADA title V, apart from the titles that apply to specific covered entities (title I for employers of fifteen or more employees, employment agencies, labor organizations, and joint labor-management committees; title II for state and local governmental entities; title III for public accommodations; and title IV for telecommunications carriers). One case that disagrees with this interpretation of the retaliation provision, however, is *Baird v. Rose,* 192 F.3d 462, 471–72 (4th Cir. 1999) (disallowing individual liability on basis of analogy to title VII of Civil Rights Act). The parallel provision for section 504 similarly forbids coercion and retaliation by anyone, not only grantees. 34 C.F.R. § 104.61 (2001) (incorporating by reference antiretaliation provision of 34 C.F.R. § 100.7(e) ("No recipient or other person shall intimidate, threaten, coerce, or discriminate against any individual for the purpose of interfering with any right or privilege secured by . . . the Act or this part. . . .")). As noted in chapter 4, a plaintiff need not be an individual with disabilities to assert a claim based on the ADA retaliation provision. *Muller v. Costello,* 187 F.3d 298, 311–12 (2d Cir. 1999) (absence of finding that plaintiff was disabled did not preclude finding that employer retaliated against him).

57. 473 U.S. 432 (1985). Commentary contending that the case actually applies a more rigorous standard includes ERWIN CHEMERINSKY, CONSTITUTIONAL LAW: PRINCIPLES AND POLICIES § 9.2.3, at 544 (1997) ("Although the Court [in *Cleburne*] expressly declared that it was applying rational basis review, it appears that there was more 'bite' to the Court's approach than usual for this level

of scrutiny.")*;* James Leonard, *The Shadows of Unconstitutionality: How the New Federalism May Affect the Anti-Discrimination Mandate of the Americans with Disabilities Act,* 52 ALA. L. REV. 91, 105 (2000) ("It is impossible to square this approach [in *Cleburne*] with traditional rational basis review."); Gayle Lynn Pettinga, Note, *Rational Basis with Bite: Intermediate Scrutiny by Any Other Name,* 62 IND. L.J. 779, 796 (1987) ("If the Court's opinion is viewed in light of what the Court actually did—not what it said it did—then Justice Marshall was correct in arguing that the Court had essentially employed intermediate scrutiny.").

58. See, e.g., *Williamson v. Lee Optical,* 348 U.S. 483 (1955) (finding no equal-protection violation in ordinance that forbade opticians from fitting eyeglasses without prescription but permitted drugstores to sell ready-to-wear glasses); *Railway Express Agency, Inc. v. New York,* 336 U.S. 106 (1949) (finding no equal-protection violation in law that forbade truck owners from advertising other businesses on sides of their trucks but permitted owners to advertise owners' business). See generally JOHN E. NOWAK & RONALD D. ROTUNDA, CONSTITUTIONAL LAW § 14.3, at 639 (6th ed. 2000) ("[I]f a classification is of this type the Court will ask only whether it is conceivable that the classification bears a rational relationship to an end of government which is not prohibited by the Constitution.")

59. 509 U.S. 312 (1993).

60. 531 U.S. 356 (2001).

61. *Id.* at 372. The Court's reasoning regarding accommodations is a stunning example of failure to see beyond one's own point of reference. It may seem rational from the viewpoint of someone without disabilities to retain or build facilities knowing that they will exclude a significant fraction of the forty-three million Americans with disabilities. From the viewpoint of someone with a disability, however, it hardly seems rational to fail to make even a reasonable accommodation, for example, making slightly wider doors and flush entrances for new buildings so that they can be used by those with wheelchairs and placing portable ramps in older facilities where feasible. As a more general matter, people without disabilities frequently overlook the large number of accommodations made for them. Chief Justice Rehnquist's chair is an accommodation for people who walk and stand. Some other people wheel their chairs with them. As Harlan Hahn has written, "[T]he basic difficulty stems from widespread ignorance of the unequal implications of everyday surroundings." Harlan Hahn, *Equality and the Environment: The Interpretation of "Reasonable Accommodations" in the Americans with Disabilities Act,* 17 J. REHABILITATION ADMIN. 101, 104 (1993).

62. See *Garrett,* 531 U.S., at 375 (Kennedy, J., concurring). Justice O'Connor joined the concurrence. Justice Breyer wrote the dissent, which Justices Stevens, Souter, and Ginsburg joined. *Garrett,* 531 U.S., at 376 (Breyer, J., dis-

senting). joined the dissent. Even in *Cleburne* itself, the six-member majority included two justices (Justice Stevens and Chief Justice Burger) who expressed skepticism that an ordinary rational-basis test applied to the case and three justices (Justices Marshall, Brennan, and Blackmun) who would have forthrightly applied elevated scrutiny. *City of Cleburne v. Cleburne Living Ctr., Inc.,* 473 U.S. 432, 453–54 (1985) (Stevens, J., concurring); *id.* at 473 (Marshall, J., concurring in part and dissenting in part).

63. See *Heller v. Doe,* 509 U.S. at 312, 319 (1993) ("Even if respondents were correct that heightened scrutiny applies, it would be inappropriate for us to apply that standard here. Both parties have been litigating this case for years on the theory of rational-basis review.").

64. See *Reed v. Reed,* 404 U.S. 71, 76 (1971) (applying rational-basis test); see also *Frontiero v. Richardson,* 411 U.S. 677, 682 (1973) (plurality opinion) (applying strict scrutiny); cf. *Craig v Boren,* 429 U.S. 190, 197 (1976) (applying intermediate scrutiny). The exact content of the intermediate scrutiny test applicable to sexually discriminatory classifications remains a subject of dispute among members of the Court. Compare *United States v. Virginia,* 518 U.S. 515, 531 (1996) (requiring "exceedingly persuasive justification" for treating sexes differently), with *id.* at 559 (Rehnquist, C.J., concurring) (criticizing use of "exceedingly persuasive justification" standard).

65. See *City of Cleburne v. Cleburne Living Ctr., Inc.,* 473 U.S. 432, 461–65 (1985) (Marshall, J., concurring in part and dissenting in part) (describing history of discrimination and other factors supporting application of elevated scrutiny). The concern that some legislation beneficial to people with disabilities might be put at constitutional risk can be handled by the flexible nature of an intermediate scrutiny test. Intermediate review is flexible and permits some classifications that benefit the members of a protected group. See NOWAK & ROTUNDA, *supra* note 58, § 14.23, at 834 (describing preservation of "benign classifications" on the basis of sex under intermediate review).

66. *Cleburne,* 473 U.S. at 447 (stating that objectives such as "'a bare . . . desire to harm a politically unpopular group' are not legitimate state interests") (quoting *United States Dep't of Agric. v. Moreno,* 413 U.S. 528, 534 (1973)). As Professor Sunstein explains:

> When the government operates to benefit A and burden B, it may do so only if it is prepared to justify its decision by reference to a public value. . . . The institution that made the discrimination must be attempting to remedy a perceived public evil, and must not be responding only to the interests or preferences of some of its constituents.

Cass R. Sunstein, *Public Values, Private Interests, and the Equal Protection Clause,* 1982 SUP. CT. REV. 127, 134. Many cases hold that indulging prejudice is not a legitimate governmental goal. See, e.g., *Romer v. Evans,* 517 U.S. 620, 635 (1996) (finding no legitimate governmental purpose in placing unique political disadvantage on gays and lesbians); *Palmore v. Sidoti*, 466 U.S. 429, 433 (1984) (finding that avoiding potential problems from racial bias in population fails to constitute permissible ground for use of race in child custody determination); see also *Cleburne*, 473 U.S. at 448 ("[M]ere negative attitudes, or fear, unsubstantiated by factors which are properly cognizable in a zoning proceeding, are not permissible bases for treating a home for the mentally retarded differently."). This reasoning is, of course, independent of the reasoning by which the Court in *Cleburne* dismissed the other justifications for the zoning decision. The dismissal of the other reasons is what might be characterized as scrutiny that is stricter than the rational-basis test.

67. Leonard, *supra* note 57, at 108 ("The principle that disadvantaging unpopular groups for its own sake violates equal protection was reasserted by the recent opinion in *Romer v. Evans.*"); see also Daniel Farber & Suzanna Sherry, *The Pariah Principle*, 13 CONST. COMMENT. 257 (1996) (contending that government violates equal protection by treating people as pariahs); Joseph S. Jackson, *Persons of Equal Worth: Romer v. Evans and the Politics of Equal Protection*, 45 UCLA L. REV. 453 (1997) (arguing that equal protection imposes principle of equal worth of individuals). See generally *Romer v. Evans*, 517 U.S. 620 (1996).

68. *Bd. of Trs. v. Garrett*, 531 U.S. 365, 366 n.4, 367 (2001).

69. *United States v. Georgia*, 126 S. Ct. 877 (2006) (upholding ADA title II claim for damages for failure to provide accommodations in prison); *Tennessee v. Lane*, 541 U.S. 509 (2004) (upholding ADA title II claim for damages against state for failure to provide accessible courtroom).

70. No. 00–284-P-C, 2001 WL 68305 (D. Me. Jan. 29, 2001).

71. *Smith v. Wade*, 461 U.S. 30 (1983) (finding punitive damages appropriate in section 1983 case). To be actionable, the offending conduct must be considered intentional. See, e.g., *Hunter v. Underwood*, 471 U.S. 222 (1985) (finding equal-protection violation on the basis of evidence of intent); *Washington v. Davis*, 426 U.S. 229 (1976) (requiring showing of intent for equal-protection violation).

72. 159 F.3d 1253 (10th Cir. 1998); see also *Maxwell v. Sch. Dist.*, 53 F. Supp. 2d 792–93 (E.D. Pa. 1999) (finding state-created-danger standard met in case involving rape by classmates when substitute teacher told unruly class she did not care what they did if they did not bother her, remained idle during attacks, and participated in locking children in classroom). The contours of this doctrine remain uncertain, but they appear to require the affirmative creation of danger, rather than inaction in the face of danger. For example, the Supreme Court found that no due process violation occurred when a social service department repeatedly received reports of a father physically abusing a child but took no action, and the father eventually beat the child so severely that he suffered permanent brain injuries leaving him profoundly mentally retarded. *De-Shaney v. Winnebago County Dep't of Soc. Servs.*, 489 U.S. 189 (1989).

73. 173 F.3d 1226 (10th Cir. 1999); see also *Waechter v. School Dist. No. 14–030*, 773 F. Supp. 1005 (W.D. Mich. 1991). In *Waechter*, the court denied a motion to dismiss a claim for violation of substantive due process against a teacher, principal, superintendent, district, and school board when the plaintiffs alleged that the teacher, who knew their son had serious heart impairments, forced the child to sprint for 350 yards for talking in line on the playground. The child suffered cardiac arrhythmia and died. The court found the child to be in the custody of the defendants and found the conduct sufficiently outrageous to violate the constitutional duty. See *id.* at 1010. Some courts, however, have rejected substantive due process claims based on abuse of children in custodial situations if the child is voluntarily enrolled at the school or if the only coercion is that of compulsory school attendance laws. E.g., *Stevens v. Umsted*, 131 F.3d 697 (7th Cir. 1997) (finding no liability and upholding Eleventh Amendment immunity of superintendent in his capacity as a state actor in case concerning sexual assaults at state school against child voluntarily enrolled there, despite superintendent's knowledge of ongoing attacks); *Maldonado v. Josey*, 975 F.2d 727 (10th Cir. 1992) (finding no liability when boy was left unsupervised, resulting in strangulation).

74. *Goss v. Lopez*, 419 U.S. 565, 566 (1975) (holding that procedural due process requires notice and hearing before suspension from public school); see also *Quackenbush v. Johnson City Sch. Dist.*, 716 F.2d 141, 145 (2d Cir. 1983) (finding due process violation based on allegation of deprivation of special education hearing rights). Though postdeprivation remedies may suffice for some school discipline cases, the procedural due process right is still applicable. See *Ingraham v. Wright*, 430 U.S. 651 (1977) (finding no due process deprivation when corporal punishment in school remained subject to later remedies). A protected interest exists in continued attendance at a public school. See *Goss*, 419 U.S. at 565.

75. *Mills v. Board of Educ.*, 348 F. Supp. 866, 875 (D.D.C. 1972) ("[M]any [children] are suspended or expelled from regular schooling or specialized instruction or reassigned without any prior hearing and are given no periodic review thereafter. Due process of law requires a hearing prior to exclusion, termination [or] classification into a special program."). The court also found that the exclusion of children with disabilities from public school violates the equal-protection component of due process. *Id.*

76. *Quackenbush*, 716 F.2d at 148 (upholding damages claim for alleged due process violation based on deprivation of special education hearing rights).

77. *Carey v. Piphus*, 435 U.S. 247 (1978) (permitting nominal damages claim for suspension that took place without hearing but with just cause).

CHAPTER 6

1. *Board of Educ. v. Rowley,* 458 U.S. 176, 192 (1982); see also *id.* at 205 ("When the elaborate and highly specific procedural safeguards embodied in [20 U.S.C.] § 1415 are contrasted with the general and somewhat imprecise substantive admonitions contained in the Act, we think that the importance Congress attached to these procedural safeguards cannot be gainsaid.").

2. The *Rowley* case involved sign-language interpretation services. *Id.* at 184–85. The catheterization case is *Irving Independent School. District v. Tatro,* 468 U.S. 883, 895–96 (1984) (affirming order for services).

3. See, e.g., 42 U.S.C.A. § 1973i (West 2005) (Voting Rights Act of 1965); 42 U.S.C.A. § 2000a-2 (West 2005) (title II of Civil Rights Act of 1964).

4. See BONNIE P. TUCKER & BRUCE A. GOLDSTEIN, LEGAL RIGHTS OF PERSONS WITH DISABILITIES 8:2–3 (1991 & Supp. 2000) ("The IDEA only protects children who, by virtue of their disabilities, require special education services. Section 504, however, prohibits discrimination against all school-age children with disabilities, regardless of whether they require special education services.") (footnotes omitted). Most children using wheelchairs would be designated as eligible under IDEA if for no other reason than their need for adaptive physical education. Nevertheless, in many jurisdictions high school children do not need to take physical education all four years, so the eligibility would not necessarily be present. A child with a visual impairment who needs only to have large-print materials or other similar adaptations would not necessarily require special education of any type. A child with Tourette's syndrome may require exceptions to ordinary discipline policies but not need any special education services. Similarly, a child with attention deficit disorder may need supplemental services but not meet the standards for eligibility under IDEA. See, e.g., *Brittan Elementary Sch. Dist.,* 16 Educ. Handicapped L. Rep. 1226 (U.S. Dep't of Educ., Off. for Civil Rights 1990) (discussing coverage under section 504 for child not eligible for services under federal special education law).

5. 381 F.3d 194 (3d Cir. 2004) (Alito, J.).

6. See *Burlington Sch. Comm. v. Department of Educ.,* 471 U.S. 359 (1985) (permitting award of tuition reimbursement when school district failed to provide appropriate education to child with disability); see also 20 U.S.C.A. § 1412(a)(10)(C)(ii) (2000) (1997 IDEA amendment permitting courts and hearing officers to award tuition reimbursement).

7. Support for the unavailability of damages other than reimbursement in the administrative process seems more or less universal. See, e.g., *Padilla v. School Dist. No. 1,* 233 F.3d 1268, 1274 (10th Cir. 2000) ("[E]ven if damages are available under the IDEA they should be awarded in civil actions, not in administrative hearings."); *Covington v. Knox County Sch. Sys.,* 205 F.3d 912, 918 (6th Cir.

2000) ("[M]oney damages . . . are unavailable through the administrative process."); see also cases cited *infra* (finding damages unavailable even in court proceedings under 20 U.S.C. § 1415); Terry Jean Seligmann, *Not as Simple as ABC: Disciplining Children with Disabilities under the 1997 IDEA Amendments*, 42 ARIZ. L. REV. 77, 85 n.32 (2000) ("Most courts passing on the question have decided that the IDEA was not intended to confer a right to money damages for violations."). Whether a court may award damages directly under the statute for violations, and if so, when, is a little less clear. See, e.g., *Witte v. Clark County Sch. Dist.*, 197 F.3d 1271, 1275 (9th Cir. 1999) ("[O]rdinarily, monetary damages are not available under that statute."); *Sellers v. School Bd.*, 141 F.3d 524, 526–27 (4th Cir. 1998) (disallowing damages under IDEA in case characterized as sounding in educational malpractice); *Hoekstra v. Independent Sch. Dist. No. 283*, 103 F.3d 624, 625–26 (8th Cir. 1996) (finding compensatory damages unavailable under IDEA); *Crocker v. Tennessee Secondary Sch. Athletic Ass'n*, 980 F.2d 382, 386–87 (6th Cir. 1992) (rejecting damages claim under IDEA); cf. *Smith v. Robinson*, 468 U.S. 992, 1020 n.24 (1984) (noting apparent consensus among courts at time that predecessor statute to IDEA did not allow damages relief). See generally TUCKER & GOLDSTEIN, *supra* note 4, at 18:4–5 (discussing availability of damages in exceptional circumstances). The failure to award compensatory damages in IDEA cases has been criticized. Stephen C. Shannon, Note, *The Individuals with Disabilities Education Act: Determining "Appropriate Relief" in a Post-Gwinnett Era*, 85 VA. L. REV. 853, 882–86 (1999) (arguing that denial of damages relief contravenes congressional intent).

    8. 42 U.S.C.A. § 1983 (West 2005). The application of a section 1983 cause of action to violations of the federal special education laws originated with the situation in which the plaintiff, because of futility, an emergency, or some other reason, was excused from exhausting the administrative procedures provided in the special education law and filed suit directly in court. The leading case of this type arose from the defendant's failure to obey the results of a due process hearing. *Robinson v. Pinderhughes*, 810 F.2d 1270 (4th Cir. 1987). The court ruled that the plaintiff did not need to re-exhaust the claim, but it found that the proper cause of action under the circumstances was not the one contemplating full use of the administrative process, that under 20 U.S.C. § 1415, but rather the cause of action for governmental violations of federal law in general, 42 U.S.C. § 1983, for violation of what is now IDEA. *Robinson*, 810 F.2d at 1273; see also *Manecke v. School Bd.*, 762 F.2d 912 (11th Cir. 1985) (applying section 1983 cause of action to case in which district failed to act on parents' request for administrative hearing).

    9. 67 F.3d 484, 488–90 (3d Cir. 1995). Although the case does not directly involve disability harassment, the court noted that in first grade the child suffered teasing because of his incontinence, a peer response that the school apparently felt no need to deal with. *Id.* at 488.

10. See *Smith v. Robinson,* 468 U.S. 992 (1984). See generally *Middlesex County Sewerage Auth. v. National Sea Clammers Ass'n,* 453 U.S. 1 (1981) (finding section 1983 remedy implicitly preempted by comprehensive enforcement mechanisms in water pollution control statutes).

11. *W.B.,* 67 F.3d at 494; see also *id.* at 493–94 n.6 (quoting 20 U.S.C. § 1415(f)) ("Nothing in this chapter shall be construed to restrict or limit the rights, procedures, and remedies available under the Constitution, title V of the Rehabilitation Act of 1973, or other Federal statutes protecting the rights of children and youth with disabilities."); H. CONF. REP. No. 99–296, at 4 (1985) ("[S]ince 1987, it has been Congress' intent to permit parents or guardians to pursue the rights of handicapped children through [IDEA], section 504, and section 1983 Congressional intent was ignored by the U.S. Supreme Court when it handed down its decision in Smith v. Robinson.").

12. *Smith v. Wade,* 461 U.S. 30 (1983).

13. 233 F.3d 1268 (10th Cir. 2000).

14. *Padilla,* 233 F.3d at 1274 (citing *Blessing v. Freestone,* 520 U.S. 329, 341 (1997); *Wright v. City of Roanoke Redev. & Hous. Auth.,* 479 U.S. 418, 423 (1987)).

15. See 131 CONG. REC. 21,391 (1985) (statement of Sen. Kennedy) ("I do not believe that Congress when it passed the Education for All Handicapped Children Act [predecessor to IDEA] intended to in any way limit handicapped children's educational rights or the remedies for protecting those rights."); 131 CONG. REC. 21,389 (1985) (statement of Sen. Weicker) ("The court's decision . . . raised questions about the extent to which rights, remedies and procedures available under section 504 of the Rehabilitation Act and other Federal civil rights statutes will be applicable to claims made under the Education of the Handicapped Act [predecessor to IDEA]. The purpose of S. 415 is simple—to overturn the Smith v. Robinson decision and thereby to clarify congressional intent regarding these matters."); 131 CONG. REC. 31,370 (1985) (statement of Rep. Williams) ("The original bill was designed to . . . reestablish statutory rights repealed by the U.S. Supreme Court in the decision Smith v. Robinson [and] to reaffirm, in light of this decision, the viability of section 504 of the Rehabilitation Act of 1973, 42 U.S.C. 1983 and the other statutes as separate vehicles for ensuring the rights of handicapped children."); see also S. REP. No. 99–112, at 3 (1986) ("Section 4 provides that the [predecessor to IDEA] does not limit the applicability of other laws which protect handicapped children and youth."). See generally Thomas F. Guernsey, *The Education for All Handicapped Children Act, 42 U.S.C. § 1983, and Section 504 of the Rehabilitation Act of 1973: Statutory Interaction Following the Handicapped Children's Protection Act of 1986,* 68 NEB. L. REV. 564, 591–92 (1989) (describing purposes and operation of HCPA). The statements of the HCPA's sponsors are utterly inconsistent with any speculation that Congress intended only a partial overruling

of *Smith*. See 132 CONG. REC. 16,824 (1986) (statement of Sen. Kerry) ("In passing the pending conference report, Congress is specifically rejecting the reasoning of the Supreme Court in Smith v. Robinson."); 132 CONG. REC. 16,823 (1986) (statement of Sen. Weicker) ("The handicapped children of this country have paid the costs for 2 years now. But today we correct this error. In adopting this legislation, we are rejecting the reasoning of the Supreme Court in Smith versus Robinson, and reaffirming the original intent of Congress. . . ."); 131 CONG. REC. 31,375 (1985) (statement Rep. Jeffords) ("There is no doubt that there is agreement among all of us that the decision rendered by the court in July 1984 must be overturned."); see also *Handicapped Children's Protection Act: Hearings on H.R. 1523 before the Subcomm. on Select Education of the House Comm. on Education and Labor*, 99th Cong. 7 (1986) (statement of Rep. Williams) (declaring rejection of *Smith*). An extended comment by Senator Simon emphasized that the law was not meant to exclude any other remedies:

> The Supreme Court reasoned that when Congress adopted the comprehensive enforcement mechanism for the protection of handicapped children's rights in Public Law 94–142 [now IDEA], we superseded and eliminated rights previously enacted under other laws. This reasoning was particularly faulty, and in passing S. 415, Congress is rejecting that reasoning. As legislative approaches to protecting the rights of handicapped persons grow, and we adopt new laws, we are building upon the existing laws, with the full knowledge of those laws and with the assumption that their provisions remain in effect as the context for new legislation. When there is an intent to modify, limit, or supersede existing law, Congress does not hesitate to do so explicitly.

132 CONG. REC. 16,825 (1986).

16. See, e.g., *Wright v. City of Roanoke Redev. and Hous. Auth.*, 479 U.S. 418, 423 (1987) (ruling that defendant must demonstrate "by express provision or other specific evidence from the statute itself that Congress intended to foreclose" the section 1983 remedy); *Maine v. Thiboutot*, 448 U.S. 1, 4 (1980) ("[T]he § 1983 remedy broadly encompasses violations of federal statutory as well as constitutional law."); ERWIN CHEMERINSKY, FEDERAL JURISDICTION § 8.8, at 529 (3d ed. 1999) ("*Wright* . . . makes clear that the presumption is in favor of the availability of § 1983 to enforce a federal statute.").

17. The cases are *Schaffer v. Weast*, 126 S. Ct. 528 (2005); *Cedar Rapids Cmty. Sch. Dist. v. Garret F.*, 526 U.S. 66 (1999); *Florence County Sch. Dist. v. Carter*, 510 U.S. 7 (1993); *Zobrest v. Catalina Foothills Sch. Dist.*, 509 U.S. 1 (1993); *Dellmuth v. Muth*, 491 U.S. 223 (1989); *Honig v. Doe*, 484 U.S. 305 (1988); *Burlington Sch. Comm. v. Department of Educ.*, 471 U.S. 359 (1985); *Irving Indep. Sch. Dist. v. Tatro*, 468 U.S. 883 (1984); *Smith v. Robinson*, 468 U.S. 992 (1984); *Board of Educ. v. Rowley*, 458 U.S. 176 (1982). None of the later cases revisited the issues decided in *Smith*.

18. That was the situation in both *Blessing* and *Wright*. *Blessing v. Freestone*, 520 U.S. 329, 341 (1997); *Wright*, 479 U.S. at 423. If one does think that the references to *Smith* were more than adventitious, one might as well conclude that they were an "I told you so" by a Court that believed it was right in *Smith* and that Congress did not reinstate the original intent of the law by passing the HCPA but instead created a wholly new rule permitting section 1983 claims. There also remains the possibility that the Supreme Court justice or clerk who provided the citations in *Blessing* and *Wright* may not have realized *Smith* was overruled, much less how thorough the overruling happened to be. On the Westlaw research service, for example, the case is described merely as "superseded by statute/rule."

19. *Marie O. v. Edgar*, 131 F.3d 610, 621–22 (7th Cir. 1997); *N.B. v. Alachua County Sch. Bd.*, 84 F.3d 1376, 1379 (11th Cir. 1996); *Angela L. v. Pasadena Indep. Sch. Dist.*, 918 F.2d 1188, 1193 n.3 (5th Cir. 1990) (dictum); *Mrs. W. v. Tirozzi*, 832 F.2d 748, 753–55 (2d Cir. 1987). But see *Padilla v. School Dist. No. 1*, 233 F.3d 1268 (10th Cir. 2000). Compare *Robinson v. Pinderhughes*, 810 F.2d 1270, 1274 (4th Cir. 1987) (permitting section 1983 action to redress school district's failure to obey administrative decision), with *J.S. v. Isle of Wight County Sch. Bd.*, 402 F.3d 468 (4th Cir. 2005) (rejecting section 1983 damages claim and distinguishing *Robinson* as case for other relief); and *Sellers v. School Bd.*, 141 F.3d 524, 532 & n.6 (4th Cir. 1998) (not permitting section 1983 action for "the more general denial of a free appropriate public education"). Two circuits have permitted actions under section 1983, but they have limited the availability of compensatory damages in the actions. *Crocker v. Tennessee Secondary Sch. Athletic Ass'n*, 980 F.2d 382, 387 (6th Cir. 1992) (denying damages under section 1983); *Digre v. Roseville Indep. Sch. Dist. No. 623*, 841 F.2d 245, 249–50 (8th Cir. 1988) (same); cf. *Birmingham v. Omaha Sch. Dist.*, 220 F.3d 850, 856 (8th Cir. 2000) (allowing section 1983 claim for compensatory education for violation of IDEA).

20. The legislative history of the law stresses the difficulty with enforcement of existing statutory rights. E.g., S. REP. NO. 94–168, at 8 (1975) (commenting on lack of enforceability of state law rights). Private enforceability by parents of statutory rights was a principal feature distinguishing the Education for All Handicapped Children Act of 1975, which became IDEA in 1990, from the grant-in-aid statutes that preceded it. This characteristic makes IDEA much different from other laws that have been found to exclude a section 1983 cause of action. See *Gonzaga Univ. v. Doe*, 536 U.S. 273 (2002) (holding section 1983 action not available to enforce Family Educational Rights and Privacy Act in light of absence of remedy other than funding cutoff and statutory emphasis on institutional policies and practices rather than individual unlawful disclosures); *Suter v. Artist M.*, 503 U.S. 347 (1992) (holding section 1983 action unavailable to enforce Adoption Assistance and Child Welfare Act in light

of conclusion that Congress intended only Secretary of Health and Human Services to enforce Act).

21. 20 U.S.C.A. § 1415(i)(2)(A) (West 2005).

22. 20 U.S.C.A. § 1415(*l*) (West 2005).

23. The legislative history of the predecessor of IDEA, the Education for All Handicapped Children Act, includes a statement by Senator Harrison Williams, its principal author, that "exhaustion of the administrative procedures established under this part should not be required . . . in cases where such exhaustion would be futile either as a legal or practical matter." 121 CONG. REC. 37,416 (1975). When the HCPA restored section 504 and other remedies to IDEA cases in 1986, the additional remedies were made subject to the same exhaustion obligation that applies to the Act. Senator Simon and Representative Miller, who managed the bill, set down what Congress understood about exhaustion in special education cases:

> It is important to note that there are certain situations in which it is not appropriate to require the exhaustion of EHA [Education of the Handicapped Act, now IDEA] administrative remedies before filing a civil law suit. These include complaints that: First, an agency has failed to provide services specified in the child's individualized educational program [IEP]; second, an agency has abridged or denied a handicapped child's procedural rights—for example, failure to implement required procedures concerning least restrictive environment or convening of meetings; three, an agency has adopted a policy or pursued a practice of general applicability that is contrary to the law, or where it would otherwise be futile to use the due process procedures—for example, where the hearing officer lacks the authority to grant the relief sought; and four, an emergency situation exists—for example, failure to provide services during the pendency of proceedings, or a complaint concerning summer school placement which would not likely be resolved in time for the student to take advantage of the program.

131 CONG. REC. 21,392–93 (1985) (statement of Sen. Simon). Representative Miller elaborated: "[N]either I nor others who wrote the law intended that parents should be forced to expend valuable time and money exhausting unreasonable or unlawful administrative hurdles. . . ." *Id.* at 31,376. Despite this authority, courts feel an irresistible compulsion to dismiss for failure to exhaust even when the authority would dictate allowing the case to proceed. Perhaps the most striking cases are those in which the plaintiffs challenge a practice of general applicability that the hearing officer (who, according to 20 U.S.C. § 1415(f)(3), must be independent of the educational agency) lacks the power to change. Despite the futility of exhaustion and applicability of the statements of Senator Simon and Representative Miller, courts in recent years have frequently dismissed cases of this type on the basis of failure to exhaust administrative

remedies. E.g., *Doe v. Arizona Dep't of Educ.*, 111 F.3d 678 (9th Cir. 1997) (requiring exhaustion in action over failure to provide special education to eligible inmates of county jail); *Gardner v. School Bd.*, 958 F.2d 108 (5th Cir. 1992) (requiring exhaustion in challenge to policy not to permit taping of individualized education program meetings); *Hayes v. Unified Sch. Dist. No. 377*, 877 F.2d 809 (10th Cir. 1989) (requiring exhaustion in case challenging use of time-out rooms for students in special education programs); *Crocker v. Tennessee Secondary Sch. Athletic Ass'n*, 873 F.2d 933 (6th Cir. 1989) (overturning preliminary injunction against operation of rule preventing participation in sports by child who transferred between schools when transfer was allegedly caused by learning disabilities; holding that lawsuit was subject to dismissal for failure to exhaust state administrative remedies); *Radcliffe v. School Bd.*, 38 F. Supp. 2d 994 (M.D. Fla. 1999) (requiring exhaustion in dispute over scheduling of individualized education program meeting outside of school hours). Contrary to what the HCPA sponsors said of congressional intent, many other cases have required exhaustion even though hearing rights or other procedural guarantees have been violated. E.g., *Doe v. Walker County Bd. of Educ.*, No. A.4:95-CV-0219-H, 1997 WL 866983 (N.D. Ga. Sept. 19, 1997) (requiring exhaustion even though district failed to develop individualized education programs to provide basis for hearing); *W.L.G. v. Houston County Bd. of Educ.*, 975 F. Supp. 1317 (M.D. Ala. 1997) (holding that claim for failure to obey settlement agreement needed to be exhausted); *Koster v. Frederick County Bd. of Educ.*, 921 F. Supp. 1453 (D. Md. 1996) (requiring exhaustion despite claimed inadequacy of notice).

24. 98 F.3d 989 (7th Cir. 1996). Claims were advanced for violations of the Constitution, section 504, title II of the ADA, and state law, but not for violations of IDEA. *Id.* at 991. In many other cases alleging harassment or similar conduct, courts have dismissed for failure to pursue an IDEA claim through all of the administrative hearing officer process. E.g., *Kubistal v. Hirsch*, No. 98 C 3838, 1999 WL 90625 (N.D. Ill. Feb. 9, 1999) (involving ridicule and humiliation by teacher of student with visual impairment); *Franklin v. Frid*, 7 F. Supp. 2d 920 (W.D. Mich. 1998) (involving aide's physical and psychological abuse of child with cerebral palsy); *Shields v. Helena Sch. Dist. No. 1*, 943 P.2d 999 (Mont. 1997) (involving exclusion from trip, humiliation, and name-calling by teachers). In two cases, courts dismissed cases brought by parents based on allegations of retaliation, despite the obvious fact that the administrative process could provide no useful relief to the parents. See *Weber v. Cranston Sch. Comm.*, 212 F.3d 41 (1st Cir. 2000); *Babicz v. School Bd.*, 135 F.3d 1420 (11th Cir. 1998). In *Weber*, the court relied on the plaintiffs' failure to allege that exhaustion was burdensome or futile. *Weber*, 212 F.3d at 52–53. In *Babicz*, the court appears not to have been aware that Congress had overruled *Smith v. Robinson*, or perhaps it was not aware that the parent was

suing on her own behalf as well as that of her children. See *Babicz,* 135 F.3d at 1422.

25. 20 U.S.C.A. § 1415(*l*) (West 2005). The context clarifies the meaning: Nothing in this chapter shall be construed to restrict or limit the rights, procedures, and remedies available under the Constitution, the Americans with Disabilities Act of 1990 . . . , title V of the Rehabilitation Act . . . , or other Federal laws . . . except that before the filing of a civil action under such laws seeking relief that is also available under this subchapter, [the administrative] procedures [required by] this section shall be exhausted to the same extent as would be required had the action been brought under this subchapter.
Id.

26. See *Covington v. Knox County Sch. Sys.,* 205 F.3d 912, 917 (6th Cir. 2000) (excusing exhaustion; distinguishing cases "simply [] appending a claim for damages"). Strangely, the *Charlie F.* opinion nearly concedes the point that services are an inadequate remedy and damages are the proper one in a harassment case. A passage at the end reads: "Perhaps Charlie's adverse reaction to the events of fourth grade cannot be overcome by services available under the IDEA and the regulations, so that in the end money is the only balm." *Charlie F.,* 98 F.3d at 993. The paragraph concludes: "[A]t least in principle relief is available under the IDEA." *Id.* The purely formal analysis, relying on relief that is available in principle, underscores the point that the court is failing to accept disability harassment, even of the most outrageous character, as an evil that works harm in fact, not merely in principle.

27. 67 F.3d 484 (3d Cir. 1995).

28. *Id.* at 496 (quoting S. Rep. No. 99–112 (1986)).

29. 205 F.3d 912, 917 (6th Cir. 2000) (citation omitted).

30. 197 F.3d 1271, 1275–76 (9th Cir. 1999).

31. *Id.* at 1276.

32. 233 F.3d 1268, 1274 (10th Cir. 2000) (citation omitted). The court ultimately held that exhaustion was not required for the ADA claim, ruling that IDEA administrative remedies could not provide relief for physical injuries such as a skull fracture and that damages are generally unavailable in IDEA administrative hearings. *Id.* at 1274–75. For this point, the court relied on W.B., 67 F.3d at 494–96, as well as *Covington v. Knox County School System,* 205 F.3d 912, 918 (6th Cir. 2000).

33. *McCormick v. Waukegan Sch. Dist. No. 60,* 374 F.3d 564 (7th Cir. 2004).

34. Sources citing these policy grounds for an exhaustion rule include Terry Jean Seligmann, *A Diller, a Dollar: Section 1983 Damage Claims in Special Education Lawsuits,* 36 GA. L. REV. 465, 520–26 (2002); Paul M. Secunda, *At the Crossroads of Title IX and a New "Idea": Why Bullying Need Not Be "A Nor-*

mal Part of Growing Up" for Special Education Children, 12 DUKE J. GENDER
L. & POL'Y 1, 25–26 (2005).

35. 20 U.S.C.A. § 1415(f)(3)(A)(i) (West 2005); *see Mayson v. Teague,* 749
F.2d 652 (11th Cir. 1984) (excluding personnel with policy-making responsibility from service as hearing officers).

36. Modest standards for knowledge of and ability to understand the law
and how to conduct hearings were incorporated into the special education law
for the first time in 2004, but they mandate nothing specific with regard to
training. See 20 U.S.C.A. § 1415(f)(3)(A)(ii)–(iv) (West 2005); cf. *Carnwath v.
Bd. of Educ.,* 33 F. Supp. 2d 431, 434 (D. Md. 1998) (finding no training requirements for due process hearing officers in IDEA).

37. Cf. *Roe v. Nevada,* 332 F. Supp. 2d 1331, 1338–39 (D. Nev. 2004) (describing hearing following incident of mistreatment of preschool children with
disabilities in which hearing officers did not address damages claims).

38. *Harlow v. Fitzgerald,* 457 U.S. 800, 815–20 (1982) (emending previous
good-faith immunity test to create objective standard, on account of difficulty of
applying subjective standard). The current doctrine of official immunity has been
subjected to severe criticism. See, e.g., PETER W. LOW & JOHN C. JEFFRIES, JR., FED-
ERAL COURTS AND THE LAW OF FEDERAL-STATE RELATIONS 944–53 (4th ed. 1998)
(summarizing arguments and collecting authorities). As Gary Gildin convincingly
demonstrates, if public officials may be found personally liable under section 504,
title II ADA, or IDEA damages claims (as opposed to section 1983 claims for constitutional violations), official immunity should not be available as a defense. Gary
S. Gildin, *Dis-qualified Immunity for Discrimination against the Disabled,* 1999
U. ILL. L. REV. 897, 900. Gildin notes that the disability statutes were not modeled
after section 1983, that common law immunities present at the time of section
1983's adoption had been limited or abolished at the time the disability statutes
were passed, and that immunity is inconsistent with the legislative purpose behind
the statutes. *Id.* But see *P.C. v. McLaughlin,* 913 F.2d 1033, 1045 (2d Cir. 1990)
(finding that immunity protects employees of state department of mental health
from section 504 and IDEA damages claims); *East Penn Sch. Dist. v. Scott B.,* No.
97–1989, 1999 WL 178361, at *4 (E.D. Pa. Mar. 25, 1999) (finding that qualified
immunity protected individual-capacity defendants from IDEA damages claim).
As noted above, although controversy exists whether individual liability is permitted under the general nondiscrimination provisions of the ADA and section 504,
individuals clearly may be liable under the retaliation and coercion provisions. For
the reasons Gildin identifies, individual defendants liable under the ADA should be
unable to claim qualified immunity to avoid that liability. The discussion in the text
in the current section of this article addresses immunity from liability for constitutional violations made actionable under section 1983.

39. Regarding blanket wrapping, see *Heidemann v. Rother,* 84 F.3d 1021,
1029 (8th Cir. 1996). The technique involved wrapping the child tightly in a

blanket so that she could not move her arms or legs. *Id.* at 1025. The defendants contended that the technique was a proper one to provide the child with warmth and stability. *Id.* The plaintiffs asserted that the technique was used for prolonged periods as a substitute for educational and habilitative programs and cited an instance in which the child's mother found the child wrapped in a blanket on the floor, with flies crawling in and around her mouth and nose. *Id.* at 1026. The court ruled that use of the technique was not a substantial departure from the application of accepted practice standards of which the defendants should have known. *Id.* at 1029. Regarding the peer sexual assault, see *Spivey v. Elliott,* 29 F.3d 1522 (11th Cir. 1994), *withdrawn in part on recons.,* 41 F.3d 1497 (11th Cir. 1995). Regarding the confinement and sexual assault by a staff member, see *P.C.,* 913 F.2d at 1033. That court also found that defendants were immune from liability on claims based on violation of procedural due process and the Fourth Amendment. *Id.* at 1043–44. In *Smith v. Maine* the court found that the individual defendants were shielded by qualified immunity from liability for the equal-protection violation, but it relied solely on the plaintiffs' failure to oppose the defense. *Smith v. Maine Admin. Sch. Dist. No. 6,* No. 00–284-P-C, 2001 WL 68305, at *7 (D. Me. Jan. 29, 2001).

40. Regarding just cause, see, e.g., *Heidemann,* 84 F.3d at 1029 ("Certainly, even if the blanket wrapping treatment did constitute a substantial departure from professional norms (which it did not), a reasonable official would not have known that to be true."); *P.C.,* 913 F.2d at 1043 ("The requirement that professional judgment be exercised is not an invitation to a court reviewing it to ascertain whether in fact the best course of action was taken.") (citations omitted). Regarding absence of deliberate indifference, see, e.g., *P.C.,* 913 F.2d at 1045 ("Again, there are simply no facts on this record showing deliberate indifference."). Regarding absence of a clearly established right to protection, see, e.g., *Spivey,* 29 F.3d at 1527. The *Spivey* court stated:

> Because no reported case addressed this kind of residential school, the district court and the parties were forced to interpret analogous cases. The district court held that no liberty interest was implicated. On the other hand, we hold that our analysis leads us to an opposite conclusion. Where there is so much room for differing interpretations, we cannot say the contours of the right were clearly established.

Id.

41. Compare *Vance v. Spencer County Pub. Sch. Dist.,* 231 F.3d 253 (6th Cir. 2000) (finding deliberate indifference when school officials responded to continued reports of peer sexual harassment by talking to offenders without taking more aggressive action), with *Soper v. Hoben,* 195 F.3d 845 (6th Cir. 1999) (finding that immunity barred sex discrimination action against individual defendants in case involving rape of student when prompt and thorough response was made to earlier complaint).

42. 159 F.3d 1253, 1262–64 (10th Cir. 1998). The court found evidence from which a reasonable jury could conclude that the defendants "acted recklessly in conscious disregard of the risk of suicide, and . . . such conduct, if true, when viewed in total, possibly could be construed as conscience-shocking. . . . In addition, these facts taken as true also could be construed to show . . . that [defendants] increased the risk of harm to Armijo." *Id.* at 1264.

43. Regarding delays, see *W.B. v. Matula*, 67 F.3d 484 (3d Cir. 1995) (denying summary judgment on basis of immunity upon finding that failure to identify and evaluate child for more than six months and other violations could be viewed as violation of clearly established law). Regarding failure to provide procedural rights, see Mason v. *Schenectady City Sch. Dist.*, 879 F. Supp. 215, 220–21 (N.D.N.Y. 1993) (holding that long delay in provision of services and failure to afford notice of procedural rights constitute violations of established rights that overcome claim of immunity); cf. *Padilla v. School Dist. No. 1*, 35 F. Supp. 2d 1260 (D. Colo. 1999) (finding no qualified immunity for behavior specialist, special education teacher, and paraprofessional when child was restrained contrary to IEP and sustained injury; upholding immunity for school nurse), *aff'd in pt., rev'd in pt. on other grounds, and remanded*, 233 F.3d 1268 (10th Cir. 2000); *Bills v. Homer Consol. Sch. Dist.*, 959 F. Supp. 507 (N.D. Ill. 1997) (holding that principal's daily interrogations of fifth grader for five days after another child admitted to conduct in question were sufficiently unreasonable that Fourth Amendment claim would not be dismissed on ground of immunity).

44. *Owen v. City of Independence*, 445 U.S. 622, 653 & n.37 (1980) (explaining distinction between individual officials and governmental entities and holding that municipal corporations do not have official immunity).

45. If suit is brought against the state officials for their own actions in directly harassing a student with disabilities, Eleventh Amendment immunity does not shield them. See *Hafer v. Melo*, 502 U.S. 21, 25–26 (1991) (finding personal liability for political firings not barred by immunity). Nevertheless, many state school employees do not have assets to pay a judgment or cannot be identified. If the plaintiff claims that the state is responsible for the conduct, the state will assert immunity, and it does not matter that state officials are sued rather than the state or state agency itself. See *Edelman v. Jordan*, 415 U.S. 651, 663 (1974) (barring action against state official when state treasury provides source of recovery). Elementary and secondary school districts are municipal corporations rather than arms of the state, so as a general rule Eleventh Amendment immunity does not protect them. *Mount Healthy City Sch. Dist. Bd. of Educ. v. Doyle*, 429 U.S. 274, 280–81 (1977) (finding Eleventh Amendment immunity not to bar suits against municipalities such as school districts). Despite the Supreme Court's holding in Mount Healthy, courts have ruled that local school districts in California, see *Eason v. Clark County Sch. Dist.*, 303 F.3d 1137 (9th

192 | *Notes to Chapter 6*

Cir. 2002), and Maryland, see *Biggs v. Bd. of Educ.*, 229 F. Supp. 2d 437 (D. Md. 2002), are sufficiently part of state government to fall under the amendment's protection. Whether these decisions are correct is beyond the scope of the current discussion, but if they are correct, the text's suggested responses to assertions of the immunity are that much more important. In general, local school districts are reluctant to claim too close an identification with state departments of education. Although an affiliation with the state might gain the districts protection from some damages claims because of the Eleventh Amendment or other immunity rules, it would subject them to prospective remedies for state violations of the law. Cf. *Milliken v. Bradley*, 414 U.S. 717 (1974) (holding local school districts not subject to desegregation remedies for segregation fostered by state education department in other districts). Eleventh Amendment immunity is an issue in cases claiming damages. Except in very limited circumstances, federal courts retain the power to enjoin ongoing violations of federal law under the doctrine of *Ex parte Young*, 209 U.S. 123 (1908).

46. The majority interpretation of the amendment traces to *Hans v. Louisiana*, 134 U.S. 1, 10–11 (1890) (describing history of Eleventh Amendment); see also id. at 18 (holding states immune from suit by same-state citizens); cf. *Edelman v. Jordan*, 415 U.S. 651 (1974) (reaffirming immunity of states from suit by same-state citizens). The case that led to passage of the amendment is *Chisholm v. Georgia*, 2 U.S. (2 Dall.) 419 (1793) (enforcing debt obligation against Georgia). Proponents of the view that the Eleventh Amendment ought to be limited in its application to cases whose jurisdiction is based on the diverse state citizenship of the plaintiff and defendant include Justices Stevens, Souter, Ginsburg, and Breyer. See ERWIN CHEMERINSKY, FEDERAL JURISDICTION § 7.3, at 407–09 (4th ed. 2003). Justice Brennan explained the position at length in *Atascadero State Hospital v. Scanlon*, 473 U.S. 234, 258–59 (1985) (Brennan, J., dissenting). So far, the majority of the Court disagrees with Justice Brennan's diversity view and holds that the Amendment stands for a broad-ranging immunity from suit, including immunity from claims by defendant-state citizens and immunity when the suit's jurisdictional basis is a federal question. E.g., *Seminole Tribe v. Florida*, 517 U.S. 44, 54 (1996) ("Although the text of the Amendment would appear to restrict only the Article III diversity jurisdiction of the federal courts, 'we have understood the Eleventh Amendment to stand not so much for what it says, but for the presupposition . . . which it confirms.'") (quoting *Blatchford v. Native Village of Noatak*, 501 U.S. 775, 779 (1991)). That position is hotly disputed by four justices. *Id.* at 130 (Souter, J., dissenting) (joined in dissent by Justices Stevens, Ginsburg, & Breyer). Much scholarship on the Eleventh Amendment supports the idea that the Amendment is limited in its operation to diversity cases. E.g., William A. Fletcher, *A Historical Interpretation of the Eleventh Amendment: A Narrow Construction of an Affirmative Grant of Jurisdiction Rather Than a Prohibition against*

Jurisdiction, 35 STAN. L. REV. 1033 (1983); John J. Gibbons, *The Eleventh Amendment and State Sovereign Immunity: A Reinterpretation*, 83 COLUM. L. REV. 1889 (1983); David L. Shapiro, *Wrong Turns: The Eleventh Amendment and the Pennhurst Case*, 98 HARV. L. REV. 61 (1984); see also *Pennsylvania v. Union Gas Co.*, 491 U.S. 1, 24 (1989), overruled by *Seminole Tribe v. Florida*, 517 U.S. 44 (1996) (Stevens, J., concurring) ("Justice Brennan's opinion in *Atascadero* and the works of numerous scholars have exhaustively and conclusively refuted the contention that the Eleventh Amendment embodies a general grant of sovereign immunity to the States . . .") (citation omitted). But see Lawrence C. Marshall, *Fighting the Words of the Eleventh Amendment*, 102 Harv. L. Rev. 1342 (1989) (challenging diversity theory); William P. Marshall, *The Diversity Theory of the Eleventh Amendment: A Critical Evaluation*, 102 HARV. L. REV. 1372 (1989) (same). Still another view is that the Amendment represents a broad federal common-law immunity that is nevertheless totally subject to congressional abrogation. See Vicki C. Jackson, *The Supreme Court, the Eleventh Amendment, and State Sovereign Immunity*, 98 YALE L.J. 1 (1988). There is a wealth of scholarship on the Eleventh Amendment. For a valuable collection of articles, see Symposium, *State Sovereign Immunity and the Eleventh Amendment*, 75 NOTRE DAME L. REV. 817 (2000).

47. 427 U.S. 445, 455 (1976).

48. 42 U.S.C.A. § 12101(b) (West 2005) (stating intention to exercise Fourteenth Amendment power in passage of ADA); see *Smith v. Robinson*, 468 U.S. 992, 1016?18 (1984) (noting "equal protection premise" of section 504). The statutes might also be considered exercises of authority over interstate commerce, and section 504 is also an exercise of conditional spending power. These additional bases of authority are important with regard to the statutes' application to nongovernmental entities, for the traditional rule has been that congressional power under the Fourteenth Amendment does not permit obligations to be imposed on private actors. See *The Civil Rights Cases*, 109 U.S. 3 (1883).

49. 521 U.S. 507 (1997).

50. 527 U.S. 627 (1999).

51. 529 U.S. 598 (2000).

52. 528 U.S. 62 (2000).

53. 531 U.S. 356 (2001). Chief Justice Rehnquist wrote the majority opinion. Justice Kennedy, joined by Justice O'Connor, filed a brief concurrence, and Justice Breyer dissented in an opinion joined by Justices Stevens, Souter, and Ginsburg.

54. See *Garrett*, 193 F.3d at 1218 (regarding title I of ADA); *id.* at 1218–19 (regarding section 504). Ironically, the holding the court of appeals relied on with regard to title I of the ADA was the other half of the Kimel case, in which the employee sued under the ADA for the same conduct that was the basis of the ADEA claim. *Kimel*, 139 F.3d 1426, 1433 (11th Cir. 1998), *aff'd*, 528 U.S. 62 (2000).

55. *Garrett*, 531 U.S. 356, 360 n.1. The Court apparently did not view the section 504 issue as covered by the grant of certiorari, for it did not mention it at all.

56. *Id.* at 367. The Court said that it would be rational for a state to hold to job qualification requirements that do not make allowances for disability.

57. *Garrett*, 531 U.S. at 369–72. The Court also stressed that private individuals remain free to enforce title I against states in actions for injunctive relief. *Id.* at 374 n.9.

58. 541 U.S. 509 (2004).

59. *Plyler v. Doe*, 457 U.S. 202 (1982) (finding violation of equal protection in exclusion of illegal alien children from public school); see also *Lau v. Nichols*, 414 U.S. 563 (1974) (finding absence of Chinese-language instruction to violate title VI of Civil Rights Act of 1964). A negative inference might also be drawn from *San Antonio Independent School District. v. Rodriguez*, 411 U.S. 1, 54–59 (1973), in which the court found no equal-protection violation in a state's unequal provision of school resources to poor areas but emphasized that there was no absolute deprivation of an education to the children in the poor neighborhoods

60. An approach other than that of the Court might view the failure to accommodate less charitably and find it the product of stereotypes about disability and the impact of the environment on disability. One does not need to adopt such an approach to consider harassment to be within the core of the conduct barred by the Fourteenth Amendment.

61. While concluding that ADA title II generally exceeds the scope of congressional authority under section 5 of the Fourteenth Amendment, the Second Circuit has ruled that monetary remedies under the title are congruent with and proportional to the reach of the Fourteenth Amendment if damages are permitted only in cases where there is discriminatory animus or ill will based on the plaintiff's disability. *Garcia v. S.U.N.Y. Health Sciences Ctr.*, 280 F.3d 98, 111 (2d Cir. 2001). So limited, title II money claims against states comport with congressional power under section 5 and are not subject to Eleventh Amendment immunity. *Id.* at *9 ("Government actions based on discriminatory animus or ill will towards the disabled are generally the same actions that are proscribed by the Fourteenth Amendment,—i.e., conduct that is based on irrational prejudice or wholly lacking a legitimate government interest."). The Second Circuit's interpretation of Eleventh Amendment immunity would thus permit damages against state entities for intentional wrongdoing such as disability harassment.

62. 126 S. Ct. 877, 882 (2006). The conduct of the state that was said to violate both the Eighth Amendment and title II included the plaintiff's confinement for twenty-three to twenty-four hours a day in a cell too narrow for him to turn his wheelchair around, denial of access to nearly all prison programs, denial of physical therapy and medical treatment, and denial of assistance with

toileting and cleanliness, which meant that on several occasions he had to sit in his own bodily waste while prison officials refused to help him. *Id.* at *2.

63. Various authority supports the point that these statutes are exercises of the power to enforce the Fourteenth Amendment. E.g., *Smith v. Robinson*, 468 U.S. 992, 1019 (1984) (finding "equal-protection premise" behind both statute now designated as IDEA and section 504); *Parks v. Pavkovic*, 753 F.2d 1397, 1407 (7th Cir. 1985) (finding statute now designated as IDEA to be valid exercise of power under Fourteenth Amendment).

64. Courts have found section 504 and IDEA to be valid exercises of congressional spending power. *Jim C. v. United States*, 235 F.3d 1079 (8th Cir. 2000) (finding section 504 to be proper exercise of spending power); *Bradley v. Arkansas Dep't of Educ.*, 189 F.3d 745 (8th Cir. 1999) (finding IDEA to be valid exercise of spending power), *vacated on other grounds, Jim C. v. Arkansas Dep't of Educ.*, 197 F.3d 958 (8th Cir. 1999); cf. *Jim C.*, 235 F.3d at 1082 ("The sacrifice of all federal education funds would be politically painful, but we cannot say that it compels Arkansas's choice."). The Court rejected a challenge to a spending-clause statute in *South Dakota v. Dole*, 483 U.S. 203 (1987), and although dicta in that case suggest that there might be some limits on Congress's spending power, the restrictions pose no threat to section 504 or IDEA. See *id.* at 207–08 (describing possible limits on spending power).

65. The Eighth Circuit found the exaction of the waivers clear and unambiguous. *Jim C.*, 235 F.3d at 1081 ("The Rehabilitation Act requires States that accept federal funds to waive their Eleventh Amendment immunity to suits brought in federal court for violations of Section 504."); *Bradley*, 189 F.3d at 753 ("When it enacted §§ 1403 and 1415, Congress provided a clear, unambiguous warning of its intent to condition a state's participation in the IDEA program and its receipt of federal IDEA funds on the state's waiver of its immunity from suit in federal court on claims made under the IDEA."), *vacated on other grounds, Jim C. v. Arkansas Dep't of Educ.*, 197 F.3d 958 (8th Cir. 1999); *Clark v. California*, 123 F.3d 1267, 1271 (9th Cir. 1997) (finding waiver of immunity under section 504 by acceptance of federal funds); see also *Marie O. v. Edgar*, 131 F.3d 610, 617–18 (7th Cir. 1997) (suggesting in case for nonmonetary relief that receipt of funds after statutory abrogation of Eleventh Amendment immunity may work as waiver of immunity). *Contra Garcia v. S.U.N.Y. Health Scis. Ctr.*, 280 F.3d 98 (2d Cir. 2001) (holding waiver ineffective on theory that state would have assumed immunity validly abrogated, and thus failed to make knowing decision). State governments may waive the immunity. See *Petty v. Tennessee-Missouri Bridge Comm'n*, 359 U.S. 275 (1959). Merely accepting federal money when the federal statute does not contain an abrogation of the immunity is not waiver, however. *Edelman v. Jordan*, 415 U.S. 651 (1974) (upholding Eleventh Amendment immunity in case brought under Social Security Act and section 1983). This rule was extended to the original version of

section 504 in *Atascadero State Hospital v. Scanlon*, 473 U.S. 234 (1985). Congress responded to the *Atascadero* decision by enacting an abrogation of immunity for section 504 suits. See Pub. L. No. 99–506, 100 Stat. 1807 (1986) (codified as amended at 29 U.S.C.A. § 701 (West 2005). Similarly, Congress prospectively overruled *Dellmuth v. Muth*, 491 U.S. 223 (1989), which found that the statute that is now IDEA did not clearly abrogate Eleventh Amendment immunity, by enacting an explicit abrogation. See Pub. L. No. 101–476, 104 Stat. 1103, 1106 (1990) (codified as amended at 20 U.S.C.A. § 1403 (West 2005)).

CHAPTER 7

1. Common-law remedies for disability harassment have received scant attention in the literature, but an early work of key importance is Frank S. Ravitch, *Beyond Reasonable Accommodation: The Availability and Structure of a Cause of Action for Workplace Harassment under the Americans with Disabilities Act*, 15 CARDOZO L. REV. 1475, 1496–99 (1994).

2. Cases include *Alcorn v. Anbro Eng'g, Inc.*, 468 P.2d 216 (Cal. 1970) (action for intentional infliction of emotional distress brought by victim of racial harassment); *Skousen v. Nidy*, 367 P.2d 248 (Ariz. 1961) (assault and battery action in context of sexual harassment). Catharine MacKinnon's early work on sexual harassment drew on the development of tort liability for harassing conduct. See CATHARINE A. MACKINNON, SEXUAL HARASSMENT OF WORKING WOMEN 164–74 (1979) (discussing tort law causes of actions applicable to sexual harassment). Nevertheless, MacKinnon considered common-law tort actions inadequate to provide protection against sex harassment. *Id.* at 173 ("To treat [sexual harassment] as a tort is less simply incorrect than inadequate."). See generally MARC A. FRANKLIN & ROBERT L. RABIN, TORT LAW AND ALTERNATIVES 825–28 (6th ed. 1996) (providing history of common-law racial and sexual harassment claims and discussing relation to statutory discrimination claims).

3. For cases in which the claim is attached to a federal statutory cause of action, see *Soodman v. Wildman, Harrold, Allen & Dixon*, No. 95 C 3834, 1997 WL 106257 (N.D. Ill. Feb. 10, 1997) (upholding claim for intentional infliction of emotional distress); *Martinez v. Monaco/Viola, Inc.*, No. 96 C 4163, 1996 WL 547258 (N.D. Ill. Sep. 18, 1996) (same); *Dutson v. Farmers Insurance Exchange*, 815 F. Supp. 349, 354 (D. Or. 1993) (same). In some jurisdictions, discharge itself may constitute intentional infliction of emotional distress. See, e.g., *Soodman*, 1997 WL 106257 at *10–11 (denying summary judgment in intentional-infliction claim based on termination of employee with condition that led to high-risk pregnancy).

4. Regarding individual liability, see *Wheeler v. Marathon Printing, Inc.*, 974 P.2d 207 (Or. App. 1998) (upholding verdict against co-worker for inten-

tional infliction of emotional distress but reversing judgment against employer). Courts have generally rejected claims of individual, personal liability under the ADA and section 504. See, e.g., *Romand v. Zimmerman*, 881 F. Supp. 806 (N.D.N.Y. 1995). But see *Johnson v. New York Hosp.*, 897 F. Supp. 83 (S.D.N.Y. 1995) (permitting individual liability against persons who play significant role in federal funding activity). Individual liability may be available under some state civil rights laws, however. See, e.g., *Hudson v. Loretex Corp.*, No. 95 CV-844 (RSP/RWS), 1997 WL 159282 (N.D.N.Y. April 2, 1997) (upholding disability discrimination claim under New York Human Rights Law against employee's supervisor). For a case dealing with the standing to sue of an independent contractor, rather than an employee, see *Dutson v. Farmers Ins. Exchange*, 815 F. Supp. 349 (D. Or. 1993) (involving insurance agent who was independent contractor). The limits on compensatory and punitive damages in ADA employment cases are found in 42 U.S.C.A. § 1981a(b)(3) (West 2005). These limits contrast with cases permitting punitive damages in intentional-infliction-of-emotional-distress causes of action. See *Norcon, Inc., v. Kotowski*, 971 P.2d 158, 174 (Alaska 1999); *Sacco v. High Country Indep. Press, Inc.*, 896 P.2d 411, 429 (Mont. 1995); *Gianoli v. Pfleiderer*, 563 N.W.2d 562, 569–69 (Wis. App. 1997). But see *Knierim v. Izzo*, 174 N.E.2d 157, 165 (Ill. 1961) (disallowing punitive damages in intentional-infliction claim).

5. RESTATEMENT (SECOND) OF TORTS § 46(1) (1965). The *Restatement*'s definition of the cause of action does not purport to define the only circumstances under which tort liability for intentional infliction of emotional distress will apply. The *Restatement* provides: "The Institute expresses no opinion as to whether there may not be other circumstances under which the actor may be subject to liability for the intentional or reckless infliction of emotional distress." *Id.*, caveat.

6. *Id.* cmt. d.

7. See *Russo v. White*, 400 S.E.2d 160 (Va. 1991) (describing tort as not favored in Virginia and refusing to extend it to plight of woman subjected to hundreds of hang-up calls by would-be suitor). See generally DAN B. DOBBS, THE LAW OF TORTS § 303 (2000) (describing widespread acceptance of intentional-infliction tort). One of the first cases is that concerning threats, *State Rubbish Collectors Ass'n v. Siliznoff*, 240 P.2d 282 (Cal. 1952). An early abusive debt collection practices case applying intentional-infliction liability is *Duty v. Gen. Fin. Co.*, 273 S.W.2d 64 (Tex. 1954). A case regarding abuse perpetrated by a job supervisor is *GTE Southwest, Inc. v. Bruce*, 998 S.W.2d 605 (Tex. 1999).

8. RESTATEMENT (SECOND) OF TORTS § 46 cmt. f, illus. 9 (1965).

9. *Id.* at illus. 9 (1965).

10. DOBBS, *supra* note 7, § 304. The *Restatement* itself embodies this idea: "The extreme and outrageous character of the conduct may arise from an abuse

by the actor of a position, or a relation with the other, or power to affect his interests." RESTATEMENT (SECOND) OF TORTS § 46 cmt. e (1965).

11. *Drejza v. Vaccaro*, 650 A.2d 1308 (D.C. 1994).

12. See Paul Sale & Doris M. Carey, *The Sociometric Status of Students with Disabilities in a Full-Inclusion School*, 62 EXCEPTIONAL CHILDREN 6, 16–17 (1995) (discussing low social prestige of students with disabilities among peers).

13. No. 96 C 4163, 1996 WL 547258 (N.D. Ill. Sep. 18, 1996).

14. See *id*. at *3. A claim for invasion of privacy was dismissed, however, based on the court's prediction that Illinois would not recognize a tort for unreasonable intrusion into the seclusion of another under the circumstances alleged. See *id*. at *2.

15. 815 F. Supp. 349, 354 (D. Or. 1993).

16. See *id*. The court granted summary judgment for defendants on the plaintiff's disability discrimination claim, relying on the fact that plaintiff was an independent contractor, rather than an employee. See *id*. at 352–53. The court also rejected a defamation claim but permitted a contract claim to proceed. See *id*. at 353–54.

17. No. Civ.A.98-CV-3304, 1999 WL 562756 (E.D. Pa. July 27, 1999).

18. *Id*. at *1.

19. The opinion, however, cautioned that to survive a motion for summary judgment, plaintiff would need to submit competent medical evidence of the causation and severity of her emotional distress and would need to submit proof that the conduct was both intentional and outrageous. *Id*. at *5–*6 & n.2.

20. 59 P.3d 611 (Wash. 2002).

21. *Id*. at 614.

22. *Id*.

23. *Id*. at 618 (discrimination), 619 (workers' compensation), 621 (intentional infliction). The court, however, affirmed reversal of entry of judgment in favor of the plaintiff on a defamation claim. *Id*. at 623.

24. *Id*. at 621.

25. *Id*. at 626–29 (Bridge, J., dissenting). There are other cases in which courts sustain intentional-infliction claims where the employee had some disabling condition but there is no clear allegation that the condition motivated the harasser to engage in the actionable conduct. See, e.g., *Steiner v. Tillamook County*, No. CV 05-809-AS, 2005 WL 2030828 (Aug. 23, 2005) (denying motion to dismiss action against supervisor of employee who eventually went on leave for emotional distress and mental health problems).

26. A surprising number of courts have found these persons not disabled on the basis of their condition, typically ruling that when the plaintiff takes the insulin the impairment does not substantially limit a major life activity. E.g., *Darst v. Vencor Nursing Ctrs., Ltd.*, No. IP 98-1621-C-M/S, 2003 WL

22016374 (S.D. Ind. July 30, 2003); *Johnson v. Penske Truck Leasing Co.*, No. CIV. A. 99–1652, 2001 WL 238181 (E.D. La. March 7, 2001).

27. *Rivera v. Cracker Barrel Old Country Store*, No. 02–4160 (JBS), 2003 WL 21077965 (D.N.J. March 3, 2003).

28. *Id.* at *6.

29. Samuel R. Bagenstos, *Subordination, Stigma and "Disability,"* 86 VA. L. REV. 397 (2000).

30. *Silk v. City of Chicago*, 194 F.3d 788, 804 (7th Cir. 1999).

31. No. 95 C 3834, 1997 WL 106257 (N.D. Ill. Feb. 10, 1997).

32. *Id.* at *10.

33. See *Smith v. Dovenmuehle Mortgage, Inc.*, 859 F. Supp. 1138 (N.D. Ill. 1994) (denying motion for summary judgment in case involving discharge of employee with AIDS); see also *Eaton v. Goodstein Mgmt., Inc.*, No. 97 CIV. 6582 TPG, 1999 WL 1037868 (Nov. 15, 1999) (upholding claim for intentional infliction of emotional distress when plaintiff alleged falsification of complaints to support removal of couch and wheelchair from building lobby, making job of building superintendent with heart impairment, diabetes, and amputation difficult, if not impossible, perform). But see *Wornick Co. v. Casas*, 856 S.W.2d 732, 735 (Tex. 1993) (holding that under Texas law, discharge alone cannot constitute outrageous behavior).

34. 70 P.3d 495, 497 (Colo. Ct. App. 2002).

35. 278 F.3d 819, 827–28 (8th Cir. 2002).

36. No. Civ. 3:04 CV 1579 PCD, 2004 WL 2750315 (D. Conn. Nov. 22, 2004). The opinion does not mention any federal claims. It is possible that there was no motion to dismiss these claims or that there was a motion but it was ruled on and discussed in some other opinion that was not published.

37. *Guckenberger v. Boston Univ.*, 957 F. Supp. 306 (D. Mass. 1997). The case relied on section 504 of the Rehabilitation Act, but the standards applied under that law are, for relevant purposes, the same as those under the ADA.

38. 192 F.3d 462 (4th Cir. 1999).

39. *Treadwell v. St. Joseph High Sch.*, No. 98 C 4906, 1999 WL 753929 at *12–*13 (N.D. Ill. Sep. 15, 1999). The court dismissed an intentional-infliction claim against a college coach who had been recruiting the student but then refused to sponsor him for admission. *Id.* at *13–*14.

40. *A.R. v. Kogan*, 964 F. Supp. 269, 272 (N.D. Ill. 1997) (applying Illinois law).

41. *Weaver v. New England Mut. Life Ins. Co.*, 52 F. Supp. 2d 127, 131–32 (D. Me. 1999).

42. 958 P.2d 202 (Or. App. 1998).

43. *Id.* at 204–05.

44. *Id.* at 205.

45. See, e.g., *Honeck v. Nicolock Paving Stones of New England, LLC*, No. Civ. 3:04CV1577 (JBA), 2005 WL 1388736 (D. Conn. June 10, 2005) (dismissing intentional-infliction claim alleging insulting and demeaning conduct against worker with health difficulties); *Daniels v. Health Ins. Plan of Greater N.Y.*, No. 02CIV6054MB, Mar. 2, 2005 WL 1138492 (S.D.N.Y. May 12, 2005) (dismissing intentional-infliction claim alleging rude behavior, overwork, failure to promote, and termination); *Sabido v. Walgreen's Drugs*, No. C 03–2857 MJJ, 2005 WL 522078 (N.D. Cal. Mar. 2, 2005) (granting employer summary judgment on intentional-infliction claim over denial of transfer and change of hours, overwork, and receipt of written warning); *Sheaffer v. County of Chatham*, 337 F. Supp.2d 709 (M.D.N.C. 2004) (granting motion to dismiss intentional-infliction claim based on verbal harassment while on sick leave and decisions regarding work activities, culminating in dismissal); *Sabrowski v. Albani-Bayeux, Inc.*, No. 1:02CV00728, 2003 WL 23018827 (M.D.N.C. Dec. 19, 2003) (dismissing intentional-infliction claim based on employer's telephone calls to third parties suggesting plaintiff used drugs, behaved dishonestly, was seriously mentally ill, and made bomb threat); *Leavitt v. Wal-Mart Stores, Inc.*, 238 F. Supp.2d 313, 316 (D. Me. 2003) (granting summary judgment to employer on claim by employee who suffered heart attack concerning shift assignments, failure to assist with transfer of work location, and comments concerning use of parking spot and early departures from work), *aff'd in part and rev'd in part on other grounds*, 74 Fed. Appx. 66 (1st Cir. 2003); *Kimble-Parham v. Minn. Mining & Mfg.*, No. CIV 00-1242, 2002 WL 31229572 at 15 (D. Minn. Oct. 2, 2002) (granting motion for summary judgment in case involving insensitive comments and alleged pattern of work decisions unfair to plaintiff); *Heasley v. D.C. Gen. Hosp.*, 180 F. Supp. 2d 158, 173 (D.D.C. 2002) (granting summary judgment to employer on intentional-infliction claim based on failure to accommodate inability to stand for prolonged periods, unpleasant remarks by co-workers, and termination on account of unjustified absence); *McCutchen v. Sunoco, Inc.*, No. CIV.A. 01–2788, 2002 WL 1896586 (E.D. Pa. Aug. 16, 2002) (granting summary judgment against employee with visual impairment when supervisors made several derogatory comments over prolonged period about his ability to see); *Robinson v. U.S. Bancorp.*, No. CIV.99-1723-ST, 2000 WL 435468 (D. Or. Apr. 20, 2000) (magistrate judge's recommendation) (dismissing claim for intentional infliction of emotional distress based on failure to provide requested accommodations to computer operator with blindness), *adopted*, 2000 WL 33141063 (D. Or. Apr. 20, 2000); *Veal v. AT & T Corp.*, No. Civ.A. 99–0370, 2000 WL 303299 (E.D. La. Mar. 22, 2000) (granting summary judgment to employer on intentional-infliction claim over unspecified harassment from supervisor); *Dupre v. Harris County Hosp. Dist.*, 8 F. Supp. 2d 908, 925–27 (S.D. Tex. 1998) (granting summary judgment against employee with bipolar disorder when conduct encompassed little beyond termination itself and employee failed to

demonstrate severity of distress); *Harris v. Middlesex County Coll.,* 801 A.2d 397, 404 (N.J. Super. Ct. App. Div. 2002) (finding comments about attitude of employee with breast cancer and about timing of her reconstructive surgery to be insufficiently outrageous); *Sasser v. Quebecor Printing (USA) Corp.,* 159 S.W.3d 579 (Tenn. Ct. App. 2004) (affirming summary judgment against employee with amputation whose computer was defaced, who had time sheets stolen, and who found grease and garbage in work space, when many employees had access to area and no specific motivation was shown); *Kirby v. City of Tacoma,* 98 P.3d 827, 837 (Wash. Ct. App. 2004) (in light of justifications for conduct, passing police officer up for promotion and other adverse conduct ruled insufficiently outrageous); see also *DiLuca v. Communications & Power Indus., Inc.,* No. 00–02000, 2003 WL 21781564 (Mass. Super. Ct. July 25, 2003) (finding emotional distress insufficiently linked to workplace conditions). Comparison to cases that succeed is difficult because the opinions' description of the offending conduct is often vague.

46. The salesman case is *McKay v. Town & Country Cadillac, Inc.,* 991 F. Supp. 966, 971 (N.D. Ill. 1997) (dismissing intentional-infliction action against former employer, who verbally abused alcoholic salesman and reduced his pay and privileges). That of the worker with multiple sclerosis is *Braunling v. Countrywide Home Loans, Inc.,* 220 F.3d 1154 (9th Cir. 2000) (affirming grant of summary judgment in action by worker with multiple sclerosis who presented evidence of tirade from human resources officer after plaintiff expressed intention to file EEOC charge). That of the employee with the brain condition is *Johnson v. Hines Nurseries, Inc.,* 950 F. Supp. 175, 178 (N.D. Tex. 1996) (granting summary judgment on intentional-infliction claim based on callous remarks regarding condition of employee following brain hemorrhage and ridicule of employee's speech).

47. 204 F.3d 494, 507–08 (3d Cir. 2000).

48. 125 F.3d 563, 569 (7th Cir. 1997).

49. E.g., *Swatzell v. Southwestern Bell Tel. Co.,* No. 7:00-CV-139-R, 2001 WL 1343429 (N.D. Tex. Oct. 31, 2001) (upholding ADA claims on summary judgment in case of individual with AIDS who experienced interrogations, appearance of latex gloves around workplace, public disclosure of medical information, and verbal harassment, but granting summary judgment on intentional-infliction claim); *Arena v. Agip, USA, Inc.,* No. 95 CIV. 1529 (WHP), 2000 WL 264312 (S.D.N.Y. Mar. 8, 2000) (rejecting intentional-infliction claim over disparaging remarks about diabetic condition of plaintiff, complaints that her diabetes treatment constituted drain on company, and interference with plaintiff's giving herself insulin shots but upholding ADA and state discrimination statute claims on summary judgment); *Davis v. York Int'l, Inc.,* No. Civ. A. HAR 92–3545, 1993 WL 524761 (D. Md. Nov. 22, 1993) (upholding ADA claim based on mimicking of gait and speech of individual with

"muscular sclerosis" and other conduct, but rejecting intentional-infliction claim).

50. 266 F.3d 916 (8th Cir. 2001); see *id.* at 925 (Hamilton, J., dissenting). The majority opinion does not contradict the description in the dissent but provides only a sanitized summary of the evidence in rejecting the appeal. See *id.* at 919. The majority adds to the account, however, that "[d]uring a basketball game . . . at which the band was playing, [the student] came to her mother and explained that [the teacher] had just told her that she could no longer play in the band because she was too stupid and that he did not have to teach students like her and that he would not. [Her mother] asked [the teacher] about it, who just laughed and said 'yeah, something like that.'" *Id.*

51. *Id.* at 925.

52. 781 N.Y.S.2d 26 (App. Div. 2004).

53. 345 F.3d 515, 519 (7th Cir. 2003) (affirming trial court decision to overturn $80,000 jury verdict in favor of customer).

54. *Hardesty v. CPRM Corp.*, No. 2:03-CV-1033-FWO, 2005 WL 1309028 (M.D. Ala. June 1, 2005).

55. E.g., *Alsbrook v. City of Maumelle*, 184 F.3d 999, 1005 n.9 (8th Cir. 1999) (en banc). An argument, however, may be advanced that if suit is brought for violation of those statutes under 42 U.S.C. § 1983, the law that provides a private right to sue for violations of federal law committed by persons with governmental authority, individual liability may be imposed. See Gary S. Gildin, *Dis-qualified Immunity for Discrimination against the Disabled,* 1999 U. ILL. L. REV. 897 (further arguing that qualified immunity should not apply to claims against individuals under ADA and section 504).

56. 272 F. Supp. 2d 1276 (N.D. Okla. 2003) (adopting magistrate judge's recommendation).

57. The court denied summary judgment on the ADA claim against Wal-Mart, noting that substantial issues existed with regard to Wal-Mart's knowledge of a need to accommodate and whether it bore responsibility for the hostile environment and a discriminatory decision to fire Campbell. *Id.* at 1287–1300, 1303–04 (opinion of magistrate judge).

58. No. 8:04CV120, 2004 WL 2451450 (D. Neb. Nov. 1, 2004).

59. The fact that the damage is emotional does not make it any less real or less deserving of compensation. See CHARLES T. McCORMICK, HANDBOOK ON THE LAW OF DAMAGES 287 (1935). Problems of determining the appropriate amount of damages are difficult, but they are no more difficult than those presented by awards of pain and suffering for physical injury. DOUGLAS LAYCOCK, MODERN AMERICAN REMEDIES: CASES AND MATERIALS 185 (2d ed. 1994) ("Dignitary torts, including assault, false imprisonment, malicious prosecution, intentional infliction of emotional distress, libel, slander, invasion of privacy, and batteries that are offensive but do no physical harm, present valuation

problems comparable to those of pain and suffering."). Exemplary (also known as punitive) damages, which are ordinarily permitted in intentional-infliction actions, are of special importance in this regard. See DOBBS, *supra* note 7, § 3.11(2) (discussing basis in punishment for exemplary damages remedy); LAY-COCK, *supra*, at 5 ("[T]here are punitive remedies: The best known is punitive damages. . . . One may question whether punitive remedies . . . remedy anything in the usual sense of correcting, repairing, or fixing. But punitive damages are sometimes necessary to make it economically feasible . . . to enforce important rights."). Even compensatory damages have effects on future behavior of persons who might be subject to liability. See DOBBS, *supra*, § 3.1, at 212 ("Even if the defendant is not subject to punitive damages, an ordinary 'compensatory' damages judgment can provide an appropriate incentive to meet the appropriate standard of behavior."); *id.* § 3.11(3) (discussing deterrence basis of punitive damages). The idea of correction of a wrong also supports the grant of damages relief, even in instances where the loss is hard to measure. See JULES L. COLEMAN, RISKS AND WRONGS 317 (1992) ("[T]he duty to compensate and the right to compensation for the invasion of rights derive from the principle of corrective justice."); ERNEST J. WEINRIB, THE IDEA OF PRIVATE LAW 135 (1995) ("With the materialization of wrongful injury, the only way the defendant can discharge his or her obligation respecting the plaintiff's right is to undo the effects of the breach of duty."). See generally Symposium, *Corrective Justice and Formalism: The Care One Owes One's Neighbors,* 77 IOWA L. REV. 403 (1992) (discussing corrective justice theories). Damages judgments are also an expression of social disapproval of harmful conduct. See DOBBS, *supra*, § 3.1, at 211 ("A sense of justice and support for rights underlies much of the legal system and would certainly seem to justify an award for pain or for the loss of a valued constitutional right.").

60. BENJAMIN N. CARDOZO, THE NATURE OF THE JUDICIAL PROCESS, Lecture IV (1921), available at http://www.constitution.org/cmt/cardozo/judproc.htm.

61. E.g., *Moysis v. DTG Datanet,* 278 F.3d 819 (8th Cir. 2002); *Metzgar v. Lehigh Valley Hous. Auth.,* No. Civ.A. 98-CV-3304, 1999 WL 562756 (E.D. Pa. July 27, 1999); *Dutson v. Farmers Ins. Exch.,* 815 F. Supp. 349 (D. Or. 1993); *Williams v. Tri-County Metro. Transp. Dist.,* 958 P.2d 202 (Apr. 29, 1998).

62. *Robel v. Roundup Corp.,* 59 P.3d 611, 620 (Wash. 2002).

63. *Id.* at 621.

64. *Id.*

65. *Id.*

66. *Doe v. Bd. of County Comm'rs,* 815 F. Supp. 1448, 1450 (S.D. Fla. 1992).

67. 974 P.2d 207 (Or. App. 1998).

68. 524 U.S. 742 (1998).

69. DOBBS, *supra* note 7, § 335 (discussing standard). Hostile-environment sexual harassment is usually distinguished from quid pro quo sexual harassment. *Meritor Sav. Bank v. Vinson*, 477 U.S. 57, 65 (1986) (drawing distinction and recognizing claim for both forms of harassment).

70. *Burlington Indus.*, 524 U.S. at 765.

71. See, e.g., *Jackson v. Righter*, 891 P.2d 1387 (Utah 1995) (discussing and applying law regarding tort of negligent supervision); *Vince v. Wilson*, 561 A.2d 103 (Vt. 1989) (discussing and applying law regarding tort of negligent entrustment).

72. See DOBBS, *supra* note 7, § 335 (proposing standard for employer tort liability in sexual harassment cases but noting usual dependence of liability on statutory standards); cf. *Faragher v. City of Boca Raton*, 524 U.S. 775, 802 (1998) (establishing vicarious liability standard for hostile-environment sexual harassment under title VII); *Burlington Indus.*, 524 U.S. at 765 (discussing defense based on reasonable care); DOBBS, *supra* at 915–16 ("Although the Court has described this liability-with-a-defense as vicarious liability, the presence of a defense sharply distinguishes it from the ordinary case of vicarious liability, where the employer cannot defend by showing [the] reasonableness of its actions.").

73. The underlying purposes of *respondeat superior* liability include the incentive effects of the rule on the employer, the fairness of imposing liability on the entity that benefits from the work, and the fact that losses are better borne by employers. DOBBS, *supra* note 7, § 334.

74. 203 F.3d 507, 516–17 (7th Cir. 2000).

75. *Id.* at 517 (describing agreement with this position of the lower court).

76. *Sanglap v. LaSalle Bank, FSB*, 345 F.3d 515, 519–20 (7th Cir. 2003).

77. 687 N.E.2d 21 (Ill. 1997).

78. *Id.* at 23–24 (discussing *Geise v. Phoenix Co. of Chicago, Inc.*, 639 N.E.2d 1273 (1994)).

79. *Id.* at 23.

80. The case for preemption will be stronger in states whose statutes have broader preemptive language. In those states, law reform might be directed to the modification of the statutes. A state in which the courts have found wide preemption of intentional infliction claims is Iowa. E.g., *Martinez v. Cole Sewell Corp.*, 233 F. Supp. 2d 1097 (N.D. Iowa 2002).

81. *McKay v. Town & Country Cadillac, Inc.*, 991 F. Supp. 966, 971 (N.D. Ill. 1997).

82. 893 F. Supp. 1092 (S.D. Ga. 1995).

83. 149 F. Supp. 2d 274 (E.D. Tex. 2001).

84. 164 F. Supp. 2d 127 (D. Mass. 2001).

85. No. Civ.A. 01–2097,2004 WL 225038 (E.D. Pa. Feb 3, 2004); see also Larson v. Indep. Sch. Dist. No. 361, Nos. Civ.02–3611(DWF/RLE), Civ.02–4095(DWF/RLE), 2004 WL 432218 (D. Minn. Mar. 2, 2004) (affording immunity to principal and social worker in intentional-infliction action).

86. See, e.g., *Gleason v. Metropolitan Council Transit Operations*, 582 N.W.2d 216, 219–21 (Minn. 1998) (holding that intentional-infliction claim against bus driver who humiliated passenger in wheelchair and refused to allow her to leave bus or secure wheelchair was not barred by statutory discretionary function immunity or official immunity).

CHAPTER 8

1. *Baty v. Willamette Indus., Inc.*, 172 F.3d 1232, 1246–47 (10th Cir. 1999); *Jenson v. Eveleth Taconite Co.*, 824 F. Supp. 847, 884 (D. Minn. 1993); *Robinson v. Jacksonville Shipyards, Inc.*, 760 F. Supp. 1486, 1534–36 (M.D. Fla. 1991). But see *DeAngelis v. El Paso Mun. Police Officers Ass'n*, 51 F.3d 591, 596 (5th Cir. 1995) (not reaching issue but describing it as "difficult"). Views of academics are more diverse. Compare J. M. Balkin, Essay, *Free Speech and Hostile Environments*, 99 COLUM. L. REV. 2295 (1999) (arguing that employer liability for hostile environments meets constitutional test); Deborah Epstein, *Can a Dumb Ass Woman Achieve Equality in the Workplace? Running the Gauntlet of Hostile Environment Harassing Speech*, 84 GEO. L.J. 399, 426 (1996) (arguing for constitutionality of existing law); Cynthia L. Estlund, *Freedom of Expression in the Workplace and the Problem of Discriminatory Harassment*, 75 TEX. L. REV. 687, 695 (1997) (same), and Suzanne Sangree, *Title VII Prohibitions against Hostile Environment Sexual Harassment and the First Amendment: No Collision in Sight*, 47 RUTGERS L. REV. 461 (1995) (same), with Kingsley R. Browne, *Title VII as Censorship: Hostile-Environment Harassment and the First Amendment*, 52 OHIO ST. L.J. 481 (1991) (challenging constitutionality of existing law) and Eugene Volokh, Comment, *Freedom of Speech and Workplace Harassment*, 39 UCLA L. REV. 1791 (1992) (same). The statement in the text should perhaps be restricted to the private employer situations. Courts have found some government agencies' general antiharassment policies unconstitutionally overbroad. E.g., *Saxe v. State Coll. Area Sch. Dist.*, 240 F.3d 200 (3d Cir. 2001); see *UWM Post, Inc. v. Board of Regents*, 774 F. Supp. 1163 (E.D. Wis. 1991) (invalidating public university student conduct code). Regarding First Amendment issues in connection with general antiharassment provisions enacted by public school authorities, see Martha McCarthy, *Anti-Harassment Policies in Public Schools: How Vulnerable Are They?* 31 J.L. & EDUC. 52 (2002).

2. Penalties for employers when they retaliate for employees' whistle-blowing or challenging discriminatory conduct are very much the exception to this norm. The other principal exception is the public employer, which will be considered in the discussion of school cases.

3. See Erwin Chemerinsky, CONSTITUTIONAL LAW § 11.3 (2d ed 2002) (collecting authorities on unprotected and lesser protected categories of speech).

4. 395 U.S. 575 (1969). The Court has also permitted regulation of an employer's implied promise of benefits during an organizing campaign. *NLRB v. Exchange Parts Co.*, 375 U.S. 405, 409 (1964) (calling implied promise "the suggestion of a fist inside the velvet glove"); *see NLRB v. Virginia Elec. & Power Co.*, 314 U.S. 469, 477 (1941) (interpreting Wagner Act to reach only coercive or threatening speech, so as to avoid First Amendment challenge, but not questioning constitutionality of prohibition on coercive or threatening speech).

5. *Gissel*, 395 U.S. at 617 (upholding regulation of verbal prediction that may have constituted implied threat to close plant if union established and strike called).

6. Eugene Volokh, *How Harassment Law Restricts Free Speech*, 47 RUTGERS L. REV. 563, 569 (1995).

7. See Balkin, *supra* note 1, at 2310–16 (emphasizing strength of captive audience argument regarding workplace); Epstein, *supra* note 1, at 422–23 (discussing argument in context of title VII liability). But see Kingsley R. Browne, *Zero Tolerance for the First Amendment: Title VII's Regulation of Employee Speech*, 27 OHIO N.U. L. REV. 563, 565–66 (2001) (decrying extension of captive audience doctrine).

8. Regarding residential picketing, see *Frisby v. Schultz*, 487 U.S. 474, 487 (1988) (upholding prohibition of targeted residential picketing). Regarding radio broadcasts, see *FCC v. Pacifica Found.*, 438 U.S. 726 (1978) (upholding restriction). Regarding transit advertising, see *Lehman v. City of Shaker Heights*, 418 U.S. 298 (1974) (permitting ban on political advertising in public transit). Regarding postal regulation, see *Rowan v. United States Post Office Dep't*, 397 U.S. 728 (1970) (permitting postal delivery to stop sexual material sent to recipient's home upon resident's request). Regarding abortion clinic picketing, see *Madsen v. Women's Health Ctr., Inc.*, 512 U.S. 753 (1994) (permitting injunction to protect users of abortion clinic). These decisions contrast with others in which the Court has ruled that those offended by the speech can simply avert their attention. E.g., *Cohen v. California*, 403 U.S. 15 (1971) (overturning conviction for disorderly conduct for wearing jacket with offensive message while in courthouse corridor).

9. See Epstein, *supra* note 1, at 434.

10. Volokh, *supra* note 1, at 1855.

11. For a discussion of this distinction, see Alan E. Brownstein, *Hate Speech and Harassment: The Constitutionality of Campus Codes That Prohibit Racial Insults*, 3 WM. & MARY BILL RTS. J. 179, 179–180 (1994).

12. See, e.g., *Gormley v. Director, Conn. State Dep't of Probation*, 632 F.2d 938, 941 (2d Cir. 1980) (upholding constitutionality of statute forbidding telephone harassment); *State v. Gattis*, 730 P.2d 497, 501 n.1 (N.M. Ct. App. 1986) (collecting cases).

13. Brownstein, *supra* note 11, at 203.

14. 485 U.S. 46 (1988).

15. See Rodney A. Smolla, *Emotional Distress and the First Amendment*, 20 ARIZ. ST. L.J. 423, 467 (1988); see also Rodney A. Smolla, *Rethinking First Amendment Assumptions about Racist and Sexist Speech*, 47 WASH. & LEE L. REV. 171, 210 (1990) (applying constitutional standards to racist and sexist speech that inflicts emotional distress); cf. Jean C. Love, *Discriminatory Speech and the Tort of Intentional Infliction of Emotional Distress*, 47 WASH. & LEE L. REV. 123, 159 (1990) (endorsing Smolla's views).

16. 538 U.S. 343 (2003).

17. See Debra D. Burke, *Workplace Harassment: A Proposal for a Bright Line Test Consistent with the First Amendment*, 21 HOFSTRA LAB. & EMP. L.J. 591, 614 (2004) ("[T]here seems to be merit in the contention that there is no valid First Amendment claim of protection just because words are used to intimidate an employee into succumbing without genuine consent to sexual overtures.").

18. Brownstein, *supra* note 11, at 184.

19. See Balkin, *supra* note 1, at 2298; see also *R.A.V. v. City of St. Paul*, 505 U.S. 377, 389 (1992) ("[A] particular content-based category of a proscribable class of speech can be swept up incidentally within the reach of a statute directed at conduct rather than speech. . . . Thus, for example, sexually derogatory 'fighting words,' among other words, may produce a violation of Title VII's general prohibition against sexual discrimination in employment practices.").

20. 505 U.S. 377, 389 (1992).

21. 538 U.S. 343, 363 (2003).

22. *Id.* Justice Souter recognized that the Court's treatment of *R.A.V.* in fact modified that precedent by recognizing an exception "when circumstances show that the statute's ostensibly valid reason for punishing particularly serious proscribable expression probably is not a ruse for message suppression. . . ." *Id.* at 384 (Souter, J., concurring in the judgment in part and dissenting in part).

23. See, e.g., *Shore Reg'l High Sch. Bd. of Educ. v. P.S.*, 381 F.3d 187 (3d Cir. 2004) (throwing rocks, hitting with padlock); *Costello v. Mitchell Pub. Sch. Dist. 79*, 266 F.3d 916 (8th Cir. 2001) (hitting in face with thrown object); *Charlie F. v. Bd. of Educ.*, 98 F.3d 989 (7th Cir. 1996) (fistfights); *Scruggs v. Meriden Bd. of Educ.*, No. 3:03CV2224(PCD), 2005 WL 2072312 (Aug. 26, 2005) (punching, kicking, having hair pulled, other conduct leading to student's suicide); *K.M. v. Hyde Park Cent. Sch. Dist.*, 381 F. Supp. 2d 343 (S.D.N.Y. 2005) (throwing to ground, body slamming, beating on head and back, hitting); *Haysman v. Food Lion, Inc.*, 893 F. Supp. 1092 (S.D. Ga. 1995) (striking with hands and kicking).

24. In discussing whether under a strict application of *R.A.V.* hate speech may permissibly be prohibited, Professor Brownstein states: "Unlike other abu-

sive speech, racial insults and other degrading comments directed at an immutable characteristic that the victim cannot change are presumptively valueless because they cannot be justified as an attempt to change the listener's behavior." Brownstein, *supra* note 11, at 211. Some authorities contend that restrictions of harassing speech would survive even the most exacting scrutiny as a content-based regulation of speech. Richard Delgado, *Words That Wound: A Tort Action for Racial Insults, Epithets, and Name-Calling*, 17 Harv. C.R.-C.L. L: Rev. 133, 172–73 (1982) (positing that tort action for racial insults would constitute permissible content-based regulation of speech); see also Morrison Torrey, *Thoughts about Why the First Amendment Operates to Stifle the Freedom and Equality of a Subordinated Majority*, 21 Women's Rights L. Rep. 21, 31 (1999) (supporting restrictions on speech that creates sexually hostile environment, noting that "the Supreme Court has thrice held that the elimination of discrimination against women is a compelling government interest permitting the government to intrude on the First Amendment freedom of association" and collecting authorities).

25. *R.A.V.*, 505 U.S. at 389.

26. *Id.*

27. *Guckenberger v. Boston Univ.*, 957 F. Supp. 306 (D. Mass. 1997).

28. *Wisconsin v. Mitchell*, 508 U.S. 476 (1993) (upholding enhanced penalties for hate crimes based on actor's motivation).

29. See *Dambrot v. Cent. Mich. Univ.*, 55 F.3d 1177 (6th Cir. 1995); *Roberts v. Haragan*, 346 F. Supp. 2d 853 (N.D. Tex. 2004); *Bair v. Shippensburg Univ.*, 280 F. Supp. 2d 357 (M.D. Pa. 2003); *UWM Post, Inc. v. Bd. of Regents of Univ. of Wis.*, 774 F. Supp. 1163 (E.D. Wis. 1991); *Doe v. Univ. of. Mich.*, 721 F. Supp. 852 (E.D. Mich. 1989).

30. A leading authority on the topic is *Hazelwood Sch. Dist. v. Kuhlmeier*, 484 U.S. 260 (1988) (articulating rule that schools may prohibit speech inconsistent with basic educational mission). See also *Bethel Sch. Dist. No. 403 v. Fraser*, 478 U.S. 675 (1986) (permitting discipline of student for making sexually suggestive speech in support of candidate for student government); *West v. Derby Unified Sch. Dist. No. 260*, 206 F.3d 1358 (10th Cir. 2000) (permitting discipline of student for display that could inflame racial tensions).

31. Compare *Pickering v. Bd. of Educ.*, 391 U.S. 563 (1968) (letter to newspaper on public budget) with *Connick v. Myers*, 461 U.S. 138 (1983) (memorandum on job conditions).

32. *O'Rourke v. City of Providence*, 235 F.3d 713 (1st Cir. 2001) (display of sexual materials); *Black v. City of Auburn*, 857 F. Supp. 1540 (M.D. Ala. 1994) (labeling argument that police officer had First Amendment right to use derogatory terms toward female co-workers frivolous), *aff'd*, 56 F.3d 1391 (11th Cir. 1995) (table).

CHAPTER 9

1. 133 F.3d 1054, 1059–60 (7th Cir. 1998). But see *Tyler v. Ispat Inland, Inc.*, 245 F.3d 969, 973–74 (7th Cir. 2001) (recognizing segregation as discrimination but finding that refusal to transfer employee with mental illness back to site where conflict with co-workers occurred failed to constitute violation when employee was integrated with other workers at new site).

2. 527 U.S. 581 (1999). For a somewhat more detailed discussion of the case, see chapter 2.

3. Most citations to the case are found in cases dealing with challenges to failure to provide placements in less restrictive settings for persons with severe disabilities in other states. E.g., *Radaszewski v. Maram*, 383 F.3d 599 (7th Cir. 2004) (claim for provision of services in home).

4. Compare *Oberti v. Bd. of Educ.*, 995 F.2d 1204 (3d Cir. 1993) (approving mainstreamed program for child with Down's syndrome) with *Beth B. v. Van Clay*, 282 F.3d 493 (7th Cir.), *cert. denied*, 123 S. Ct. 412 (2002) (rejecting mainstreamed placement for child with Rhett syndrome). See generally Mark C. Weber, *The Least Restrictive Environment Obligation as an Entitlement to Educational Services: A Commentary*, 5 U.C.-DAVIS J. JUVENILE L. & POL'Y 147 (2001) (discussing interpretation of obligation to educate children with disabilities in least restrictive environment); Joshua Andrew Wolfe, Note, *A Search for the Best Idea: Balancing the Conflicting Provisions of the Individuals with Disabilities Education Act*, 55 VAND. L. REV. 1627 (2002) (comparing approaches of circuit courts in cases regarding placement of students in the least restrictive environment).

5. Michael Ashley Stein, *Employing People with Disabilities: Some Cautionary Thoughts for a Second-Generation Civil Rights Statute*, in EMPLOYMENT, DISABILITY, AND THE AMERICANS WITH DISABILITIES ACT 51, 53 (Peter David Blanck ed., 2000). An exception, although it can hardly be called a monumental effort in light of the results, is the integration mandate in IDEA.

6. See Mark C. Weber, *Towards Access, Accountability, Procedural Regularity and Participation: The Rehabilitation Act Amendments of 1992 and 1993*, JOURNAL OF REHABILITATION, July, 1994, at 21 (describing increased emphasis on programs that involve placement of individuals in competitive employment with job coaches and other supports).

7. See Peter D. Blanck et al., *The Emerging Workforce of Entrepreneurs with Disabilities: Preliminary Study of Entrepreneurship in Iowa*, 85 IOWA L. REV. 1583 (2000) regarding small-business creation programs.

8. Innovative programs of this type include a Canadian one providing catering and executive gifts, see *Bow Catering—About Us*, at http://bowcatering.ca/aboutus.html (visited Feb. 6, 2006), and one in Maryland

furnishing organic vegetables, see *Red Wiggler Foundation Mission,* at http://www.redwiggler.org/aboutus/organization.html (visited Feb. 7, 2006).

9. For detailed description of the relevant laws and proposals, see Mark C. Weber, *Beyond the Americans with Disabilities Act: A National Employment Policy for People with Disabilities,* 46 BUFF. L. REV. 123, 142–74 (1998).

10. See, e.g., Bonnie Poitras Tucker, *The ADA's Revolving Door: Inherent Flaws in the Civil Rights Paradigm,* 62 OHIO ST. L.J. 335, 386–87 (2001).

11. See SPECIAL TASK FORCE, SEC'Y OF HEALTH, EDUC. & WELFARE, WORK IN AMERICA 34–36 (1973) (describing economic status as most important determinant of social acceptance).

12. See Lisa Waddington, *Reassessing the Employment of People with Disabilities in Europe: From Quotas to Anti-Discrimination Laws,* 18 COMP. LAB. L.J. 62, 69 (1996) (noting success of German system of job quotas but pointing out continuing problems with compliance).

13. 20 U.S.C.A. § 1412(a)(5)(A) (West 2005).

14. See MARK C. WEBER, SPECIAL EDUCATION LAW AND LITIGATION TREATISE § 9:3–:6 (2d ed. 2002 & supp. III 2005) (collecting cases). For an argument in favor of the interpretation of the statutory language as an affirmative entitlement to services to promote integration, see Weber, *supra* note 4.

15. Mark C. Weber, *Disability and the Law of Welfare,* 2000 U. ILL. L. REV. 889, 943–47. Objections to this proposal, including cost, are considered at length in that source.

16. Michael Stein elaborates on this point:
[T]he campaign for the ADA's passage "brought this fragmented population together in a fight against discrimination." As noted at the time by ADA lobbyist Liz Savage, "People with epilepsy now will be advocates for the same piece of legislation as people who are deaf. . . . That has never happened before. And that's really historic."
Michael Ashley Stein, *From Crippled to Disabled: The Legal Empowerment of Americans with Disabilities,* 43 EMORY L.J. 245, 255 (1994) (footnotes omitted) (quoting JOSEPH P. SHAPIRO, NO PITY: PEOPLE WITH DISABILITIES FORGING A NEW CIVIL RIGHTS MOVEMENT 126–27 (1993)).

17. See Steven D. Baderian et al., *Managing Employment Risks in Light of the New Rulings in Sexual Harassment Law,* 21 W. NEW ENG. L. REV. 343, 364–67 (1999) (describing components of effective policies against sexual harassment).

18. See MARTHA MINOW, MAKING ALL THE DIFFERENCE: INCLUSION, EXCLUSION, AND AMERICAN LAW 173–224 (1990) (suggesting movement away from emphasis on categories of people towards emphasis on social relations); cf. MARTHA MINOW, NOT ONLY FOR MYSELF: IDENTITY, POLITICS, AND THE LAW 30–58 (1997) (suggesting uses and limits of group identity).

19. See Laura L. Rovner, *Perpetuating Stigma: Client Identity in Disability*

Rights Litigation, 2001 UTAH L. REV. 247 (discussing contradictions inherent in portraying person who experienced denial of accommodations as victim).

20. Rosemarie Garland Thomson, *Seeing the Disabled: Visual Rhetorics of Disability in Popular Photography,* in THE NEW DISABILITY HISTORY 335, 368 (Paul K. Longmore & Lauri Umansky eds., 2001) (describing "rhetoric of the ordinary"). In Thomson's article, this passage is accompanied by a reproduction of a clothing advertisement that features a good-looking male who has a prosthesis in place of a right hand. See *id.* at 369.

21. Simon Ungar, *Disability and the Built Environment,* at http://www.surrey.ac.uk/~pss1su/lecturenotes/sun/LectureNotes/city/ (visited Feb. 7, 2006).

22. Samuel R. Bagenstos, *The Future of Disability Law,* 114 YALE L.J. 1, 4 (2004).

Index